Consistency, Choice,
and Rationality

# Consistency, Choice, and Rationality

Walter Bossert

*and*

Kotaro Suzumura

Harvard University Press

Cambridge, Massachusetts

London, England

2010

*Library of Congress Cataloging-in-Publication Data*

Bossert, Walter.
Consistency, choice, and rationality / Walter Bossert and Kotaro Suzumura.
p.   cm.
Includes bibliographical references and index.
ISBN 978-0-674-05299-4 (alk. paper)
1. Rational choice theory.   2. Social choice—Mathematical models.
3. Welfare economics.   I. Suzumura, Kotaro, 1944–   II. Title.
HM495.B67   2010
302'.13015118—dc22        2010012972

# Contents

Preface                                                                    *ix*

## I. Foundations

1   Historical Background                                                    *3*

   1.1   Suzumura Consistency   *3*
   1.2   Rational Choice as Purposive Behavior   *6*
   1.3   Samuelson's Weak Axiom   *7*
   1.4   Houthakker's Axiom   *12*
   1.5   General Choice Functions   *15*
   1.6   Rational Choice: An Outlook   *20*
   1.7   Reference-Dependent Choice   *21*
   1.8   External Norms   *23*
   1.9   Welfare Economics and Social Choice Theory   *26*
   1.10  Beyond Finite-Population Social Choice   *29*

2   Mathematical Background                                                  *32*

   2.1   Binary Relations   *32*
   2.2   Greatest and Maximal Elements   *41*
   2.3   Extensions of Relations   *42*
   2.4   Filters and Ultrafilters   *52*

## II. Rationalizability on General Domains

3   Definitions of Rationalizability                                        *57*

   3.1   Preliminaries   *57*
   3.2   Greatest-Element Rationalizability   *61*

3.3    Maximal-Element Rationalizability    *72*

3.4    A Synthesis    *75*

4    Characterizations                                                77

4.1    A Preliminary Result    *77*

4.2    Three Special Cases    *78*

4.3    A Unified Approach    *81*

4.4    Summary    *109*

## III.  Rationalizability on Specific Domains

5    Domain Closedness Properties                              115

5.1    Additional Choice Coherence Axioms    *115*

5.2    Logical Relationships    *119*

5.3    Closedness under Intersection    *121*

5.4    Closedness under Union    *122*

6    Cardinality-Complete Domains                             128

6.1    Base Domains    *128*

6.2    Logical Relationships on Base Domains    *128*

6.3    Characterizations on Base Domains    *130*

6.4    Base Domains and Closedness under Union    *134*

## IV.  Alternative Notions of Rationalizability

7    Non-deteriorating Choice                                  139

7.1    Individual Non-deteriorating Choice    *139*

7.2    Characterizations of ND-Rationalizability    *144*

7.3    The Multi-agent Case    *146*

7.4    Characterizing Efficient and Non-deteriorating Choice    *153*

8    External Norms and Rational Choice                       162

8.1    Internal Coherence of Choice    *162*

8.2    Norm-Conditional Choice    *163*

8.3    Norm-Conditional Rationalizability    *164*

8.4    Characterization Results    *165*

# V. Topics in Social Choice Theory

**9**    Collective Choice Rules     *173*

    9.1    Weakening Social Coherence Properties    *173*

    9.2    Earlier Results    *177*

    9.3    Generalizations of the Pareto Rule    *178*

    9.4    A Characterization    *180*

**10**   Decisiveness and Infinite Populations     *185*

    10.1    Decisive Coalitions, Filters, and Ultrafilters    *185*

    10.2    Decisiveness without Social Richness Assumptions    *187*

    10.3    Intergenerational Social Choice    *193*

    10.4    Multi-profile Stationarity    *198*

References     *205*

Index     *215*

# Preface

The theme of this monograph revolves around three basic questions. The first of these is, What should we mean by choice, individual or collective, being *rational*? Since the concept of rationality of choice lies at the heart of social choice theory and microeconomic theory in general, it is no surprise that there is a wide range of possible formulations of this concept. However, we think that there should be an essential core meaning of this term that is shared by most, if not all, proposed notions of rational choice behavior. In the first part of this monograph, we identify such a fundamental definition of rationality and characterize this concept by means of revealed preference axioms and related properties. It is fairly straightforward to trace our basic notion of rational choice back to the classical theory of consumer's behavior along the lines pursued by authors such as Ragnar Frisch, John Hicks, and Paul Samuelson. It asserts that a set of observable choices is rational if and only if there exists an underlying preference relation such that the choice from every feasible set within a specified domain can be construed to result from optimizing this relation subject to the implied feasibility constraint. In other words, by rationality of choice we mean throughout this monograph a choice that is *rationalizable* by a preference relation. For mnemonic convenience, we refer to a relation that rationalizes a given set of choices as a *rationalization* thereof.

The second question we address is, How should the concept of rationality *by itself* be related to the imposition of *other* properties on a rationalizing relation, such as the *coherence* property of transitivity or the *richness* properties of reflexivity and completeness? This question is meaningful, as there are many statements in the literature on individual and social choice theory that closely associate the term *rationality* with coherence and richness properties of a preference relation. As we see it, the concept of rational choice as rationalizable choice merely requires the existence of *some* underlying relation, the optimization of which subject to the feasibility constraint recovers the observed objects of choice in each choice situation. In other words, *additional* properties of a rationalization such as coherence or richness requirements have nothing *intrinsically* to do with the existence of a rationalization per se. Having said this, however, we may go one step further and allow for different *forms* of rationality depending on the additional coherence and richness properties that a rationalization can be required to possess.

The standard richness requirements imposed on preference relations are *reflexivity* and *completeness,* and not much needs to be said about these properties at this stage. The classical coherence requirement is that of *transitivity* and, as far as our analysis in this monograph is concerned, this is the strongest coherence property we consider. There are several weakenings thereof that have been discussed extensively in the literature, most notably *quasi-transitivity* and *acyclicity.* More recently, the concept of *Suzumura consistency,* developed by Kotaro Suzumura, has been added as an alternative weakening of transitivity. To conclude our discussion of the second question, the conceptual framework of our analysis of rationalizable choice is expanded by examining the consequences of imposing various combinations of richness and coherence requirements in addition to the basic property of rationalizability itself.

Finally, we turn to our third question, which is, Why should we examine coherence and richness properties of a rationalization at all instead of settling for mere rationalizability? A standard answer to this question, when the relevant concept of coherence is that of transitivity, is often provided by a variation of one of the following three arguments, namely, those of *path independence,* the existence of *maximal elements* in any finite feasible set, and the absence of a *money pump.* These are important considerations. However, while it is true that transitivity indeed is sufficient for all of these three properties, it is *not necessary* for any of them and, thus, weaker coherence properties are of considerable interest as well.

Path independence demands that the choice from a set can be recovered by means of a two-stage procedure where the original set is partitioned into two non-empty subsets. The first stage consists of making choices from the two subsets, followed by the second stage in which a choice is made from the union of the two sets chosen in the first stage. If the resulting choice coincides with the choice made directly from the original set for all choice situations, the choice is said to be path independent. As is well-known, the property of rationalizability by a quasi-transitive relation is all that is required for path-independent choice and the full force of transitivity is not needed.

Another well-known observation is that the existence of maximal elements according to a relation in any finite feasible set is guaranteed by the acyclicity of that relation. Again, a weaker coherence property than transitivity turns out to be necessary *and* sufficient for the desired attribute of a relation.

As to the third argument, although the transitivity of a relation is sufficient to rule out the existence of a money pump, it again fails to be necessary: what is necessary and sufficient for the absence of a money pump is the property of Suzumura consistency.

Beginning with an attempt to address these basic questions, the focus of this monograph moves into several directions. The subject matter of rational choice as rationalizable choice is interesting in itself and deeply rooted in the theory of revealed preference theory, but there are non-rationalizable choices that can nevertheless satisfy some important choice coherence properties. Along with rationalizable choices, we analyze what we refer to as *non-deteriorating* choices. We also explore the implications of Suzumura consistency in the context of social choice problems. Our hope is that this monograph serves both as an up-to-date treatment of the subject matter considered here and as an encouragement to other researchers to follow up on the analysis of consistency, choice, and rationality.

The plan of this monograph took concrete shape while we were working on the theory of rationalizability of individual and social choice over the past decade at the University of Montreal, Quebec, Canada, and Hitotsubashi University, Tokyo, Japan. We are most grateful for the financial support from a Grant-in-Aid for Scientific Research from the Ministry of Education, Culture, Sports, Science and Technology of Japan and from the Social Sciences and Humanities Research Council of Canada. Thanks are also due to the University of Montreal and Hitotsubashi University for their warm hospitality while we were visiting each other's home institutions. We also gratefully acknowledge the hospitality of Bocconi University, Milan, Italy, where Walter Bossert spent a sabbatical year in the course of the preparation of this monograph. In some of our joint work we had the good fortune of counting Yves Sprumont as another member of our research team. It didn't take long before we realized that our joint research should be coherently integrated into a research monograph. In the meantime, we have published several articles in professional journals such as *Analyse & Kritik, Economic Theory, Economica, Economics and Philosophy,* the *Journal of Economic Theory, Mathematical Social Sciences, Order, Social Choice and Welfare,* and *Theory and Decision,* as well as in a *Festschrift* in honor of Amartya Sen, which eventually formed the basic structure of this monograph. Many of these preliminary articles were presented in seminars and conferences. We have benefited from the thought-provoking and constructive comments and questions provided by numerous audience members, to whom we are most grateful. In addition, we thank the reviewers of these earlier publications as well as those of Harvard University Press who enabled us to make this a much better book than it would have been without their valuable suggestions.

Our interest in as well as our views on the issues covered in this monograph were strongly influenced by the interactions we enjoyed with many scholars over the years. They include Kenneth Arrow, Geir Asheim, Nicholas Baigent, Salvador Barberà, Kaushik Basu, Charles Blackorby, Douglas Blair, George Bordes, Susumu Cato, Rajat Deb, David Donaldson, Bhaskar Dutta, Lars Ehlers, Marc Fleurbaey, Wulf Gaertner, Frank Hahn, Peter Hammond, Chiaki Hara, Aanund Hylland, Jerry Kelly, Michel Le Breton, Prasanta Pattanaik, Hans Peters, John Roemer, Donald Saari, Tatsuyoshi Saijo, Maurice Salles, Thomas Schwartz, Amartya Sen, Tomoichi Shinotsuka, Yves Sprumont, Koichi Tadenuma, William Thomson, John Weymark, and Yongsheng Xu. We are most grateful for their helpful comments, criticisms, and discussions. Our apologies to anyone who may inadvertently have been left out of this list; all oversights of that nature are entirely due to our faulty memories. Of course, the responsibility for any remaining shortcomings should be exclusively attributed to us.

*Walter Bossert and Kotaro Suzumura*
*Montreal and Tokyo*

— I —

# Foundations

# — 1 —

# Historical Background

## 1.1  Suzumura Consistency

Binary relations play a major role in much of microeconomic theory, both in individual decision theory and in the context of social choice problems. Arrow (1951, 1963) is to be credited with introducing the axiomatics of relations to economic theory in general and to social choice theory in particular. In an interview conducted by Kelly (1987), Arrow attributed much of his own interest in this topic to a course he took with Tarski, whose fundamental textbook (Tarski, 1941) continues to be one of the classics on mathematical logic. Arrow recalls (see Kelly, 1987, p. 44): "... I *knew* that Alfred Tarski was a great and famous logician and there he was in my last term in school and obviously I was going to take a course with Alfred Tarski. ... The other course he gave was in the calculus of relations. To say it was in the *calculus* of relations meant that he gave an axiomatic treatment of relations. ... He had an axiomatic theory like an axiomatic treatment of set theory."

Perhaps the most fundamental coherence requirement imposed on a relation is the well-known *transitivity* axiom. If a relation is interpreted as a preference relation, transitivity postulates that whenever one alternative is at least as good as a second and the second alternative is, in turn, at least as good as a third, then the first alternative must be at least as good as the third. However, from an empirical as well as a conceptual perspective, transitivity is frequently considered too demanding, especially in group decision problems. As a consequence, weaker notions of coherence have been proposed in the literature, most notably *quasi-transitivity* and *acyclicity*. Quasi-transitivity demands that the strict preference associated to a relation is transitive, whereas acyclicity rules out the presence of strict preference

3

cycles. Quasi-transitivity is implied by transitivity and implies acyclicity. The reverse implications are not valid.

Suzumura (1976b) introduced an alternative weakening of transitivity and showed that it can, in many ways, be considered a more intuitive property than quasi-transitivity. This notion of coherence, called *consistency* by Suzumura (1976b), excludes the presence of cycles with at least one instance of strict preference. Thus, the axiom is stronger than acyclicity and weaker than transitivity. It is equivalent to transitivity in the presence of *reflexivity* and *completeness* but it neither implies nor is implied by quasi-transitivity. Because the term *consistency* is used under a variety of different meanings, we refer to Suzumura's variant as *Suzumura consistency* throughout this monograph.

To appreciate the importance of the axiom, note first that Suzumura consistency is exactly what is needed to avoid the phenomenon of a *money pump*. If an agent's preferences are not Suzumura consistent in the above-described sense, there exists a cycle with at least one instance of strict preference. If this occurs, the agent is willing to trade a first alternative for a second alternative (where "willingness to trade" is identified with being at least as well-off after an exchange as before), the second alternative for a third, and so on until an alternative is reached such that getting back the original alternative is strictly preferred to retaining possession of the last alternative in the chain. Thus, at the end of such a chain of exchanges, the agent is willing to give up the last alternative and, in addition, to pay a positive amount in order to get back the original alternative—the classical definition of a money pump. An illustrative example of a money pump is given by Raiffa (1968). In the example, Mr. Jones is a decision maker who has cyclical preferences over three properties $A$, $B$, and $C$ that could, for instance, be the result of aggregating three characteristics such as cost, space, and location by making pairwise comparisons on the basis of the number of characteristics that are better. For the sake of argument, suppose Jones considers $A$ to be better than $B$, $B$ better than $C$, and $C$ better than $A$. The example goes as follows (see Raiffa, 1968, p. 78): "Suppose, Mr. Jones, that you have just been given the deed to property $A$ and now the realtor offers you $C$ for a small premium. If your preferences mean anything, they certainly mean that you would be willing to pay this tiny premium to exchange $A$ for $C$.... Okay, now you have $C$. Next suppose the realtor offers you $B$ for another tiny premium. Certainly you should be willing to pay this premium to get $B$ rather than stay with $C$.... Okay, now you have $B$. But why stay with $B$ when for a small premium you can switch to $A$? After all, you say you prefer $A$ to $B$. . . . Okay, now you have $A$. But why stop here? Do you still insist you prefer $C$ to $A$? You do? . . . Well, for a small premium . . . Are you sure, Mr. Jones, you don't want to change your mind?" Raiffa (1968) used cyclical preferences in his example but it is clear that, with our definition of willingness to trade, the example is easily amended so as to apply to preferences that are not Suzumura consistent.

In his seminal contribution, Szpilrajn (1930) showed that, for any asymmetric and transitive relation, there exists an asymmetric, transitive, and complete relation that contains the original relation. An analogous result applies if asymmetry is dropped as an assumption and reflexivity is added as a property of the extension—that is, any transitive relation has an *ordering extension*. Suzumura (1976b) strengthened this result considerably by establishing that the transitivity assumption can be weakened to Suzumura consistency without changing the conclusion regarding the existence of an ordering extension. Moreover, he showed that Suzumura consistency is the *weakest possible* property that guarantees this existence result. Because extension theorems are of considerable importance in many applications of set theory, this is a fundamental result and illustrates the significance of the property. Szpilrajn's (1930) extension theorem has proven to be useful in a variety of disciplines including mathematics, economics, and political sciences, and we hope that this monograph succeeds in persuading many readers that Suzumura's (1976b) strengthening thereof is worth exploring further.

It is an important task to revisit some classical results and, moreover, to examine new possibilities in a setting where transitivity is replaced with Suzumura consistency. In the absence of reflexivity and completeness, transitivity not only implies Suzumura consistency but the implication is actually *strict* and, thus, there is a strong promise for arriving at a considerably enriched set of possibilities. Various types of indeterminacies such as incompleteness, vagueness, and incommensurabilities have long been considered to be significant and, thus, the study carried out in this monograph indeed has the potential of opening up previously undiscovered paths along which new attractive and plausible choice and decision rules can be discovered, both in individual and collective settings. Thus, many of the observations collected here can also be viewed as contributions to individual and collective choice in a more general framework where preferences need not be complete.

Early applications of Suzumura consistency as an attractive weakening of transitivity may be found in the theory of individual rights; see, for

example, Suzumura (1978; 1983, chapter 7). However, in spite of its significance, Suzumura consistency has received relatively little attention and
contributions employing it as an attractive weakening of transitivity have
only just started to emerge; see Bossert (2008) for a brief survey. Among the
fields where it has been analyzed recently are the theory of rational choice
and some variants thereof (see, for instance, Bossert, Sprumont, and Suzumura, 2005a,b; Bossert and Suzumura, 2007a, 2009a) and social choice
theory (see Bossert and Suzumura, 2008a). The classical status of Suzumura consistency is vindicated by some of the principal proponents of the
*behavioral* approach to welfare economics. Bernheim and Rangel (2009,
p. 53) attempt to "develop a generalized welfare criterion that respects choice
directly, without reference to the decision maker's underlying objectives, . . .
thereby avoid[ing] the thorny problems associated with formulating and
justifying rationalizations." However, as Bernheim and Rangel (2009, p. 61,
footnote 14) themselves recognize, their natural generalizations of revealed
preference turn out to be closely related to Suzumura consistency; see also
Bernheim (2009, p. 298, footnote 31). In this monograph, we provide a
unified treatment of the use of Suzumura consistency and place it in the context of other coherence properties. Our purpose is to argue that it provides
a promising alternative to the classical transitivity axiom that allows us
to resolve some impossibilities without giving up too much in terms of the
coherence of the relation under consideration. Our main motivations (as
discussed above) are its equivalence to the absence of a money pump, its
crucial role as a sufficient *and* necessary condition for the existence of an
ordering extension, and its resulting unique position as a minimal coherence
property once completeness is dropped as a requirement.

## 1.2   Rational Choice as Purposive Behavior

What do we mean by choice behavior being rational? Whatever else we may
additionally mean, we should at least mean that *rational choice behavior can
be coherently construed as purposive behavior.*

We need not search for long before we may confirm that this simple view
on the rationality of choice is indeed deeply rooted in the history of standard economic theory. Suffice it to quote a neat passage from Robbins (1935,
p. 93): "[T]here is a sense in which the word rationality can be used which
renders it legitimate to argue that at least some rationality is assumed before
human behaviour has an economic aspect—the sense, namely, in which it

is equivalent to 'purposive.' ... [I]t is arguable that if behaviour is not conceived of as purposive, then the conception of the means-end relationships which economics studies has no meaning. So if there were no purposive action, it could be argued that there were no economic phenomena." It is precisely this classical conception of the notion of rationality of choice that we are going to examine in later chapters of this monograph.

Before setting about pursuing this target, there is one more lesson to be learned from Robbins (1935, p. 93): "To say [that rational choice is tantamount to purposive behaviour] is not to say in the least that all purposive action is completely consistent. It may indeed be urged that the more that purposive action becomes conscious of itself, the more it necessarily becomes consistent. But this is not to say that it is necessary to assume *ab initio* that it always is consistent or that the economic generalizations are limited to that, perhaps, tiny section of conduct where all inconsistencies have been resolved." This being the case, we are led to introduce an analytical framework which allows us to talk sensibly about different *forms of rationality* among those choice behaviors which are rational in the sense specified above. Large parts of this monograph are intended to provide such an analytical framework and explore the axiomatic structure of choice with various forms of rationality. In particular, we aim at defining and analyzing notions of rationality that differ in the additional properties that "purposive" behavior may entail. These additional properties include richness properties such as reflexivity and completeness as well as coherence properties such as transitivity and weakenings thereof. Throughout the monograph, we identify "purposive" behavior with the existence of a preference relation such that all chosen alternatives weakly dominate all feasible alternatives (the case of *greatest-element rationalizability*) or none of the chosen alternatives is strictly dominated by any feasible alternative (*maximal-element rationalizability*). Without neglecting other possibilities, we pay close attention to variants that involve what we refer to as *Suzumura-consistent rationalizations*.

## 1.3 Samuelson's Weak Axiom

The first attempt to give analytical substance to this conception of rational choice behavior as purposive action was made by Samuelson (1938a,b) within the specific context of what he refers to as the *pure theory of consumer's behavior*. According to Georgescu-Roegen (1954; 1966, p. 216), Frisch (1926) laid the foundations of modern theories of rational choice: "In the Fisher-Pareto theory, choice merely reflects ophelimity; therefore, ophelimity is the primary and choice is the secondary concept. With Frisch, choice becomes the basic element of the theory of the consumer; the indifference curves are a derived concept introduced to facilitate the rationalization of choice." It is clear that Frisch's approach is precisely what Samuelson (1938a) was about to explore, although Samuelson (1950, pp. 369–370) himself attributed the original inspiration of his revealed preference theory to a discussion with Haberler and to Leontief's analysis of indifference curves. Georgescu-Roegen (1954; 1966, p. 217) went further and traced the origin of revealed preference theory to nobody other than Pareto: "[T]he basic idea goes back to Pareto who in the *Manuel* and, especially, in his article 'Economie Mathematique,' not only tells us that the family of indifference curves and the family of offer curves provide two equally good foundations for a theory of the consumer, but also shows us how we could pass from one to the other." Despite the existence of these conspicuous precursors, it seems fair to say that the analytical, as compared with the doctrinal, origin of the modern theory of rationalizability should be unambiguously attributed to Samuelson.

To orient our analysis of the rationality of observable choice, let us examine Samuelson's theory of revealed preference in detail. His first exploration of revealed preference theory started with a historical observation to the effect that "[f]rom its very beginning the theory of consumer's choice has marched steadily towards greater generality, sloughing off at successive stages unnecessarily restrictive conditions" (Samuelson, 1938a, pp. 61–62). The focus of his sloughing-off operation was the concept of utility per se, but "much of even the most modern [as of the time of Samuelson's own writing] analysis shows vestigial traces of the utility concept." It was in view of this state of the art that Samuelson proposed to "start anew in direct attack upon the problem, dropping off the last vestiges of the utility analysis." In trying to do so, he intended to get rid of the notion of utility altogether and replace it with a simple behavioral hypothesis that could be phrased in terms of the values of demand functions in competitive markets at two price-income situations and nothing else. In his discussion of Samuelson's revealed preference approach, Little (1949, p. 97) went as far as to suggest that ". . . the new formulation is scientifically more respectable. If an individual's behaviour is consistent, then it must be possible to explain that behaviour without reference to anything other than behaviour."

At this stage, a few remarks regarding the numerical representability of a binary relation $R$ may be in order. There are two concepts to be distinguished. The first concept, which is relevant in the case where the relation $R$ is complete, is that of *complete representability*. It requires the existence of a real-valued function $u$ on the universal set of alternatives such that, for any two alternatives $x$ and $y$,

$$(x, y) \in R \Leftrightarrow u(x) \geq u(y)$$

holds. The second concept, which is relevant in the case where $R$ need not satisfy completeness, is that of *representability*, and it reads as follows: there exists a real-valued function $u$ such that, for any two alternatives $x$ and $y$,

$$[(x, y) \in R \Rightarrow u(x) \geq u(y)] \text{ and } [(x, y) \in P(R) \Rightarrow u(x) > u(y)]$$

hold, where $P(R)$ denotes the asymmetric (strict) factor of $R$. See, for instance, Majumdar and Sen (1976) for a discussion of various notions of representability.

It should be clear that a binary relation $R$ is completely representable only if $R$ is an ordering, that is to say, it satisfies reflexivity, completeness, and transitivity. The case of representability is subtly different. It is easy to check that $R$ being Suzumura consistent is a necessary condition for representability. Conversely, assume that $R$ is Suzumura consistent. As we have already observed, we are then assured that there exists an ordering extension $R^*$ of $R$. Conditions under which an ordering $R^*$ has a complete representation $u$ are well-known; see, for example, Debreu (1959). Assume that $u$ completely represents $R^*$ under such a set of conditions. This implies that, for any two alternatives $x$ and $y$,

$$[(x, y) \in R \Rightarrow (x, y) \in R^* \Leftrightarrow u(x) \geq u(y)]$$

and

$$[(x, y) \in P(R) \Rightarrow (x, y) \in P(R^*) \Leftrightarrow u(x) > u(y)]$$

hold. We are thus assured that a Suzumura-consistent relation $R$ has a representation if one of its ordering extensions $R^*$ has a complete representation.

We do not explicitly include representation issues in this monograph because we frequently deal with relations that do not necessarily allow for the existence of a (complete) representation. However, because the use of the term *utility* has been standard for a long time, it will continue to appear in our discussion of the historical background of the matter at hand.

To prepare the ground for Samuelson's theory of revealed preference with special emphasis on the theory of rationalizability, consider a competitive economy involving $\ell$ commodities, where $\ell$ is an integer greater than one. Let $X$ be the *commodity space,* a subset of the set of $\ell$-dimensional non-negative vectors, let $p$ be a positive $\ell$-dimensional *price vector,* and let $Y$ be the positive *income* or *budget* of a consumer. Let $\mathbf{Z}$ denote the family of competitive budget sets, the typical element of which is given by

$$Z(p, Y) = \{x \in X \mid px \leq Y\}.$$

Let $h$ be the *demand function* of a competitive consumer, which is a single-valued function from $\mathbf{Z}$ into $X$ such that, for all $Z(p, Y) \in \mathbf{Z}$, $h(p, Y) \in Z(p, Y)$. The intended interpretation is that, given a competitive price vector $p$ and an income $Y$, $h(p, Y) \in Z(p, Y)$ denotes the commodity bundle that the consumer chooses from the budget set $Z(p, Y) \in \mathbf{Z}$. In the Pareto-Hicks theory of consumer's behavior based on an ordinal utility function, $h$ is derived from maximizing the utility subject to the constraint $x \in Z(p, Y)$ by choice of the consumption bundle $x$.

Classical revealed preference theory in the context of consumer choice problems is linked to numerous developments in demand analysis. For instance, the issue of designing and applying suitable *price indices* based on price and demand data has a long tradition, as documented by contributions such as Laspeyres (1871), Paasche (1874), Fisher (1922), and Samuelson (1947, chapters 5 and 6). Keeping in mind the focus and the structure of this monograph, we do not pursue these applications here although we are aware of their relevance and significance.

Samuelson chose a demand function $h$ rather than an ordinal utility function as the primitive concept of his theoretical framework, and tried to generate almost all, if not literally all, properties of $h$ by means of a weak hypothesis that could be expressed solely in terms of this demand function. To formalize his analytical scenario, we employ a *revealed preference relation* $R_h$, which is a binary relation on $X$ defined as follows. For all $x, y \in X$, $(x, y) \in R_h$ if and only if there exists a budget set $Z(p, Y) \in \mathbf{Z}$ such that

$$x = h(p, Y) \text{ and } y \in Z(p, Y) \setminus \{h(p, Y)\}.$$

In plain words, $x$ is revealed preferred to $y$ if and only if there exists a price-income situation in which $x$ is chosen, whereas $y$ is feasible, but not in fact chosen.

In Samuelson's (1950, p. 370) characteristic parlance, the *weak axiom of revealed preference* was phrased as follows: "Weak axiom: If at the price and income of situation $A$ you could have bought the goods actually bought at a different point $B$ and if you actually chose not to, then $A$ is defined to be 'revealed to be better than' $B$. The basic postulate is that $B$ is never to reveal itself to be *also* 'better than' $A$." Formulated in terms of the revealed preference relation $R_h$, Samuelson's (1938a) hypothesis reads as follows.

**Samuelson's weak axiom of revealed preference**  For all $x, y \in X$,

$$(x, y) \in R_h \Rightarrow (y, x) \notin R_h.$$

Samuelson's (1938a,b, 1947, 1948) tour de force was to show that almost all restrictions on the demand function of a competitive consumer, which the Hicksian theory of consumer's behavior had derived from the constrained maximization of the consumer's ordinal utility function, could be derived from Samuelson's weak axiom of revealed preference and nothing else. The Pareto-Hicks theory of consumer's behavior, the evolution of which owes much to several great scholars including Pareto (1906), Slutsky (1915), Hicks and Allen (1934), and many others, culminated in part I of Hicks's (1939) classic, *Value and Capital*. See also Samuelson (1947, chapters 5–7) for a synthesis of the Pareto-Hicks theory and the status of his own revealed preference theory vis-à-vis Pareto-Hicks.

Samuelson's intended use of Ockham's razor would have resulted in a perfectly happy ending with the complete elimination of the utility concept if only his weak axiom of revealed preference could have entailed the treacherous property of integrability as well. According to Samuelson (1950, p. 116), "[t]he assumption that [the matrix of the Slutsky-Hicks substitution terms] be symmetrical and negative semi-definite completely exhausts the [remaining] empirical implications of the utility analysis. All other demand restrictions can be derived as theorems from the [weak axiom of revealed preference]. These are bold statements, but they are substantiated by the fact that it is possible to work backwards from the assumption [that the matrix of the Slutsky-Hicks substitution terms be symmetrical and negative semi-definite] to an integrable preference field displaying the properties necessary for a maximum."

Thus, the fate of revealed preference theory as a full-fledged *substitute* to the Pareto-Hicks theory hinges squarely on the answer to the following question: Can the weak axiom of revealed preference be sufficiently strong to bring about an integrable preference field? From the beginning, Samuelson (1950, p. 370) had his own doubts: "I soon realized that [the weak axiom of revealed preference] could carry us almost all the way along the path of providing new foundations for utility theory. But not quite all the way. The problem of integrability, it soon became obvious, could not yield to this weak axiom alone. I held up publication on the conjecture that if the axiom were strengthened to exclude non-contradictions of revealed preference for a chain of three or more situations, then non-integrability could indeed be excluded." The answer to this crucial question had to wait until Houthakker (1950) arrived on the scene and proposed his *semi-transitivity* axiom.

## 1.4   Houthakker's Axiom

Recollect that whatever pitfalls the non-integrability problem may entail to the Pareto-Hicks theory of consumer's behavior cannot but be present in Samuelson's revealed preference theory as well, unless some axiom expressed within the latter theory can explicitly avoid the occurrence of the counterpart of non-integrability. It was in his justly famous classic that Houthakker (1950) neatly generalized Samuelson's weak axiom of revealed preference into what he named *semi-transitivity*, thereby complementing Samuelson's weak axiom of revealed preference while preserving the methodological idiosyncrasy of revealed preference theory. To make this verdict transparent, we must answer the following three questions. The first question: What is the counterpart of the integrability problem within the framework of revealed preference theory? The second question: What do we mean by the methodological idiosyncrasy of revealed preference theory? The third question: What precisely does Houthakker's semi-transitivity axiom mean and accomplish, and what is the analytical upshot of his contribution to the overall status of revealed preference theory vis-à-vis the traditional Pareto-Hicks theory? Let us answer these questions in turn.

We begin with our first question. In a different but related context, Arrow (1963, p. 120) made the following observation on the importance of the transitivity condition: "Those familiar with the integrability controversy in the field of consumer's demand theory will observe that the basic problem . . . is the independence of the final choice from the path to it. Transitivity will insure this independence. . . ." However, it may be verified that Samuelson's weak axiom of revealed preference does *not* guarantee transitivity of the revealed preference relation $R_h$. While Rose (1958) has shown that, in the case of two commodities, $R_h$ is transitive in the presence of Samuelson's weak axiom of revealed preference, Gale (1960) has established that this is not the case if there are more than two goods. As shown by Blackorby, Bossert, and Donaldson (1995), the assumption that demand is single valued is not crucial for Rose's result: the theorem remains true if demands are allowed to be multi-valued. Peters and Wakker (1994) showed that if *bargaining problems* involving compact, convex, and comprehensive feasible sets rather than consumer choice problems only are considered, Gale's observation survives: transitivity of the revealed preference relation does not follow from a suitably formulated version of the weak axiom in the case of problems of dimension three or higher.

Samuelson was fully aware of the fact that "the relations of better or worse as revealed by the value sums are not transitive" (Samuelson, 1947, p. 151). He had also tried to find an appropriate strengthening of his weak axiom of revealed preference that is capable of guaranteeing transitivity of the relation $R_h$. It was Houthakker who arrived at the desired strengthening of the weak axiom of revealed preference ahead of anybody else.

At this juncture, let us turn to the second question. Recollect that the original integrability problem was posed and answered in terms of the total differential form, the integrability of which is precisely the focal issue. Thus, the whole problem of integrability was an exercise in infinitesimal calculus. In contrast, the methodological idiosyncrasy of revealed preference theory was "to deduce implications of our integrability conditions which can be expressed in finite form, i.e., be conceivably refutable merely by a finite number of point observations" (Samuelson, 1947, p. 107, footnote 13). In his monumental work, Houthakker (1950, p. 160) reminded us of "the preponderant use of finite differences" in Samuelson's revealed preference theory. This is because "it is felt that differential expressions should be avoided because they do not directly correspond to real phenomena. This, together with the use of value sums, makes for a formulation of consumption theory in immediately observable quantities." This, then, is the self-imposed constraint under which Houthakker had to phrase his own answer to the question left open by Samuelson.

Finally, let us answer the third question by stating Houthakker's semi-transitivity axiom and the impact thereof on the whole spectrum of Samuelson's revealed preference theory. The basic idea is to apply the concept underlying Samuelson's weak axiom of revealed preference not only to pairs of consumption bundles but to *chains* of arbitrary finite length. To be precise, suppose there exist a positive integer $K$, consumption bundles $x^0, \ldots, x^K \in X$ where at least two of these bundles are distinct, positive price vectors $p^0, \ldots, p^K$ and positive incomes $Y^0, \ldots, Y^K$ such that, for all $k \in \{0, \ldots, K\}$, $x^k = h(p^k, Y^k)$ and $p^k x^k = Y^k$, and for all $k \in \{1, \ldots, K\}$, $p^{k-1} x^{k-1} \geq p^{k-1} x^k$. Then the semi-transitivity axiom requires that $p^K x^K < p^K x^0$.

This somewhat complex axiom was rephrased by Samuelson (1950, pp. 370–371) as follows: "If $A$ reveals itself to be 'better than' $B$, and if $B$ reveals itself to be 'better than' $C$, and if $C$ reveals itself to be 'better than' $D$, etc., then I extend the definition of 'revealed preference' and say that $A$ can be defined to be 'revealed to be better than' $Z$, the last in the chain. In such cases it is postulated that $Z$ must never *also* be 'revealed to be better' than $A$."

Samuelson's alternative formulation is what he referred to as the *strong axiom of revealed preference*. It has been widely accepted as the right version of Houthakker's axiom. It is true, however, that Houthakker's semi-transitivity axiom and Samuelson's strong axiom of revealed preference are subtly different, and Samuelson (1950, p. 371, footnote 1) had his own reservations: "I have glossed over a few delicate points. Thus, not all of the situations have to be different ones. Also, there is the question of how to handle two situations which at $A$'s prices *cost the same*, but where $A$ was chosen. If we rule out the possibility that $B$ is 'indifferent to $A$,' then we rule out some realistic cases of multiple equilibrium points. Even when $B$ costs less than $A$ at $A$'s prices, in ruling that $A$ is 'better than B' we are making some implicit assumptions about the absence of 'saturation effects.' Throughout this [rephrasing] I have dodged delicate problems of this sort, taking refuge in over-strong assumptions about regularity of curvature." As long as we are concerned with the analysis of *single-valued* demand functions, this subtle difference does not create any substantial difference. In the more general context, which we discuss later in this chapter, however, these two related but distinct axioms generate remarkably contrasting implications.

What, then, is the major consequence of strengthening Samuelson's weak axiom of revealed preference to Houthakker's semi-transitivity axiom (or the strong axiom of revealed preference in Samuelson's terminology)? The best way to answer this question is to cite a brief passage from Houthakker (1950, p. 173): "We have shown that a theory based on semi-transitive revealed preference entails the existence of ordinal utility, while the property of semi-transitivity itself was derived from utility considerations. The 'revealed preference' and 'utility function' (or 'indifference surface') approaches to the theory of consumer's behavior are therefore formally the same. . . . This solves the problem suggested by Professor Samuelson, viz., to deduce integrability from a generalization of his 'fundamental hypothesis.'" (See Uzawa, 1960, and Stigum, 1973, among others, for modified versions of the proof of Houthakker's main theorem.) In other words, what started as an attempt "to develop the theory of consumer's behavior freed from any vestigial traces of the utility concept" (Samuelson, 1938a, p. 71) resulted in the theory that generates an ordinal utility function that can coherently rationalize the demand function if only we are prepared to accept Houthakker's axiom of semi-transitivity. Thus, the Samuelson-Houthakker theory of revealed preference turns out to be *equivalent* to the Pareto-Hicks ordinalist utilitarian theory of consumer's behavior. In view of the declared purpose of freeing the theory of consumer's behavior from the utility concept, this culmination outcome may be regarded as a pathetic collapse. However, as an afterthought, this should have been expected. Indeed, Samuelson's (1948, p. 243) early remark to the following effect not only summarizes the essential nature of revealed preference theory, but also beautifully presages this eventual outcome: "[T]he individual guinea-pig, by his market behaviour, reveals his preference pattern—if there is such a consistent pattern."

It is clear that Samuelson's weak axiom of revealed preference is *not stronger* than his strong axiom, which follows immediately from the definition of these two axioms. A natural question to ask is whether his weak axiom is *strictly weaker* than the strong axiom. The answer to this question is, again, provided by Rose (1958) and Gale (1960): in the case of two commodities, the two axioms are equivalent; if there are three or more goods, however, the weak axiom is indeed strictly weaker than the strong axiom.

## 1.5  General Choice Functions

While Samuelson and Houthakker restricted attention to the case of a competitive consumer, the question of rationality of observable choice behavior can be posed in more general environments, such as individual choices of arbitrary options and social choices of policies. However, a general conceptual framework for the analysis of rational choice can be modeled after the pure theory of consumer's behavior. Let $X$ be the universal set of alternatives. Unlike in the theory of consumer's behavior, we do not require that $X$ is a subset of some finite-dimensional Euclidean space—all we require is that $X$ is non-empty. It may be finite, it may be countably infinite, or it may be uncountably infinite. Let $\Sigma$ be a non-empty family of non-empty subsets of $X$. The intended interpretation of a set $S \in \Sigma$ is that $S$ denotes a set of available alternatives that could be presented to the agent in charge of making a choice under a specified choice environment. A *choice function* $C$ is a function defined on the domain $\Sigma$, which assigns to each $S \in \Sigma$ a non-empty subset $C(S)$ of $S$, which is to be called the *choice set* of $S$. It is clear that the theory of consumer's behavior is a special case of this general framework, where $X$ is a subset of the set of all non-negative consumption bundles, $\Sigma = Z$, and for each $Z(p, Y) \in Z$, $C(Z(p, Y)) = \{h(p, Y)\}$. The general version of this conceptual framework is what we utilize in what follows; see Uzawa (1956) and Arrow (1959). Houthakker (1965) made use of a special case of this setting in his analysis of the logic of preference and choice.

We now use generalized versions of revealed preference relations to formulate three revealed preference axioms within this general framework. To do so, we need the notion of the *transitive closure $tc(R)$* of a relation $R$ on $X$. The transitive closure is *the smallest transitive relation containing $R$*. The way this transitive closure can be defined is to declare a pair $(x, y)$ to be in $tc(R)$ if there exists a finite chain of preferences according to $R$ leading from $x$ to $y$. Clearly, $R$ is contained in $tc(R)$ for any relation $R$ because whenever $(x, y) \in R$, there is a one-link chain from $x$ to $y$ and thus $(x, y) \in tc(R)$. If $R$ itself is transitive, $R = tc(R)$ but if $R$ is not transitive, the set inclusion is strict—$R$ is a strict subset of $tc(R)$. See Chapter 2 for a detailed and rigorous discussion.

The *direct revealed preference relation $R_C$* of a choice function $C$ with domain $\Sigma$ is defined as

$$R_C = \{(x, y) \mid \exists S \in \Sigma \text{ such that } [x \in C(S) \text{ and } y \in S]\}.$$

The *(indirect) revealed preference relation* of a choice function $C$ is the transitive closure $tc(R_C)$ of the direct revealed preference relation $R_C$.

The *direct revealed strict preference relation* of a choice function $C$ is the relation $R_C^s$ defined by

$$R_C^s = \{(x, y) \mid \exists S \in \Sigma \text{ such that } [x \in C(S) \text{ and } y \in S \setminus C(S)]\}.$$

The *(indirect) revealed strict preference relation* of a choice function $C$ is the transitive closure $tc(R_C^s)$ of the direct revealed strict preference relation $R_C^s$.

In words, $(x, y) \in R_C$ holds if and only if there exists a feasible set $S$ such that $x$ is chosen from $S$ and $y$ could be chosen from $S$. Likewise, $(x, y) \in tc(R_C)$ means that we can find a chain of direct revealed preferences from $x$ to $y$. Finally, $(x, y) \in R_C^s$ holds if and only if there exists a feasible set $S$ such that $x$ is chosen from $S$ and $y$ could be chosen, but is not actually chosen from $S$. Again, $(x, y) \in tc(R_C^s)$ is true whenever $x$ and $y$ can be linked via a chain of direct revealed strict preferences.

We are now ready to introduce three revealed preference axioms by means of $R_C$, $tc(R_C)$, $R_C^s$, and $tc(R_C^s)$. The first axiom is a natural generalization of Samuelson's weak axiom of revealed preference.

**Weak axiom of revealed preference**    For all $x, y \in X$,

$$(x, y) \in R_C^s \Rightarrow (y, x) \notin R_C.$$

If the scope of this axiom is extended to certain chains of revealed preferences, the following two axioms can be obtained.

**Strong axiom of revealed preference**    For all $x, y \in X$,

$$(x, y) \in tc(R_C^s) \Rightarrow (y, x) \notin R_C.$$

**Houthakker's axiom of revealed preference**    For all $x, y \in X$,

$$(x, y) \in tc(R_C) \Rightarrow (y, x) \notin R_C^s.$$

The above definition of the weak axiom of revealed preference is subtly different from Samuelson's weak axiom of revealed preference defined in the context of consumer's behavior in competitive markets. However, in the case studied by Samuelson and by Houthakker, choices are single valued and, in this case, there is no real difference between $R_C$ and $R_C^s$ when applied to pairs of distinct alternatives, and the seeming difference between the two forms of the weak axiom of revealed preference disappears. It also follows that the strong axiom and Houthakker's axiom are in fact equivalent under the same specification of the choice situation.

After Samuelson and Houthakker had laid the foundations of revealed preference theory, the evolution of rational choice theory branched into several paths, depending on the specification of the domain of the choice function. Following Pollak's (1990, p. 146) summary evaluation of Houthakker's contributions to the theory of consumer's behavior, let us begin with three domain specifications.

The first specification, which Pollak called the standard domain version of revealed preference theory, "places restrictions on choices from all budget sets, but not on choices from any other type of feasible sets. Thus, the class of admissible feasible sets consists of all budget sets." We have nothing further to add to the standard domain version of revealed preference theory.

The second specification, which Pollak labeled the extended domain version of revealed preference theory, "exploits the observation that revealed preference theory can be applied to finite sets as well as to budget sets." It was Arrow (1959) who pioneered the extended domain version of revealed preference theory. In Arrow's (1959, p. 122) own parlance, "the demand-function point of view would be greatly simplified if the range over which the choice functions are considered to be determined is broadened to include all finite sets. Indeed, as Georgescu-Roegen has remarked, the intuitive justification of such assumptions as the Weak Axiom of Revealed Preference has no relation to the special form of the budget constraint sets but is based rather on implied consideration of two-element sets." Sen (1971) followed Arrow's lead and rightly observed that the great simplification of revealed preference theory rendered by the extended domain approach can be afforded at a lower price than that paid to include *all* finite sets in the domain of the choice function. Indeed, if the weak axiom is assumed to hold for all two-element and all three-element sets in addition to all budget sets, then the weak axiom can be shown to imply the strong axiom. Sen (1973, p. 246) went further and stated: "[I]n the revealed preference literature, it had been customary to assume, usually implicitly, that the Weak Axiom holds only for those choices that can be observed in the market and not necessarily for other choices. ... Treated as an axiom in the light of which consumer's choices are analysed and interpreted, rather than as a hypothesis which is up for verification, there is no case for restricting the scope of the Weak Axiom arbitrarily to budget sets only, and in the absence of this invidious distinction, transitivity follows directly from the Weak Axiom of Revealed Preference." If we subscribe to this viewpoint, the equivalence between the weak axiom of revealed preference and the existence of an ordering that rationalizes the choice function can be demonstrated by very elementary methods. As Arrow (1959, p. 126) observed, "[i]t is true that very interesting mathematical problems are bypassed by this point of view, but this should not perhaps be a compelling consideration." There are many who employed this simplifying device and tried to explore many other issues in rational choice theory including the characterization of lesser degrees of rationality than full rationalization by an ordering. See, among others, Plott (1973), Blair, Bordes, Kelly, and Suzumura (1976), Bordes (1976), and Schwartz (1976).

The third specification, which Pollak named the restricted domain version of revealed preference theory, adopts the following viewpoint: "Unlike the extended domain version, which expands the class of admissible feasible sets, the restricted domain version contracts it. Under the restricted domain version, the class of admissible feasible sets consists of budget sets, but instead of including all budget sets, it contains only a fixed, finite number." (Pollak, 1990, p. 146.) This domain restriction is motivated by due respect for the methodological idiosyncrasy of Samuelson's revealed preference theory that makes preponderant use of finite inferences. Recollect that Samuelson (1953, p. 1) observed that "[i]n its narrow version the theory of 'revealed preference' confines itself to a finite set of observable price-quantity competitive demand data, and attempts to discover the full empirical implications of the hypothesis that the individual is consistent." In contrast with the standard domain that consists of a continuum of budget sets, the restricted domain makes finite inferences possible by restricting the class of admissible feasible sets to a finite number of budget sets. According to Pollak (1990, p. 148), "[t]he restricted domain version is often described as a technique for constructing 'an approximation to a decision-maker's utility function' (Diewert, 1973, p. 419) or a 'nonparametric approach to demand analysis' (Varian, 1982) rather than as a version of revealed preference theory.... Unlike empirical demand analysis, the restricted domain version of revealed preference theory provides a systematic procedure for determining whether a finite set of price-quantity observations is consistent with the preference hypothesis, an algorithm for constructing a utility function that generates the observed data."

This monograph does not say anything more about the standard domain and the extended domain in the context of revealed preference theory. Instead, we focus on yet another important domain assumption and aspire to develop the theory of rational choice in terms of the underlying class of choice functions. In addition, we discuss some specific restricted domains that are of interest especially in the context of applying the notion of Suzumura consistency. The domain we are primarily interested in may be called the *general domain*, which means that $\Sigma$ can be *any* arbitrary non-empty family of non-empty subsets of $X$. This is by far the weakest restriction on the domain of a choice function, so that the theory of rational choice functions developed on the general domain can be applied to whatever choice situations we may care to specify. Richter (1966, 1971), Hansson (1968), and Suzumura (1976a, 1977) are among the early contributions that explored the structure of rational choice functions on the general domain.

The domain of a choice function is of crucial importance when it comes to identifying the relationships among different definitions of rationalizability and the equivalence (or lack thereof) of different revealed preference axioms. For instance, the weak axiom, the strong axiom, and Houthakker's axiom are equivalent if a choice function $C$ is defined on the extended domain. These are Arrow's (1959) classical results; see also Sen (1971). The situation is dramatically different if the choice function $C$ is defined on the general domain. It is shown by Suzumura (1977; 1983, chapter 2, appendix A) that the choice function $C$ on the general domain is rationalizable by an ordering if and only if it satisfies Houthakker's axiom of revealed preference. Besides, the strong axiom does not imply Houthakker's axiom, and neither does the weak axiom imply the strong axiom on a general domain. See Suzumura (1983, chapter 2, appendix B) for details on these results.

## 1.6   Rational Choice: An Outlook

What should our final verdict be on the lasting importance of Samuelson's revealed preference theory? From the beginning, Samuelson's original insight and his unique sense of nomenclature served occasionally as a will-o'-the-wisp. Even the very name of "revealed preference" served as a dazzler for such expert readers as Robertson (1952, p. 19), who wrote about his first encounter with revealed preference theory as follows: "[T]he logicians and behaviorists, having tasted the blood of cardinal utility, were spurred to fresh efforts of purgation, which have resulted . . . in the development of the doctrine of 'revealed preference.' Dare I confess that when I first heard this term . . . I thought that perhaps to some latter-day saint, in some new Patmos off the coast of Massachusetts, the final solution of all these mysteries had been revealed in a new apocalypse? But alas! it does not mean that; all it means is that we are to construct an account of the consumer's behavior simply by observing, or rather imagining ourselves to observe, all the acts of choice which he performs in the market, without making any assumption about what goes on in his mind when he makes them." Since the declared purpose of Samuelson's revealed preference theory was to free the theory of consumer's behavior from the notion of utility, Robertson's view of the nature of this theory is understandable. But Samuelson's (1948, p. 243) own remark regarding the revelation of a preference pattern by individual market behavior (already quoted in the next-to-last paragraph of Section 1.4) reminds us of the fact that his theory is not really unconcerned with what goes on in the consumer's mind when he or she performs in the competitive markets.

Despite this and other ambiguities that surrounded the evolution of revealed preference theory, an important fact remains. As Mas-Colell (1982, p. 72) rightly observed, "[r]evealed preference is as foundational and purely theoretical a subject as one can find, and one cannot help thinking that this is part of its fascination. Indeed, of how many topics can it be said, to paraphrase what Samuelson wrote in the Georgescu-Roegen Festschrift, people will be discussing them a hundred years from now? Certainly, the pure theory of rational choice is one." It is Samuelson's revealed preference theory that not only opened the gate toward a general theory of rational choice, but also devised the most fundamental axiom around which the whole subsequent work evolved over seventy years. Mas-Colell's summary evaluation of the revealed preference approach was echoed in a recent paper by Varian (2006, p. 99), who observed that ". . . revealed preference must count as one of the most influential ideas in economics. At the time of its introduction, it was a major contribution to the pure theory of consumer behavior, and the basic idea has been applied in a number of other areas of economics."

Although much progress has been made regarding the rationalizability of choice functions on general domains if the rationalizing relation is required to be transitive (see, in particular, Richter, 1966), weaker coherence properties have been analyzed in a comprehensive manner only recently. We provide a thorough discussion of these contributions in Part II of this monograph. Part III is devoted to specific restricted domains that are of importance in many applications. These parts constitute a progress report of our work along the lines laid out by Samuelson and Houthakker.

## 1.7   Reference-Dependent Choice

In traditional choice theory, the decision maker chooses from any feasible set the greatest or maximal elements according to a preference relation. The testable restrictions implied by this optimization hypothesis are the subject matter discussed in the theory of revealed preference. In spite of its normative appeal, this optimization hypothesis may be considered too demanding in some circumstances and systematic violations have been recorded in several contexts; see, for instance, the surveys by Camerer (1995), Shafir and Tversky (1995), and Rabin (1998). In addition to violations of transitivity (which we address in Parts II and III of this monograph by allowing for rationalizability under less restrictive—or even no—coherence properties), the very postulate of preference-based choice has been called into question. For example, demand behavior frequently displays what are commonly referred to as *endowment effects* or *status quo biases*, claiming that a decision maker is more likely to choose an alternative $x$ over another alternative $y$ if $x$ is perceived as the status quo than if $y$ is. This phenomenon, first described by Thaler (1980), appears in experimental studies such as those of Knetsch (1989) and Kahneman, Knetsch, and Thaler (1991) as well as in non-experimental empirical work; see, for instance, Samuelson and Zeckhauser (1988).

In view of these observations, alternatives to the optimization hypothesis are worthwhile to explore. One possibility is to relax the assumption that a *single* preference relation underlies all observed choices, and to allow for the possibility that a decision maker seeks to optimize *context-dependent* preferences. This is explored in contributions such as those of Tversky and Kahneman (1991), Munro and Sugden (2003), and Sagi (2006), for example. In these approaches, the preference relation to be optimized may vary with the status quo and specific assumptions, such as the *loss-aversion hypothesis*, are made regarding the way in which preferences vary with the status quo alternative; see, for instance, Sagi (2006) for an axiom that explicitly introduces a status quo bias on the part of the decision maker.

The structure of such theories is not simple: choice depends on *several* preference relations; preferences may change with the status quo according to rather specific patterns; and preferences are optimized. Due to this complexity, it can be difficult to disentangle the role of the various assumptions. In particular, the role of the optimization hypothesis is hard to assess: indeed, it has no behavioral implications if preferences may vary *arbitrarily* with the choice context; this point emerges, for instance, in Kalai, Rubinstein, and Spiegler (2002) who analyze choices based on preference relations that vary with the feasible set (and not with a reference alternative). Duggan (1997) illustrates how restrictions on the way preferences may change with the feasible set can be imposed; see also Tyson (2008).

Assuming multiple preferences represents a drastic departure from classical theories of choice. Optimizing behavior imposes a strong form of coherence of choice across contexts. It is not obvious *how* drastic a deviation from the standard theory is required to account for the empirical evidence quoted above, and it may be useful to seek a "simplest" explanation of choices that is able to accommodate this evidence. For example, Kalai, Rubinstein, and Spiegler (2002) search for the smallest number of context-dependent preference relations whose maximization is compatible with a given choice function.

A second possible departure from classical revealed preference theory is to maintain the assumption that a *single* preference relation underlies all observable choices and to weaken the optimization hypothesis. This is the approach we discuss in Chapter 7 of this monograph. The theory we develop in detail is based on contributions by Bossert and Sprumont (2003, 2009) and Bossert and Suzumura (2007b). As in Tversky and Kahneman (1991) and much of the subsequent literature, we assume that, in any choice situation, a reference alternative exists. We depart from the reference-dependent preference approach by postulating a single preference relation. The central hypothesis is that an agent should not select an option that would make her or him worse off than the reference alternative—that is, choices should be what we call *non-deteriorating*. Non-deteriorating choice can be regarded as a "minimal" form of rationality. Stronger requirements may be considered too demanding and, in this context, Simon's (1955) notion of *satisficing* behavior, for instance, has received considerable attention. The approach followed here is related to Zhou (1997) and Masatlioglu and Ok (2005). Both of these contributions study reference-dependent choice functions but they do not examine the implications of the non-deterioration hypothesis.

## 1.8   External Norms

In his presidential address to the Econometric Society, Sen (1993) presented a criticism against a priori imposition of the requirement of internal consistency of choice such as the weak axiom of revealed preference. On the face of it, Sen's criticism may seem to run squarely against rational choice theory altogether. The gist of Sen's criticism can be phrased very simply as follows: "[C]an a set of choices really be seen as consistent or inconsistent on purely internal grounds *without* bringing in something *external* to choice, such as the underlying objectives or values that are pursued or acknowledged by choice?" To make Sen's point unambiguously, consider the following pair of choice sets:

$$C(\{x, y\}) = \{x\} \text{ and } C(\{x, y, z\}) = \{y\}. \tag{1.1}$$

By definition, we obtain $(x, y) \in R_C^s$ and $(y, x) \in R_C$, which is a clear violation of the weak axiom of revealed preference. As Sen (1993, p. 501) rightly pointed out, however, this seeming inconsistency can be easily resolved if only we understand more about the person's choice situation: "Suppose the person faces a choice at a dinner table between having the last remaining apple in the fruit basket $(y)$ and having nothing instead $(x)$, forgoing the nice-looking apple. She decides to behave decently and picks nothing $(x)$, rather than the one apple $(y)$. If, instead, the basket had contained two apples, and she had encountered the choice between having nothing $(x)$, having one nice apple $(y)$ and having another nice one $(z)$, she could reasonably enough choose one $(y)$, without violating any rule of good behavior. The presence of another apple $(z)$ makes one of the two apples decently choosable, but the combination of choices would violate the standard consistency condition ... even though there is nothing particularly 'inconsistent' in this pair of choices...."

There is another interpretation that may explain the choices expressed in (1.1), namely, that the feasible set itself conveys information about the nature of the options contained therein. This is what Sen (1993, p. 502) refers to as the *epistemic value* of a menu. The observation that feasible sets may have epistemic value has been made before. Luce and Raiffa (1957, p. 288) provide the following illuminating example: "A gentleman wandering in a strange city at dinner time chances upon a modest restaurant which he enters uncertainly. The waiter informs him that there is no menu, but that this evening he may have either broiled salmon at $2.50 or steak at $4.00. In a first-rate restaurant his choice would have been steak, but considering his unknown surroundings and the different prices he elects the salmon. Soon after the waiter returns from the kitchen, apologizes profusely, blaming the uncommunicative chef for omitting to tell him that fried snails and frog's legs are also on the bill of fare at $4.50 each. It so happens that our hero detests them both and would always select salmon in preference to either, yet his response is 'Splendid, I'll change my order to steak.' ... Yet can we argue that he is acting unreasonably? He, like most of us, has concluded from previous experience that only 'good' restaurants are likely to serve snails and frog's legs, and so the risk of a bad steak is lessened in his eyes." See also Bossert (2001) and Bossert and Suzumura (forthcoming 2010) for discussions.

What is the upshot of Sen's criticism against rationality of choice in terms of axioms such as the weak axiom of revealed preference? Sen's basic point is that "internal" consistency conditions on choice behavior may be incapable of capturing *external norms* (such as the maxim "Do not choose the last remaining apple"). In Chapter 8 of this monograph, we illustrate how Sen's concerns regarding external norms can be taken care of in the spirit of Samuelson-Houthakker revealed preference theory.

An early suggestion to deal with external norms was proposed by Baigent and Gaertner (1996). In response to Sen's (1993) criticism, they define a non-standard notion of rationalizability that obeys the restriction imposed by the external norm not to choose the *uniquely* greatest element according to some relation but conforms to the traditional version of rationalizability when the set of greatest objects contains at least two elements. According to Baigent and Gaertner (1996, p. 244), a choice function $C$ is *non-standard rationalizable* if there exists a transitive relation $R$ on $X$ such that, for all feasible sets $S$, $C(S)$ consists of the set of greatest elements of the subset of $S$ that is obtained if the unique greatest element is removed; if there is no unique greatest element, the choice function selects all greatest elements according to $R$ as in the traditional setting. The characterization of non-standard rationalizability established by Baigent and Gaertner (1996) applies to the extended domain consisting of all non-empty subsets of $X$ and they assume $X$ to be finite. The set of chosen elements is assumed to be non-empty and, thus, they implicitly exclude singleton sets from their domain.

External norms can be taken into consideration by specifying all pairs consisting of a feasible set and an element of this set with the interpretation that this element is prohibited from being chosen from this set by the relevant system of external norms. *Norm-conditional rationalizability* then requires the existence of a preference relation such that, for each feasible set in the domain of the choice function, the chosen elements are at least as good as all elements in the set except for those that are prohibited by the external norm. We discuss this general method of accommodating external norms in Chapter 8. See Xu (2007) for a discussion of some special cases of this approach.

## 1.9   Welfare Economics and Social Choice Theory

Little (1949, p. 98) expresses an optimistic view as to the potential of revealed preference theory to serve as a foundation of welfare economics: "No one would to-day want to *identify* 'an increase in welfare' with 'a higher level of satisfaction as anticipated by the individual.' The transition to welfare economics can still be made in various ways depending on one's views. One could, for instance, say that a person is, on the whole, likely to be happier the more he is able to have what he would choose. Or, alternatively, one can say that it is a good thing that he should be able to have what he would choose."

Another early response to the emergence of revealed preference theory came from none other than Hicks. Recollect that the declared purpose of Samuelson's theory was to provide a substitute to the ordinalist utilitarian Pareto-Hicks theory of consumer's behavior. Hicks, one of the major proponents of the latter theory, accepted the research program of revealed preference theory and set about revising his own theory of consumer's behavior presented in *Value and Capital* (Hicks, 1939). In *A Revision of Demand Theory* (Hicks, 1956, preface, p. vi), he recollected as follows: "In the autumn of 1951 I gave a course of public lectures at the London School of Economics, on 'Demand and Welfare'; in one of these lectures I gave a sketch of what was to become the central part of [*A Revision of Demand Theory*]." This, in itself, is somewhat surprising, as Samuelson himself took extra care to dissociate his revealed preference theory from welfare analysis. Indeed, Samuelson (1938a, p. 71) concluded his first article on revealed preference theory with the following remark: "[N]othing said here in the field of consumer behavior affects in any way or touches upon at any point the problem of welfare economics, except in the sense of revealing the confusion in the traditional theory of these distinct subjects."

However, Hicks was confident that any new theory of demand should open a novel gate toward welfare application: "If one starts from a theory of demand like that of Marshall and his contemporaries, it is exceedingly natural to look for a welfare application. If the general aim of the economic system is the satisfaction of consumers' wants, and if the satisfaction of individual wants is to be conceived of as a maximizing of Utility, cannot the aim of the system be itself conceived of as a maximizing of utility, Universal Utility as Edgeworth called it? If this could be done, and some measure of universal utility could be found, the economist's function could be widened out, from the understanding of cause and effect to the judgment of the effects—whether, from the point of view of want-satisfaction they are to be judged as successful or unsuccessful, good or bad. Economists have always felt that such judgement or assessment was in some way a part of their business" (Hicks, 1956, p. 6). As a manifesto on the role economists should play, Hicks's statement to this effect has a strong appeal. But the real test is how "some measure of universal utility" can be constructed. Hicks went on to observe that "[d]emand theory, in its Marshallian form, appeared to offer a strikingly simple and powerful way of making such judgements. . . . It must be admitted—and indeed emphasized—that the econometric theory of demand provides no such easy and natural transition to welfare economics as the Marshallian theory appeared to give us. The econometric theory of demand does study human beings, but only as entities having certain patterns of market behavior; it makes no claim, no pretense, to be able to see inside their heads. But welfare economics has a strong tendency to go farther—if we like, to aim higher. There is therefore a chasm which has to be passed, a bridge which needs to be built" (Hicks, 1956, p. 6). Hicks was convinced that it is not impossible to build such a bridge, and he expressed his intention "to make as precise a statement as [he] can of the way in which [he] would now endeavor to build it" (Hicks, 1956, p. 6). Unfortunately, this intention was left unaccomplished not only in *A Revision of Demand Theory*, but also in his subsequently published work.

There are two unpublished manuscripts, namely, Hicks (n.d., ca. 1955) and Hicks (n.d., ca. 1963), which are supposed to be preliminary drafts of the synthesis of his welfare economics, but something important seems to have happened to Hicks in between these two manuscripts. In his preface to *Essays in World Economics* (Hicks, 1959, pp. viii–ix), Hicks declared his farewell to the traditional approach to welfare economics: "The view which, now, I do not hold I propose . . . to call 'Economic Welfarism': for it is one of the tendencies which has taken its origin from that great and immensely influential work, the *Economics of Welfare* of Pigou. . . . The line between Economic Welfarism and its opposite is not concerned with what economists call utilities; it is concerned with the transition from Utility to the more general good. . . ." Why was Hicks led to this conversion? According to Hicks (1959, pp. x–xi), it was because he came to the strong belief that "when the economist makes a recommendation, he is responsible for it in the round; all aspects of that recommendation, whether he chooses to label them economic or not, are his concern." Despite this declaration against Economic Welfarism, Hicks was not ready to jump to the other polar extreme: "I have ... no intention, in abandoning Economic Welfarism, of falling into the 'fiat libertas, ruat caelum' which some latter-day liberals seem to see as the only alternative. What I do maintain is that the liberal goals are goods; that they are values which, however, must be weighed up against other values." This seems to explain the great shift of emphasis in between the two unpublished manuscripts of Hicks. Indeed, Hicks (n.d., ca. 1963) exhibited a conspicuous resemblance to the classical economists who emphasized materialistic opulence rather than subjective happiness.

Considering more recent developments in welfare economics and its link to decision analysis, we note that behavioral approaches to welfare economics have started to attract the attention of choice theorists; see, for instance, Bernheim and Rangel (2007), Gul and Pesendorfer (2007), and Kőszegi and Rabin (2007). Although this may well turn out to become an active area of research, we do not include a detailed discussion here owing to the different theme we have chosen as the focus of this monograph. More generally, we do not pursue the welfare implications of rational choice theory. However, concerning Hicks's problem of how to construct some measure of universal utility, we do have something to say on how Suzumura consistency can play an important role in establishing the existence of collective choice rules with additional appealing properties in Chapter 9. Following Arrow's (1951, 1963) impossibility theorem, one way of escape has been to relax the requirements imposed on social rankings. Because this opens up the possibility of non-dictatorial rules, there is the potential to impose further plausible properties on collective choice rules. Some pioneering work in that regard has been done by Sen (1969, 1970), Mas-Colell and Sonnenschein (1972), Plott (1973), Brown (1975), Blair and Pollak (1982), Weymark (1984), and Banks (1995), among others. Sen (1969, 1970) weakened Arrow's transitivity assumption to quasi-transitivity (see also Plott, 1973) while retaining the richness properties of reflexivity and completeness. Together with a strengthening of weak Pareto and an anonymity condition that requires individuals to be treated impartially (thus ruling out dictatorships), he obtained a characterization of the Pareto extension rule. The *Pareto rule* generates transitive but not necessarily complete social relations for all possible profiles of individual preferences. It declares an alternative at least as good as another if everyone in society agrees that the former is at least as good as the latter. As such, it is clear that it generates a substantial amount of non-comparability: whenever at least two agents disagree on the strict ranking of two alternatives, the social rule is silent regarding their comparison. The *Pareto extension rule* replaces non-comparability with indifference, thus generating complete social relations at the expense of transitivity. Although not transitive, the resulting relations are always quasi-transitive. Weymark (1984) retained transitivity of the social relation as a requirement but dropped completeness, thereby arriving at a characterization of the Pareto rule. However, replacing transitivity with quasi-transitivity does not help us much in finding an escape route from Arrow's (1951, 1963) impasse as long as Arrow's other assumptions are retained and slightly strengthened in certain ways; see Mas-Colell and Sonnenschein (1972), for instance. Acyclical social preferences have been analyzed by authors such as Brown (1975), Blair and Pollak (1982), and Banks (1995), among others. It should be noted that additional properties such as variants of *non-negative responsiveness* are frequently invoked in these earlier contributions.

In Chapter 9, we follow in the footsteps of these explorations by examining the consequences of weakening transitivity to Suzumura consistency and dropping the completeness assumption on social relations. It turns out that we obtain a richer set of collective choice rules as compared to the Pareto rule, provided that the set of alternatives is "small" relative to the set of individuals. This is, for example, the case in elections where a large number of voters make selections from a small number of political parties or candidates.

## 1.10   Beyond Finite-Population Social Choice

Arrow's (1951, 1963) theorem establishing the existence of a dictator as a consequence of a set of seemingly innocuous properties of a social welfare function is the most fundamental result in the theory of social choice. Its conclusion depends crucially on the assumption that the population under consideration is finite and alternative methods of proof provided by authors such as Fishburn (1970), Sen (1979), and Suzumura (2000) highlight the important role played by this finiteness property. Kirman and Sondermann (1972) and Hansson (1976) consider the structure of *decisive coalitions* in the Arrovian framework. A coalition (that is, a subset of the population) is decisive if its members can always guarantee a strict social preference for any alternative over any other if all coalition members have a strict preference for the former. Kirman and Sondermann (1972) and Hansson (1976) establish that, in the general case where the population may be finite or infinite, the set of decisive coalitions forms an *ultrafilter*, given that social relations are assumed to be orderings and Arrow's axioms of unrestricted domain, weak Pareto, and independence of irrelevant alternatives are satisfied. In the finite-population case, all ultrafilters are *principal* ultrafilters—that is, they are generated by a singleton. This singleton is, by definition of the decisiveness property, a dictator. Thus, the results of these two papers generate Arrow's theorem as a corollary. In contrast, if the population is infinite, there exist non-principal ultrafilters and these ultrafilters correspond to decisive coalition structures that are non-dictatorial. Kirman and Sondermann (1972) argue that sets of decisive coalitions that are non-principal ultrafilters still have a dictatorial flavor when expressed in a different space (leading to what they refer to as "invisible" dictators) but this does not make the underlying social welfare functions themselves dictatorial; see Hansson (1976) for a discussion. As in the original Arrovian setting, Hansson assumes in his first set of results that a collective choice rule always generates orderings. Moreover, he considers the case where social preferences are merely quasi-transitive but not necessarily transitive while retaining the richness properties of reflexivity and completeness. In this case, the family of decisive coalitions does not necessarily form an ultrafilter but it always is a *filter*.

There has been some renewed interest in specific applications of infinite-population Arrovian social choice, particularly in the context of infinite-horizon social choice problems where the unidirectional flow of time permits some natural domain restrictions. Treating generations equally is one of the fundamental principles in the utilitarian tradition of moral philosophy. As Sidgwick (1907, p. 414) observed, "the time at which a man exists cannot affect the value of his happiness from a universal point of view; and ... the interests of posterity must concern a Utilitarian as much as those of his contemporaries." This view, which is formally expressed by the anonymity axiom, was also endorsed quite forcefully by Ramsey (1928). Following the lead of Koopmans (1960), Diamond (1965) established that anonymity is incompatible with strong Pareto when ordering infinite utility streams. Moreover, he showed that if anonymity is weakened to *finite* anonymity—which restricts the application of the standard anonymity requirement to situations where utility streams differ in at most a finite number of components—and a continuity requirement is added, an impossibility results again. Basu and Mitra (2003) show that strong

Pareto, finite anonymity, and representability by a real-valued function are incompatible.

Asheim and Tungodden (2004) provide a characterization of an infinite-horizon version of the leximin principle by adding an equity-preference condition and a preference-continuity property to strong Pareto and finite anonymity. An infinite-horizon version of utilitarianism is characterized by Basu and Mitra (2007) by adding an information-invariance condition to the two fundamental axioms. Focusing on equity properties such as the (*strict*) *transfer principle*, Bossert, Sprumont, and Suzumura (2007) characterize extensions of an infinite-horizon formulation of the well-known generalized Lorenz quasi-ordering. See also Asheim, Mitra, and Tungodden (2007) and Hara, Shinotsuka, Suzumura, and Xu (2008) for equity properties in the infinite-horizon context. A choice-theoretic approach to infinite-horizon resource allocation problems is pursued in Asheim, Bossert, Sprumont, and Suzumura (2010).

Ferejohn and Page (1978) and Packel (1980) follow a multi-profile approach to intergenerational infinite-horizon social choice. They analyze the consequences of imposing a stationarity property and come up largely with negative results.

In Chapter 10, we reexamine the infinite-population approach from two different angles. First, we relax the properties imposed on social preferences by Hansson (1976) and then we follow up on Ferejohn and Page's (1978) and Packel's (1980) model involving stationary multi-profile intergenerational social choice.

# — 2 —

# Mathematical Background

## 2.1 Binary Relations

Clearly, binary relations are at the very heart of the subject matter investigated in this monograph. While particular attention is devoted to Suzumura-consistent relations, other coherence properties and, in fact, numerous additional aspects of the theory of binary relations are of essential importance. We therefore begin our review of the fundamental mathematical techniques relevant for this monograph with a discussion of binary relations, their properties, and some important methods and results concerning their application to individual and collective choice problems.

Consider a non-empty (but otherwise arbitrary) set of alternatives $X$ and let $R \subseteq X \times X$ be a (binary) relation on $X$. The following are some standard properties of such a relation.

**Symmetry**   For all $x, y \in X$,

$$(x, y) \in R \Rightarrow (y, x) \in R.$$

**Asymmetry**   For all $x, y \in X$,

$$(x, y) \in R \Rightarrow (y, x) \notin R.$$

**Antisymmetry**   For all $x, y \in X$,

$$[(x, y) \in R \text{ and } (y, x) \in R] \Rightarrow x = y.$$

The *symmetric factor* $I(R)$ of $R$ is defined by

$$I(R) = \{(x, y) \mid (x, y) \in R \text{ and } (y, x) \in R\}.$$

The *asymmetric factor* $P(R)$ of $R$ is defined by

$$P(R) = \{(x, y) \mid (x, y) \in R \text{ and } (y, x) \notin R\}.$$

The *non-comparable factor* $NC(R)$ of $R$ is defined by

$$NC(R) = \{(x, y) \in X \times X \mid (x, y) \notin R \text{ and } (y, x) \notin R\}.$$

If $R$ is interpreted as a *weak preference relation*, that is, $(x, y) \in R$ means that $x$ is considered at least as good as $y$, $P(R)$, $I(R)$, and $NC(R)$ can be interpreted as the *strict preference relation*, the *indifference relation*, and the *non-comparability relation* corresponding to $R$, respectively. Clearly, $I(R)$ and $NC(R)$ are symmetric and $P(R)$ is asymmetric for any binary relation $R$. The *diagonal relation* on $X$ is given by $\Delta = \{(x, x) \mid x \in X\}$.

Two fundamental properties of a binary relation $R$ are those of *reflexivity* and *completeness*. They are defined as follows.

**Reflexivity**   $\Delta \subseteq R$.

**Completeness**   For all $x, y \in X$ such that $x \neq y$,

$$(x, y) \in R \text{ or } (y, x) \in R.$$

These two properties are what we refer to as *richness* conditions imposed on a binary relation. The use of this term is motivated by the observation that the properties in this group require that, at least, some pairs must belong to the relation. In the case of reflexivity, all pairs of the form $(x, x)$ are required to be in the relation, whereas completeness demands that, for any two *distinct* alternatives $x$ and $y$, at least one of $(x, y)$ and $(y, x)$ must be in $R$. In some contributions, reflexivity and completeness are merged into a single condition, requiring that, for all $x, y \in X$, we have $(x, y) \in R$ or $(y, x) \in R$ without the qualification that $x$ and $y$ are distinct. We prefer to follow the approach introduced above in separating the two properties because we think that there are conceptual differences between the comparability of an alternative with itself and the comparability of two distinct (and possibly quite heterogeneous) alternatives.

A third fundamental property of a binary relation is *transitivity*. It requires that if $(x, y)$ and $(y, z)$ are in $R$ for any three alternatives $x, y, z \in X$, then the pair $(x, z)$ must be in $R$ as well.

**Transitivity**   For all $x, y, z \in X$,

$$[(x, y) \in R \text{ and } (y, z) \in R] \Rightarrow (x, z) \in R.$$

A reflexive and transitive relation is called a *quasi-ordering* and a complete quasi-ordering is called an *ordering*.

An important notion that is used frequently throughout this monograph is that of the *transitive closure* of a binary relation (see also our discussion in Chapter 1). The transitive closure $tc(R)$ of a relation $R$ on $X$ is

$$tc(R) = \{(x, y) \mid \exists K \in \mathbb{N} \text{ and } x^0, \ldots, x^K \in X \text{ such that}$$
$$[x = x^0 \text{ and } (x^{k-1}, x^k) \in R \text{ for all } k \in \{1, \ldots, K\} \text{ and } x^K = y]\}.$$

$$(2.1)$$

To illustrate this definition, consider the following example. Let $X = \{x, y, z, v\}$ and $R = \{(x, y), (x, z), (z, v)\}$. The transitive closure of $R$ is given by

$$tc(R) = \{(x, y), (x, z), (x, v), (z, v)\} = R \cup \{(x, v)\} \supseteq R.$$

In this example, the relation $R$ is a subset of its transitive closure $tc(R)$. This is no coincidence but a general result that applies to any closure operation; see, for instance, Berge (1963, p. 12) for details. We gather some important properties of the closure operator $tc$ on the set of all binary relations on $X$ in the following theorem.

**Theorem 2.1**  *Let $R$ and $R'$ be relations on $X$.*

*(i) $R \subseteq tc(R)$.*
*(ii) $R$ is transitive if and only if $R = tc(R)$.*
*(iii) $tc(R)$ is the smallest transitive relation containing $R$.*
*(iv) If $R \subseteq R'$, then $tc(R) \subseteq tc(R')$.*

**Proof**  (i) Let $(x, y) \in R$ for some $x, y \in X$. Setting $K = 1$ in (2.1) immediately yields $(x, y) \in tc(R)$.

(ii) In view of part (i), it is sufficient to prove that $tc(R) \subseteq R$ if $R$ is transitive. Let $(x, y) \in tc(R)$ for some $x, y \in X$. By (2.1), there exist $K \in \mathbb{N}$ and $x^0, \ldots, x^K \in X$ such that

$$x = x^0 \text{ and } (x^{k-1}, x^k) \in R \text{ for all } k \in \{1, \ldots, K\} \text{ and } x^K = y.$$

By (repeated if necessary) application of the transitivity of $R$, we obtain $(x, y) = (x^0, x^K) \in R$.

(iii) We begin by establishing the transitivity of $tc(R)$. Let $x, y, z \in X$ be such that $(x, y) \in tc(R)$ and $(y, z) \in tc(R)$. By definition of the transitive closure, $(x, y) \in tc(R)$ means that there exist $K \in \mathbb{N}$ and $x^0, \ldots, x^K \in X$ such that

$$x = x^0 \text{ and } (x^{k-1}, x^k) \in R \text{ for all } k \in \{1, \ldots, K\} \text{ and } x^K = y.$$

Analogously, $(y, z) \in tc(R)$ implies that there exist $L \in \mathbb{N}$ and $y^0, \ldots, y^L \in X$ such that

$$y = y^0 \text{ and } (y^{\ell-1}, y^\ell) \in R \text{ for all } \ell \in \{1, \ldots, L\} \text{ and } y^L = z.$$

Define $J = K + L$ and let the alternatives $z^0, \ldots, z^J \in X$ be such that $x = x^0 = z^0$, $z^j = x^j$ for all $j \in \{1, \ldots, K\}$, $z^j = y^{j-K}$ for all $j \in \{K+1, \ldots, K+L\}$ and $z^J = y^L = z$. According to (2.1), we obtain $(x, z) \in tc(R)$.

Now suppose that $Q$ is an arbitrary transitive relation containing $R$. To complete the proof of part (iii), we establish that $tc(R) \subseteq Q$. Suppose that $(x, y) \in tc(R)$ for some $x, y \in X$. Because $R \subseteq Q$, it follows that there exist $K \in \mathbb{N}$ and $x^0, \ldots, x^K \in X$ such that

$$x = x^0 \text{ and } (x^{k-1}, x^k) \in Q \text{ for all } k \in \{1, \ldots, K\} \text{ and } x^K = y,$$

and the transitivity of $Q$ implies $(x, y) \in Q$.

(iv) Suppose $R \subseteq R'$ and $(x, y) \in tc(R)$. This conjunction implies that there exist $K \in \mathbb{N}$ and $x^0, \ldots, x^K \in X$ such that

$$x = x^0 \text{ and } (x^{k-1}, x^k) \in R' \text{ for all } k \in \{1, \ldots, K\} \text{ and } x^K = y.$$

By definition, $(x, y) \in tc(R')$.   ∎

In spite of its predominant position in theories of individual and collective choice, violations of transitivity are quite likely to be observed in practical choice situations. For instance, Luce's (1956) well-known coffee-sugar example provides a plausible argument against assuming that indifference is always transitive: the inability of a decision maker to perceive "small" differences in alternatives is bound to lead to intransitivities. As this example illustrates, transitivity frequently is too strong an assumption to impose in the context of individual choice. In collective choice problems, it is even more evident that the plausibility of transitivity can be called into question. For that reason, weakenings of transitivity have been proposed in the literature. Two of the most prominent ones are *quasi-transitivity* and *acyclicity*, defined as follows.

**Quasi-transitivity**   $P(R)$ is transitive.

**Acyclicity**   For all $x, y \in X$,

$$(x, y) \in tc(P(R)) \Rightarrow (y, x) \notin P(R).$$

Clearly, an equivalent definition of acyclicity is obtained by writing out the transitive closure relationship between $x$ and $y$ explicitly. That is, acyclicity can alternatively be defined as follows. For all $x, y \in X$, for all $K \in \mathbb{N}$, and for all $x^0, \ldots, x^K \in X$,

$$[x = x^0 \text{ and } (x^{k-1}, x^k) \in P(R) \text{ for all } k \in \{1, \ldots, K\} \text{ and } x^K = y]$$
$$\Rightarrow (y, x) \notin P(R).$$

Quasi-transitivity is an obvious way of weakening transitivity: transitivity is restricted to the asymmetric factor of $R$ and, in particular, indifference need not be transitive. The term was coined by Sen (1969; 1970, chapter 1*), and it has been employed in numerous approaches to the theory of individual and social choice, including issues related to rationalizability.

Acyclicity rules out the presence of strict preference cycles. One of its important implications is that it, together with reflexivity and completeness, is not only sufficient for the existence of greatest elements in any arbitrary finite subset of a universal set, but it is also necessary for the existence of such elements in all finite subsets of the universal set; see Sen (1970, chapter 1*) and our discussion of greatest and maximal elements later in this chapter.

An alternative weakening of transitivity is *Suzumura consistency*, an axiom introduced by Suzumura (1976b). In contrast to acyclicity, it rules out not only strict preference cycles but all cycles with at least one strict preference.

**Suzumura consistency**    For all $x, y \in X$,

$$(x, y) \in tc(R) \Rightarrow (y, x) \notin P(R).$$

As is the case for acyclicity, Suzumura consistency can alternatively be defined by explicit use of the relevant transitive closure relationship to obtain the following equivalent formulation. For all $x, y \in X$, for all $K \in \mathbb{N}$, and for all $x^0, \ldots, x^K \in X$,

$$[x = x^0 \text{ and } (x^{k-1}, x^k) \in R \text{ for all } k \in \{1, \ldots, K\} \text{ and } x^K = y]$$
$$\Rightarrow (y, x) \notin P(R).$$

The four properties of transitivity, quasi-transitivity, acyclicity, and Suzumura consistency are *coherence* properties. They require that if certain pairs belong to $R$, then certain other pairs must belong to $R$ as well (as is the case for transitivity and quasi-transitivity) or certain other pairs cannot belong to $R$ (which applies to the cases of acyclicity and Suzumura consistency). Quasi-transitivity and Suzumura consistency are independent. A transitive relation is quasi-transitive, and a quasi-transitive relation is acyclical. Moreover, a transitive relation is Suzumura consistent, and a

Suzumura-consistent relation is acyclical. We summarize these observations in the following theorem. For convenience, a diagrammatic representation is employed in its statement. An arrow pointing from one box $b$ to another box $b'$ indicates that the axiom in $b$ implies that in $b'$, and the converse implication is not true. In addition, of course, all implications resulting from chains of arrows depicted in the diagram are valid.

**Theorem 2.2** *Let $R$ be a relation on $X$. Then*

**Proof** (a) Suppose $R$ is transitive and let $x, y, z \in X$ be such that $(x, y) \in P(R)$ and $(y, z) \in P(R)$. Because $P(R) \subseteq R$, the transitivity of $R$ implies $(x, z) \in R$. By way of contradiction, suppose it is also true that $(z, x) \in R$. Because $(x, y) \in P(R) \subseteq R$, the transitivity of $R$ implies $(z, y) \in R$, in contradiction to the assumption that $(y, z) \in P(R)$ and thus $(z, y) \notin R$. Therefore, $(z, x) \notin R$ and thus $(x, z) \in P(R)$.

(b) To see that transitivity implies Suzumura consistency, suppose $R$ is transitive and $x, y \in X$ are such that $(x, y) \in tc(R)$. Because $R$ is transitive, we obtain $(x, y) \in R$, which immediately implies $(y, x) \notin P(R)$. Thus, $R$ is Suzumura consistent.

(c) Now suppose $R$ is quasi-transitive and $(x, y) \in tc(P(R))$ for some $x, y \in X$. By applying quasi-transitivity (repeatedly if necessary), we obtain $(x, y) \in P(R)$ and thus $(y, x) \notin P(R)$.

(d) The remaining implication follows from the set inclusion $P(R) \subseteq R$ and the resulting set inclusion $tc(P(R)) \subseteq tc(R)$ established in part (iv) of Theorem 2.1.

To establish that no further implications other than those resulting from the arrows in the theorem statement are valid, it is sufficient to provide examples showing that (e) quasi-transitivity does not imply Suzumura consistency; (f) Suzumura consistency does not imply quasi-transitivity; (g) acyclicity does not imply quasi-transitivity and acyclicity does not imply Suzumura consistency. For all of these examples, we assume that the universal set is given by $X = \{x, y, z\}$.

(e) Let $R = \{(x, y), (y, x), (y, z), (z, x), (z, y)\}$. This relation is quasi-transitive but not Suzumura consistent.

(f) Now let $R = \{(x, y), (y, z)\}$. $R$ is Suzumura consistent but not quasi-transitive.

(g) Finally, let $R = \{(x, y), (x, z), (y, z), (z, x)\}$. $R$ is acyclical but not Suzumura consistent and not quasi-transitive. ∎

The discrepancy between transitivity and Suzumura consistency established in the previous theorem disappears for relations that are reflexive and complete; see Suzumura (1983, p. 244). This equivalence result is an immediate consequence of the following theorem.

**Theorem 2.3** *If a relation R on X is reflexive, complete, and Suzumura consistent, then R is transitive, hence an ordering.*

**Proof** Suppose $R$ is reflexive, complete, and Suzumura consistent. Let $x, y, z \in X$ be such that $(x, y) \in R$ and $(y, z) \in R$. If $x = z$, $(x, z) \in R$ follows from reflexivity. Now suppose $x \neq z$. By Suzumura consistency, $(z, x) \notin P(R)$. Because $x \neq z$, $(x, z) \in NC(R)$ conflicts with completeness. Therefore, $(x, z) \notin NC(R)$. Together with the observation $(z, x) \notin P(R)$, this implies $(x, z) \in R$ and $R$ is transitive. Thus, $R$ is an ordering. ∎

The concept of Suzumura consistency has some important characteristics that distinguish it from the other two weakenings of transitivity. For example, this property is precisely what is required to prevent the existence of a "money pump." If Suzumura consistency is violated, there exists a preference cycle with at least one strict preference. In this case, an agent with such preferences is willing to trade (where "willingness to trade" is assumed to require that the alternative acquired in the trade is at least as good as that relinquished) an alternative $x^K$ for another alternative $x^{K-1}$, $x^{K-1}$ for an alternative $x^{K-2}$, and so on until we reach an alternative $x^0$ such that the agent *strictly prefers* getting back $x^K$ to retaining possession of $x^0$. Thus, at the end of a chain of exchanges, the agent is willing to pay a positive amount in order to get back the original alternative—a classical example of a money pump.

There is yet another reason for the importance of the concept of Suzumura consistency. As shown in Suzumura (1976b; 1983, chapter 1), Suzumura consistency is necessary and sufficient for the existence of an ordering that subsumes all the pairwise information contained in the binary relation. See Theorem 2.8 stated and proven later in this chapter.

In analogy to the transitive closure of a relation $R$, there exists a unique smallest Suzumura-consistent relation containing $R$—the *Suzumura-consistent closure* of $R$. As is the case for the transitive closure, this operation plays a fundamental role in our analysis. In contrast, there is no analogue for quasi-transitivity and for acyclicity; these two coherence properties do not permit an unambiguous minimal way of capturing the nature of a relation by means of a superset that satisfies the requisite coherence condition. The Suzumura-consistent closure $sc(R)$ of a binary relation $R$ is defined by

$$sc(R) = R \cup \{(x, y) \mid (x, y) \in tc(R) \text{ and } (y, x) \in R\}. \qquad (2.2)$$

To illustrate the definition of the Suzumura-consistent closure and its relationship to the transitive closure, consider the following examples. Let $X = \{x, y, z\}$, and define two relations $R$ and $R'$ on $X$ by $R = \{(x, x), (x, y), (y, y), (y, z), (z, x), (z, z)\}$ and $R' = \{(x, y), (y, z)\}$. We obtain $sc(R) = tc(R) = X \times X$, $sc(R') = R'$ and $tc(R') = \{(x, y), (y, z), (x, z)\}$. The Suzumura-consistent closure of $R$ coincides with the transitive closure thereof, whereas the Suzumura-consistent closure of $R'$ is a strict subset of the transitive closure of $R'$. In general, for any relation $R$ on $X$, $R$ is always a subset of $sc(R)$, which, in turn, is always a subset of $tc(R)$; see part (i) of Theorem 2.4 below. Moreover, Theorem 2.4 establishes additional important properties of the Suzumura-consistent closure of a relation $R$ analogous to those of the transitive closure reported in Theorem 2.1.

**Theorem 2.4** *Let $R$ and $R'$ be relations on $X$.*

(i) $R \subseteq sc(R) \subseteq tc(R)$.
(ii) $R$ is Suzumura consistent if and only if $R = sc(R)$.
(iii) $sc(R)$ is the smallest Suzumura-consistent relation containing $R$.
(iv) If $R \subseteq R'$, then $sc(R) \subseteq sc(R')$.

**Proof** (i) The set inclusions follow immediately from the definition of $sc(R)$ and part (i) of Theorem 2.1.

(ii) In view of the first set inclusion established in part (i), it is sufficient to prove that $sc(R) \subseteq R$ if $R$ is Suzumura consistent. Let $(x, y) \in sc(R)$ for some $x, y \in X$. By (2.2), $(x, y) \in R$ or $[(x, y) \in tc(R)$ and $(y, x) \in R]$. If $(x, y) \in R$, we are done. In the other case, the assumption $(x, y) \notin R$

immediately implies $(y, x) \in P(R)$ in view of $(y, x) \in R$, contradicting the Suzumura consistency of $R$. Thus, $(x, y) \in R$ in all cases.

(iii) We first prove that $sc(R)$ is Suzumura consistent. Suppose $x, y \in X$ are such that $(x, y) \in tc(sc(R))$. We have to establish that $(y, x) \notin P(sc(R))$. Using part (i) and the transitivity of $tc(R)$, we obtain $(x, y) \in tc(R)$. If $(y, x) \notin sc(R)$, we immediately obtain $(y, x) \notin P(sc(R))$ and we are done. If $(y, x) \in sc(R)$, we must have $(y, x) \in R$ or $[(y, x) \in tc(R)$ and $(x, y) \in R]$.

If $(y, x) \in R$, $(x, y) \in tc(R)$ and the definition of $sc(R)$ together imply $(x, y) \in sc(R)$ and, thus, $(y, x) \notin P(sc(R))$. If $(y, x) \in tc(R)$ and $(x, y) \in R$, $(x, y) \in sc(R)$ follows because $R \subseteq sc(R)$. Again, this implies $(y, x) \notin P(sc(R))$ and the proof that $sc(R)$ is Suzumura consistent is complete.

To show that $sc(R)$ is the smallest Suzumura-consistent relation containing $R$, suppose that $Q$ is an arbitrary Suzumura-consistent relation containing $R$. To complete the proof, we establish that $sc(R) \subseteq Q$. Suppose that $(x, y) \in sc(R)$. By the definition of $sc(R)$,

$$(x, y) \in R \text{ or } [(x, y) \in tc(R) \text{ and } (y, x) \in R].$$

If $(x, y) \in R$, $(x, y) \in Q$ follows because $R$ is contained in $Q$ by assumption. If $(x, y) \in tc(R)$ and $(y, x) \in R$, part (i) and the assumption $R \subseteq Q$ together imply that $(x, y) \in tc(Q)$ and $(y, x) \in Q$. If $(x, y) \notin Q$, we obtain $(y, x) \in P(Q)$ in view of $(y, x) \in Q$. Since $(x, y) \in tc(Q)$, this contradicts the Suzumura consistency of $Q$. Therefore, we must have $(x, y) \in Q$.

(iv) Suppose $R \subseteq R'$ and $(x, y) \in sc(R)$. By definition of $sc(R)$, $(x, y) \in R$ or $[(x, y) \in tc(R)$ and $(y, x) \in R]$.

If $(x, y) \in R$, the assumption $R \subseteq R'$ implies $(x, y) \in R'$ and, by part (i), $(x, y) \in sc(R')$ and we are done.

If $(x, y) \in tc(R)$ and $(y, x) \in R$, the conjunction of the assumption $R \subseteq R'$ and part (iv) of Theorem 2.1 implies $(x, y) \in tc(R')$, and the assumption $R \subseteq R'$ implies $(y, x) \in R'$. Thus, $(x, y) \in sc(R')$ by definition of the Suzumura-consistent closure.  ∎

There is a reason why we do not introduce an analogous closure operation for quasi-transitivity and for acyclicity. Intuitively, when moving from $R$ to $tc(R)$ or to $sc(R)$, pairs are added that are *necessarily* in any transitive or Suzumura-consistent relation containing $R$. As soon as there exist alternatives $x^0, \ldots, x^K$ connecting $x$ and $y$ via a chain of preferences, transitivity demands that the pair $(x, y)$ is included in any transitive relation that contains $R$. Analogously, a chain of that nature implies that if, in addition, the pair $(y, x)$ is in $R$, $(x, y)$ must be added if the resulting relation is to be Suzu-mura consistent. In contrast, there are no necessary additions to a relation in order to transform it into a quasi-transitive relation by augmenting it. For instance, suppose we have $(x, y) \in P(R)$, $(y, z) \in P(R)$, and $(z, x) \in P(R)$. In order to define a quasi-transitive relation that contains $R$, at least two of the three strict preferences must be converted into indifferences but *any two* will do. Thus, there is no unique smallest quasi-transitive relation contain-ing $R$. Similarly, if we have a cycle of strict preferences, an acyclical relation containing $R$ merely has to have the property that *at least one* of the pairs along the cycle, representing a strict preference, must be converted into an indifference. But there is nothing that forces this indifference on a specific pair along the cycle. As a consequence, there is, in general, no unique small-est acyclical relation containing an arbitrary relation $R$. Incidentally, this also explains why some versions of rationalizability by a quasi-transitive or an acyclical relation are more difficult to characterize than versions of rationalizability involving transitivity or Suzumura consistency. We return to this issue in Chapter 4.

## 2.2   Greatest and Maximal Elements

Our next task is that of introducing the concepts of greatestness and maxi-mality with respect to a relation. Let $\mathcal{X}$ be the set of all non-empty subsets of $X$. Given a relation $R$ on $X$ and a set $S \in \mathcal{X}$, we define the set $G(S, R)$ of all *R-greatest elements* of $S$ by

$$G(S, R) = \{x \in S \mid (x, y) \in R \text{ for all } y \in S\}$$

and the set $M(S, R)$ of all *R-maximal elements* of $S$ by

$$M(S, R) = \{x \in S \mid (y, x) \notin P(R) \text{ for all } y \in S\}.$$

The sets $G(S, R)$ and $M(S, R)$ are related as follows.

**Theorem 2.5**  *Suppose $R$ is a relation on $X$ and $S \in \mathcal{X}$.*

 *(i) $G(S, R) \subseteq M(S, R)$.*
 *(ii) If $R$ is reflexive and complete, then $G(S, R) = M(S, R)$.*

**Proof**  (i) Because $(x, y) \in R$ excludes the possibility of $(y, x) \in P(R)$, $M(S, R)$ must be a superset of $G(S, R)$.

To prove part (ii), we have only to note that $(y, x) \notin P(R)$ implies $(x, y) \in R$ if $R$ is reflexive and complete.   ■

The next theorem provides simple and intuitive sufficiency conditions for the existence of $R$-maximal elements and $R$-greatest elements.

**Theorem 2.6**   *Suppose $R$ is a relation on $X$ and $S \in \mathcal{X}$.*

(i) *If $R$ is acyclical and $S$ is finite, then $M(S, R) \neq \emptyset$.*
(ii) *If $R$ is reflexive, complete, and acyclical, and $S$ is finite, then $G(S, R) \neq \emptyset$.*

**Proof**   (i) We use an induction argument on the number $|S|$ of the elements in $S$. If $|S| = 1$, the statement is obviously true. Suppose that the result is true when $|S| = k \geq 1$, and consider the case where $|S| = k + 1$. Take any $x^0 \in S$, and let $S^0 = S \setminus \{x^0\}$. By the induction hypothesis, there exists an $x^* \in M(S^0, R)$. If $(x^0, x^*) \notin P(R)$, we obtain $x^* \in M(S, R)$, and we are done. If $(x^0, x^*) \in P(R)$, the acyclicity of $R$ implies $x^0 \neq x^*$. If $x^0 \in M(S, R)$, we are done. If $x^0 \notin M(S, R)$, there exists an $x^1 \in S$ such that $(x^1, x^0) \in P(R)$. Because $R$ is acyclical, $x^1 \notin \{x^0, x^*\}$. If $x^1 \in M(S, R)$, we are done. If not, we have $(x^2, x^1) \in P(R)$ for some $x^2 \in S$. Because $R$ is acyclical, $x^2 \notin \{x^1, x^0, x^*\}$. Because $S$ is a finite set, this algorithm must terminate and lead us to an element of $M(S, R)$.

Part (ii) follows immediately from combining part (i) and part (ii) of Theorem 2.5.   ■

## 2.3   Extensions of Relations

We are now ready to discuss some extension theorems for binary relations that play indispensable roles in later chapters of this monograph. A binary relation $R^*$ is an *extension* of a binary relation $R$ if and only if we have

$$R \subseteq R^* \text{ and } P(R) \subseteq P(R^*).$$

Conversely, $R$ is said to be a *subrelation* of $R^*$ if and only if $R^*$ is an extension of $R$. When this relationship between $R$ and $R^*$ obtains, we say that $R$ and $R^*$ are *compatible* binary relations.

The following classical theorem, which is a variant of the basic theorem due to Szpilrajn (1930), specifies a sufficiency condition for the existence of an extension that is an ordering, to be called an *ordering extension*. This convenient variant of Szpilrajn's theorem was stated by Arrow (1951, p. 64) without a proof, whereas Hansson (1968) provided a full proof thereof on the basis of Szpilrajn's original theorem.

**Theorem 2.7**  *Any quasi-ordering R on X has an ordering extension.*

The proof of Theorem 2.7 requires an auxiliary proposition called Zorn's lemma. Let $\succeq$ be a relation on a non-empty set $\Xi$. We say that the pair $(\Xi, \succeq)$ is *inductive* if and only if, for every non-empty subset $\Xi^* \subseteq \Xi$ such that

$$[(x, y) \in \succeq \text{ or } (y, x) \in \succeq] \text{ for all } x, y \in \Xi^*,$$

we have

$$\{x \in \Xi \mid (x, y) \in \succeq \text{ for all } x \in \Xi^*\} \neq \emptyset.$$

Zorn's lemma provides sufficient conditions for the existence of $\succeq$-maximal elements in a set $\Xi$.

**Zorn's Lemma**   *Suppose that $\succeq$ is a quasi-ordering on $\Xi$ and $(\Xi, \succeq)$ is inductive. Then $M(\Xi, \succeq) \neq \emptyset$.*

Although the validity of Zorn's lemma may not be intuitively clear immediately, it is demonstrably equivalent to the important *axiom of choice*, a fundamental axiom of set theory, which is accepted nowadays by most mathematicians. The axiom of choice requires that it is possible to select an element from each of a collection of sets.

**Axiom of choice**   Suppose that $\mathcal{T}$ is a collection of non-empty sets. Then there exists a function $\varphi \colon \mathcal{T} \to \cup_{T \in \mathcal{T}} T$ such that $\varphi(t) \in t$ for all $t \in \mathcal{T}$.

**Proof of Theorem 2.7**   Let $R$ be a quasi-ordering on $X$ and let $\Xi$ be the collection of all extensions of $R$ that are themselves quasi-orderings. $\Xi$ is non-empty because $R \in \Xi$. Let $\Xi^*$ be any subcollection of $\Xi$ such that

$$[R' \subseteq R \text{ or } R \subseteq R'] \text{ for all } R, R' \in \Xi^*,$$

and define $R^{\Xi^*} = \cup_{R^* \in \Xi^*} R^*$. It is clear that

$$R^{\Xi^*} \in \{R^* \in \Xi \mid R^* \supseteq R' \text{ for all } R' \in \Xi^*\}$$

for any such $\Xi^*$, which implies that $(\Xi, \supseteq)$ is inductive. In view of the fact that $\supseteq$ is a quasi-ordering on $\Xi$, we can now apply Zorn's lemma to assert the existence of a $\supseteq$-maximal element in $\Xi$; that is, there exists an $R^{**} \in \Xi$ such that $R^{**} \in M(\Xi, \supseteq)$. Because $R^{**} \in \Xi$, $R^{**}$ is a quasi-ordering, thus reflexive and transitive. We establish that $R^{**}$ is also complete, thus an ordering. Suppose, to the contrary, that there exist $x^0$ and $y^0$ in $X$ satisfying $x^0 \neq y^0$, $(x^0, y^0) \notin R^{**}$, and $(y^0, x^0) \notin R^{**}$. Let the relation $R^0$ be defined by

$$R^0 = R^{**} \cup \{(x, y) \mid (x, x^0) \in R^{**} \text{ and } (y^0, y) \in R^{**}\}. \qquad (2.3)$$

It is clear that $R^{**} \subseteq R^0$. Because $(x^0, y^0) \in R^0$ and $(x^0, y^0) \notin R^{**}$, it is in fact true that $R^{**} \subset R^0$. To show the transitivity of $R^0$, let $(x, y) \in R^0$ and $(y, z) \in R^0$. If

$$(x, y) \in R^{**} \text{ and } (y, z) \in R^{**},$$

we have $(x, z) \in R^{**} \subseteq R^0$, thanks to the transitivity of $R^{**}$. If

$$(x, y) \in R^{**} \text{ and } [(y, x^0) \in R^{**} \text{ and } (y^0, z) \in R^{**}],$$

we obtain $(x, x^0) \in R^{**}$ and $(y^0, z) \in R^{**}$, which implies $(x, z) \in R^0$ in view of (2.3). The case where

$$[(x, x^0) \in R^{**} \text{ and } (y^0, y) \in R^{**}] \text{ and } (y, z) \in R^{**}$$

can be similarly treated. Finally, the case where

$$[(x, x^0) \in R^{**} \text{ and } (y^0, y) \in R^{**}] \text{ and } [(y, x^0) \in R^{**} \text{ and } (y^0, z) \in R^{**}]$$
$$(2.4)$$

cannot occur, because (2.4) entails $(y^0, x^0) \in R^{**}$, a contradiction. Therefore, $R^0$ is transitive.

To show that $R^0$ is an extension of $R$, notice first that $R \subseteq R^{**} \subseteq R^0$. Let $(x, y) \in P(R) \subseteq P(R^{**})$. We then have $(x, y) \in R^{**}$ and $(y, x) \notin R^{**}$. If it is true that $(y, x^0) \in R^{**}$ and $(y^0, x) \in R^{**}$, it follows that $(y^0, x^0) \in R^{**}$, a contradiction. Therefore, $(y, x) \notin R^0$ is the case, which implies $(x, y) \in P(R^0)$, and hence $P(R) \subseteq P(R^0)$.

It now follows that $R^0 \in \Xi$ and $R^{**} \subset R^0$, in contradiction to the $\supseteq$-maximality of $R^{**}$ in $\Xi$. ∎

A relation's being a quasi-ordering is sufficient for the existence of an ordering extension thereof, as is asserted by Szpilrajn's theorem, but it is not necessary. In our subsequent analysis, it is often useful to have an extension theorem that identifies a condition that is both sufficient *and* necessary for the existence of an ordering extension. The next theorem, which is due to Suzumura (1976b), provides a condition to that effect: it establishes that Suzumura consistency is precisely what is required. This result is one of our major motivations in studying this notion of coherence in detail. Suzumura consistency is *the* crucial property of a (not necessarily reflexive and complete) relation $R$ when it comes to the question of whether $R$ can possibly be compatible with an ordering. Thus, it provides a precise dividing line and allows for some non-transitive relations while, at the same time, retaining the important property of avoiding incompatibility results regarding $R$'s agreement with *some* ordering.

**Theorem 2.8**   *A relation $R$ on $X$ has an ordering extension if and only if $R$ is Suzumura consistent.*

**Proof**   Suppose first that $R$ is not Suzumura consistent. Then there exist $x, y \in X$ such that $(x, y) \in tc(R)$ and $(y, x) \in P(R)$. Let $R^*$ be an extension of $R$. Because $R \subseteq R^*$ and $P(R) \subseteq P(R^*)$ by definition, we immediately know that $R^*$ cannot be Suzumura consistent and thus cannot be transitive. Thus, $R^*$ cannot be an ordering extension of $R$.

Conversely, suppose that $R$ is Suzumura consistent. Let a relation $R^0$ be defined by

$$R^0 = tc(R) \cup \Delta. \tag{2.5}$$

We show that $R^0$ is a quasi-ordering on $X$. $R^0$ being obviously reflexive, we have only to establish transitivity. Let $x, y, z \in X$ be such that $(x, y) \in R^0$ and $(y, z) \in R^0$. If both $(x, y)$ and $(y, z)$ belong to $tc(R)$, we obtain $(x, z) \in tc(R) \subseteq R^0$ by virtue of the transitivity of $tc(R)$. If $(x, y) \in \Delta$ (respectively $(y, z) \in \Delta$), we have $x = y$ (respectively $y = z$), so that $(x, z) \in R^0$ is implied by $(y, z) \in R^0$ (respectively $(x, y) \in R^0$). Now that $R^0$ has turned out to be a quasi-ordering, it has an ordering extension $R^*$ by virtue of Theorem 2.7. If we can show that $R^0$ is an extension of $R$, we are done. By (2.5), $R \subseteq R^0$ is obviously true. To show the validity of $P(R) \subseteq P(R^0)$, take any $(x, y) \in P(R)$. It follows from $(x, y) \in R$ that $(x, y) \in R^0$, so that we have only to prove that $(y, x) \notin R^0$ follows from $(x, y) \in P(R)$. Assume, therefore, that $(y, x) \in R^0$. Clearly, $(y, x) \notin \Delta$, because otherwise $(x, y) \in P(R)$ could not have been the case in the first place. It then follows that $(y, x) \in tc(R)$. When $(x, y) \in P(R)$ is added to this, we obtain a contradiction to the Suzumura consistency of $R$. This completes the proof.   ∎

The message of Theorem 2.8 is simple and straightforward. It is because of this theorem that Suzumura consistency can be considered a weakening of transitivity that is *minimal* in the sense that it cannot be weakened further without abandoning all hope of finding an ordering extension of a relation. It should also be pointed out that quasi-transitivity, being logically independent of Suzumura consistency, has nothing to do with the possibility of extending a binary relation to an ordering.

The usefulness of Theorem 2.8 may be established in several distinct contexts. As an illustrative example, consider Dushnik and Miller's (1941) classical result and some of its generalizations. Dushnik and Miller (1941) show that every transitive and asymmetric relation $R$ is the intersection of a collection of complete, transitive, and asymmetric relations. Donaldson and Weymark (1998) employ Suzumura's extension theorem to establish the conclusion of Dushnik and Miller's (1941) theorem in a setting where asymmetry is replaced with reflexivity. More precisely, they use Theorem 2.8 to show that every quasi-ordering $R$ is the intersection of all ordering extensions of $R$. Bossert (1999) provides an alternative proof of their theorem, and a generalization can be found in Duggan (1999), along with various other extension results.

There is another direction toward which we can generalize Szpilrajn's basic extension theorem. It was Arrow (1951, pp. 64–68) who explored this alternative possibility. To do so, we define the *restriction* of a relation $R$ on $X$ to a (not necessarily non-empty) subset $S$ of $X$ to be given by $R \cap (S \times S)$. Now suppose there is an ordering $T$ of the alternatives in a (not necessarily non-empty) subset $S$ of $X$ that is fixed in advance. Consider a quasi-ordering $Q$ on $X$ such that any two distinct elements in $S$ are non-comparable according to $Q$. Then, given *any* ordering $T$ of the elements in $S$, there is a way of ordering all the alternatives in $X$ that are compatible with the given ordering $T$ on $S$. In other words, if we know there is some predefined ordering on a subset $S$ of $X$ and a quasi-ordering $Q$ does not rank any distinct pairs in $S$, there is an ordering extension $R$ of $Q$ the restriction of which to $S$ coincides with $T$. To be precise, Arrow's generalization of Szpilrajn's theorem reads as follows.

**Arrow's Lemma**   *Let $Q$ be a quasi-ordering on $X$, let $S$ be a subset of $X$ such that, if $x \neq y$ and $x, y \in S$, then $(x, y) \notin Q$, and let $T$ be an ordering on $S$. Then there exists an ordering extension $R$ of $Q$ such that the restriction of $R$ to $S$ coincides with $T$.*

To illustrate the message of Arrow's lemma, suppose that $Q$ is a quasi-ordering on $X$ that keeps silence on a subset $S$ of $X$. Then, given *any* ordering $T$ on the set $S$ of non-comparable alternatives, there exists a compatible ordering $R$ on $X$ that coincides with $T$ on $S$.

It is clear that Arrow's lemma implies Szpilrajn's theorem as a special case where $S = \emptyset$. We conclude this section with a result that generalizes Arrow's lemma. This generalization, which is due to Suzumura (2004), subsumes Theorem 2.8, just as Arrow's lemma subsumes Theorem 2.7. In order to proceed, we require the following definition. For any two relations $R$ and $R'$ on $X$, the *composition of $R$ and $R'$* is given by

$$R \circ R' = \{(x, y) \mid \exists z \in X \text{ such that } [(x, z) \in R \text{ and } (z, y) \in R']\}.$$

Suzumura's (2004) theorem generalizes Arrow's lemma. The structure of its proof is modeled after Inada (1954), who constructed a simple alternative proof of Arrow's lemma.

**Theorem 2.9** *Let $Q$ be a binary relation on $X$, let $S$ be a subset of $X$ such that, if $x \neq y$ and $x, y \in S$, then $(x, y) \notin tc(Q)$, and let $T$ be an ordering on $S$. Then there exists an ordering extension $R$ of $Q$ such that the restriction of $R$ to $S$ coincides with $T$ if and only if $Q$ is Suzumura consistent.*

**Proof** Suppose first that there exists an ordering extension $R$ of $Q$ such that the restriction of $R$ to $S$ coincides with the given ordering $T$ on $S$. Let $x, y \in X$ be such that

$$(x, y) \in tc(Q). \tag{2.6}$$

In view of $Q \subseteq R$, it follows from part (iv) of Theorem 2.1 and (2.6) that $(x, y) \in tc(R)$, which implies $(x, y) \in R$ by (repeatedly if necessary) invoking the transitivity of $R$. Then we have $(y, x) \notin P(R)$, which implies $(y, x) \notin P(Q)$ because $R$ is an ordering extension of $Q$. Thus, $Q$ must be Suzumura consistent.

Now suppose $Q$ is Suzumura consistent. Starting from $Q$, define a binary relation $Q^*$ by

$$Q^* = tc(Q) \cup \Delta. \tag{2.7}$$

It is clear that $Q^*$ is reflexive. To show that $Q^*$ is transitive, let $(x, y) \in Q^*$ and $(y, z) \in Q^*$ for some $x, y, z \in X$. If $(x, y) \in tc(Q)$ and $(y, z) \in tc(Q)$, we obtain $(x, z) \in tc(Q) \subseteq Q^*$. If $(x, y) \in \Delta$ (respectively $(y, z) \in \Delta$), we obtain $x = y$ (respectively $y = z$), so that $(x, z) \in Q^*$ follows from $(y, z) \in Q^*$ (respectively $(x, y) \in Q^*$). Thus, $Q^*$ is a quasi-ordering.

Using this $Q^*$ and the ordering $T$ on $S$, we now define

$$Q^{**} = Q^* \cup (Q^* \circ T) \cup (Q^* \circ T \circ Q^*) \cup (T \circ Q^*) \cup T. \qquad (2.8)$$

The proof is completed by means of the following five steps.

**Step 1**   $Q^{**}$ is a quasi-ordering on $X$.

It follows from (2.7) and (2.8) that $Q^{**}$ is reflexive. To show that $Q^{**}$ is transitive, suppose that $(x, y) \in Q^{**}$ and $(y, z) \in Q^{**}$ for some $x, y, z \in X$. We go through all possible cases.

(a) If $(x, y) \in Q^*$ and $(y, z) \in Q^*$, then $(x, z) \in Q^* \subseteq Q^{**}$ by virtue of the transitivity of $Q^*$.

(b) If $(x, y) \in Q^*$ and $(y, z) \in Q^* \circ T$, there exists $s \in X$ such that $(x, y) \in Q^*, (y, s) \in Q^*$, and $(s, z) \in T$. By virtue of the transitivity of $Q^*$, we have $(x, s) \in Q^*$ and $(s, z) \in T$, that is to say, $(x, z) \in Q^* \circ T \subseteq Q^{**}$.

(c) If $(x, y) \in Q^*$ and $(y, z) \in Q^* \circ T \circ Q^*$, there exist $s, t \in X$ such that $(x, y) \in Q^*, (y, s) \in Q^*, (s, t) \in T$, and $(t, z) \in Q^*$. Invoking the transitivity of $Q^*$, we then obtain $(x, s) \in Q^*, (s, t) \in T$, and $(t, z) \in Q^*$, that is to say, $(x, z) \in Q^* \circ T \circ Q^* \subseteq Q^{**}$.

(d) If $(x, y) \in Q^*$ and $(y, z) \in T \circ Q^*$, we obtain $(x, z) \in Q^* \circ T \circ Q^* \subseteq Q^{**}$.

(e) If $(x, y) \in Q^*$ and $(y, z) \in T$, we obtain $(x, z) \in Q^* \circ T \subseteq Q^{**}$.

(f) If $(x, y) \in Q^* \circ T$ and $(y, z) \in Q^*$, we obtain $(x, z) \in Q^* \circ T \circ Q^* \subseteq Q^{**}$.

(g) If $(x, y) \in Q^* \circ T$ and $(y, z) \in Q^* \circ T$, there exist $s, t \in X$ such that $(x, s) \in Q^*, (s, y) \in T, (y, t) \in Q^*$, and $(t, z) \in T$. It follows from $(s, y) \in T$ and $(t, z) \in T$ that both $y$ and $t$ belong to $S$. Combined with $(y, t) \in Q^*$, this fact implies $y = t$. It then follows that $(s, z) \in T$, which implies $(x, z) \in Q^* \circ T \subseteq Q^{**}$ in view of $(x, s) \in Q^*$.

(h) If $(x, y) \in Q^* \circ T$ and $(y, z) \in Q^* \circ T \circ Q^*$, there exist $s, t, u \in X$ such that $(x, s) \in Q^*, (s, y) \in T, (y, t) \in Q^*, (t, u) \in T$, and $(u, z) \in Q^*$. It follows from $(s, y) \in T$ and $(t, u) \in T$ that both $y$ and $t$ belong to $S$. Combined with $(y, t) \in Q^*$, this fact implies $y = t$. It then follows that $(s, u) \in T$, which implies $(x, z) \in Q^* \circ T \circ Q^* \subseteq Q^{**}$ in view of $(x, s) \in Q^*$ and $(u, z) \in Q^*$.

(i) If $(x, y) \in Q^* \circ T$ and $(y, z) \in T \circ Q^*, (x, z) \in Q^* \circ T \circ Q^* \subseteq Q^{**}$ holds.

(j) If $(x, y) \in Q^* \circ T$ and $(y, z) \in T$, there exists $s \in X$ such that $(x, s) \in Q^*, (s, y) \in T$, and $(y, z) \in T$ hold. It follows that $(x, s) \in Q^*$ and $(s, z) \in T$, so that $(x, z) \in Q^* \circ T \subseteq Q^{**}$.

(k) If $(x, y) \in Q^* \circ T \circ Q^*$ and $(y, z) \in Q^*$, there exist $s, t \in X$ such that $(x, s) \in Q^*, (s, t) \in T, (t, y) \in Q^*$, and $(y, z) \in Q^*$ hold. It follows that $(x, s) \in Q^*, (s, t) \in T$, and $(t, z) \in Q^*$, so that $(x, z) \in Q^* \circ T \circ Q^* \subseteq Q^{**}$.

(l) If $(x, y) \in Q^* \circ T \circ Q^*$ and $(y, z) \in Q^* \circ T$, there exist $s, t, u \in X$ such that $(x, s) \in Q^*, (s, t) \in T, (t, y) \in Q^*, (y, u) \in Q^*$, and $(u, z) \in T$. It follows from $(t, y) \in Q^*$ and $(y, u) \in Q^*$ that $(t, u) \in Q^*$, whereas $(s, t) \in T$ and $(u, z) \in T$ imply that both $t$ and $u$ belong to $S$. It follows that $t = u$, so that we obtain $(x, z) \in Q^* \circ T \subseteq Q^{**}$.

(m) If $(x, y) \in Q^* \circ T \circ Q^*$ and $(y, z) \in Q^* \circ T \circ Q^*$, there exist $s, t, u, v \in X$ such that $(x, s) \in Q^*, (s, t) \in T, (t, y) \in Q^*, (y, u) \in Q^*$ and $(u, v) \in T$, and $(v, z) \in Q^*$. It follows from $(t, y) \in Q^*$ and $(y, u) \in Q^*$ that $(t, u) \in Q^*$, whereas $(s, t) \in T$ and $(u, v) \in T$ imply that both $t$ and $u$ belong to $S$. It follows that $t = u$, so that we obtain $(x, s) \in Q^*, (s, v) \in T$, and $(v, z) \in Q^*$, where we invoked the transitivity of $T$. Thus, $(x, z) \in Q^* \circ T \circ Q^* \subseteq Q^{**}$.

(n) If $(x, y) \in Q^* \circ T \circ Q^*$ and $(y, z) \in T \circ Q^*$, there exist $s, t, u \in X$ such that $(x, s) \in Q^*, (s, t) \in T, (t, y) \in Q^*, (y, u) \in T$, and $(u, z) \in Q^*$. It follows from $(s, t) \in T$ and $(y, u) \in T$ that both $t$ and $y$ belong to $S$, which, combined with $(t, y) \in Q^*$, implies $t = y$. We then have $(x, s) \in Q^*$, and $(s, u) \in T$ and $(u, z) \in Q^*$, where we invoked the transitivity of $T$. It follows that $(x, z) \in Q^* \circ T \circ Q^* \subseteq Q^{**}$.

(o) If $(x, y) \in Q^* \circ T \circ Q^*$ and $(y, z) \in T$, there exist $s, t \in X$ such that $(x, s) \in Q^*, (s, t) \in T, (t, y) \in Q^*$, and $(y, z) \in T$. It follows from $(s, t) \in T$ and $(y, z) \in T$ that both $t$ and $y$ belong to $S$, which, combined with $(t, y) \in Q^*$, implies $t = y$. We then have $(x, s) \in Q^*, (s, t) \in T$, and $(t, z) \in T$, from which we can conclude that $(x, z) \in Q^* \circ T \subseteq Q^{**}$, where use is made of the transitivity of $T$.

(p) If $(x, y) \in T \circ Q^*$ and $(y, z) \in Q^*$, we obtain $(x, z) \in T \circ Q^* \subseteq Q^{**}$ in view of the transitivity of $Q^*$.

(q) If $(x, y) \in T \circ Q^*$ and $(y, z) \in Q^* \circ T$, there exist $s, t \in X$ such that $(x, s) \in T, (s, y) \in Q^*, (y, t) \in Q^*$, and $(t, z) \in T$. By virtue of the transitivity of $Q^*$, we have $(x, s) \in T, (s, t) \in Q^*$, and $(t, z) \in T$. It follows from $(x, s) \in T$ and $(t, z) \in T$ that both $s$ and $t$ belong to $S$, which, combined with $(s, t) \in Q^*$, implies $s = t$. Thus, we have

$(x, s) \in T$ and $(s, z) \in T$, which further implies $(x, z) \in T \subseteq Q^{**}$ by virtue of the transitivity of $T$.

(r) If $(x, y) \in T \circ Q^*$ and $(y, z) \in Q^* \circ T \circ Q^*$, there exist $s, t$, $u \in X$ such that $(x, s) \in T, (s, y) \in Q^*, (y, t) \in Q^*, (t, u) \in T$, and $(u, z) \in Q^*$. By virtue of the transitivity of $Q^*$, we have $(s, t) \in Q^*$, whereas $(x, s) \in T$ and $(t, u) \in T$ imply that both $s$ and $t$ belong to $S$. It follows that $s = t$, so that we obtain $(x, u) \in T$ in view of the transitivity of $T$. Thus, $(x, z) \in T \circ Q^* \subseteq Q^{**}$.

(s) If $(x, y) \in T \circ Q^*$ and $(y, z) \in T \circ Q^*$, there exist $s, t \in X$ such that $(x, s) \in T, (s, y) \in Q^*, (y, t) \in T$, and $(t, z) \in Q^*$. It follows from $(x, s) \in T$ and $(y, t) \in T$ that both $s$ and $y$ belong to $S$. In view of $(s, y) \in Q^*$, we then obtain $s = y$, so that $(x, t) \in T$ and $(t, z) \in Q^*$, where use is made of the transitivity of $T$. Thus, $(x, z) \in T \circ Q^* \subseteq Q^{**}$.

(t) If $(x, y) \in T$ and $(y, z) \in Q^*$, we have $(x, z) \in T \circ Q^* \subseteq Q^{**}$.

(u) If $(x, y) \in T$ and $(y, z) \in Q^* \circ T$, we have $(x, y) \in T, (y, s) \in Q^*$, and $(s, z) \in T$ for some $s \in X$. It follows from $(x, y) \in T$ and $(s, z) \in T$ that both $y$ and $s$ belong to $S$, which implies $y = s$ in view of $(y, s) \in Q^*$. Taking the transitivity of $T$ into consideration, we then obtain $(x, z) \in T \subseteq Q^{**}$.

(v) If $(x, y) \in T$ and $(y, z) \in Q^* \circ T \circ Q^*$, there exist $s, t \in X$ such that $(y, s) \in Q^*, (s, t) \in T$, and $(t, z) \in Q^*$. It follows from $(x, y) \in T$ and $(s, t) \in T$ that both $y$ and $s$ belong to $S$, so that $(y, s) \in Q^*$ implies that $y = s$. By virtue of the transitivity of $T$, we then obtain $(x, t) \in T$ and $(t, z) \in Q^*$, that is, $(x, z) \in T \circ Q^* \subseteq Q^{**}$.

(w) If $(x, y) \in T$ and $(y, z) \in T \circ Q^*$, there exists $s \in X$ such that $(y, s) \in T$ and $(s, z) \in Q^*$. $T$ being transitive, we then obtain $(x, s) \in T$ and $(s, z) \in Q^*$, that is, $(x, z) \in T \circ Q^* \subseteq Q^{**}$.

(x) If $(x, y) \in T$ and $(y, z) \in T$, we obtain $(x, z) \in T \subseteq Q^{**}$ by virtue of the transitivity of $T$.

(y) The case $(x, y) \in T \circ Q^*$ and $(y, z) \in T$ is analogous to (w) with the roles of $(x, y)$ and $(y, z)$ interchanged.

**Step 2**   $Q^{**}$ is an extension of $Q^*$.

Since $Q^* \subseteq Q^{**}$ holds by definition, we have only to prove that $(x, y) \in P(Q^*)$ must imply $(y, x) \notin Q^{**}$. Suppose that $(x, y) \in P(Q^*)$ and $(y, x) \in Q^{**}$ for some $x, y \in X$. We show that this is actually impossible.

(a) Suppose that $(y, x) \in Q^*$. This is incompatible with $(x, y) \in P(Q^*)$.

(b) Suppose that $(y, x) \in Q^* \circ T$, that is, $(y, s) \in Q^*$ and $(s, x) \in T$ for some $s \in X$. $Q^*$ being transitive, we then obtain $(x, s) \in Q^*$. Since $(s, x) \in T$, both $s$ and $x$ belong to $S$, so that $s = x$ in view of $(x, s) \in Q^*$. Then we have $(x, y) \in P(Q^*)$ and $(y, x) \in Q^*$, which is impossible.

(c) Suppose that $(y, x) \in Q^* \circ T \circ Q^*$. Then there exist $s, t \in X$ such that $(y, s) \in Q^*, (s, t) \in T$, and $(t, x) \in Q^*$. It follows from $(x, y) \in Q^*$ and $(y, s) \in Q^*$ that $(x, s) \in Q^*$, which implies $(t, s) \in Q^*$ in view of $(t, x) \in Q^*$. Since both $s$ and $t$ belong to $S$ in view of $(s, t) \in T, (t, s) \in Q^*$ implies $t = s$. Then $(y, s) \in Q^*$ and $(t, x) \in Q^*$ imply $(y, x) \in Q^*$, in contradiction to $(x, y) \in P(Q^*)$.

(d) Suppose that $(y, x) \in T \circ Q^*$. Then there exists $s \in X$ such that $(y, s) \in T$ and $(s, x) \in Q^*$. It follows from $(x, y) \in Q^*$ and $(s, x) \in Q^*$ that $(s, y) \in Q^*$. In view of $(y, s) \in T$, which implies that both $y$ and $s$ belong to $S, (s, y) \in Q^*$ implies $s = y$. But $(x, y) \in P(Q^*), (s, x) \in Q^*$, and $s = y$ are contradictory.

(e) Suppose that $(y, x) \in T$, which implies that both $x$ and $y$ belong to $S$. Since $(x, y) \in Q^*$ holds, it follows that $x = y$. But this is incompatible with $(x, y) \in P(Q^*)$.

**Step 3**   For all $x, y \in S, (x, y) \notin T$ implies $(x, y) \notin Q^{**}$.

Suppose that $(x, y) \notin T$ and $(x, y) \in Q^{**}$ for some $x, y \in S$.

(a) If $(x, y) \in Q^*$, then $x = y$ must be true in contradiction with $(x, y) \notin T$ and the reflexivity of $T$.

(b) If $(x, y) \in Q^* \circ T$, there exists $s \in X$ such that $(x, s) \in Q^*$ and $(s, y) \in T$, which implies that $x = s$ in view of $x \in S$. But $(x, y) \notin T$, $(s, y) \in T$, and $x = s$ are contradictory.

(c) If $(x, y) \in Q^* \circ T \circ Q^*$, there exist $s, t \in X$ such that $(x, s) \in Q^*$, $(s, t) \in T$, and $(t, y) \in Q^*$. It follows from $(s, t) \in T$ that both $s$ and $t$ belong to $S$. Since $x, y \in S$ by definition, it follows from $(x, s) \in Q^*$ and $(t, y) \in Q^*$ that $x = s$ and $t = y$. Thus $(s, t) \in T$ implies $(x, y) \in T$ in contradiction with $(x, y) \notin T$.

(d) If $(x, y) \in T \circ Q^*$, there exists $s \in X$ such that $(x, s) \in T$ and $(s, y) \in Q^*$. It follows from $(x, s) \in T$ that both $x$ and $s$ belong to $S$, whereas $y \in S$ by definition. Thus, $(s, y) \in Q^*$ cannot but imply $s = y$, which in turn implies $(x, y) \in T$ in contradiction with $(x, y) \notin T$.

(e) If $(x, y) \in T$, this is directly contradictory with $(x, y) \notin T$.

**Step 4**   There exists an ordering extension $R$ of $Q$.

$Q^{**}$ being a quasi-ordering by virtue of Step 1, there exists an ordering extension $R$ thereof by virtue of Theorem 2.7. $Q^{**}$ being an extension of $Q^*$ by virtue of Step 2, $R$ is an ordering extension of $Q^*$. To complete the proof of this step, we have only to prove that $Q^*$ is an extension of $Q$, that is, $Q \subseteq Q^*$ and $P(Q) \subseteq P(Q^*)$. The former is obvious by the definition of $Q^*$; see (2.7). To prove the latter, assume that $(x, y) \in P(Q)$, that is, $(x, y) \in Q$ and $(y, x) \notin Q$. It follows from $(x, y) \in Q$ that $(x, y) \in Q^*$. Assume that $(y, z) \in Q^*$. Clearly $(y, x) \notin \Delta$, since otherwise $(x, y) \in P(Q)$ could not be true. Thus, we must obtain $(y, x) \in tc(Q)$. When $(x, y) \in P(Q)$ is added to this, we have a contradiction to the Suzumura consistency of $Q$.

**Step 5**   For all $x, y \in S, (x, y) \in R$ holds if and only if $(x, y) \in T$.

By virtue of (2.8) and Step 4, we have $T \subseteq Q^{**} \subseteq R$. Thus, we have only to show that $(x, y) \in R$ implies $(x, y) \in T$. Suppose to the contrary that $(x, y) \notin T$ for some $x, y \in S$. Thanks to Step 3, we then obtain $(x, y) \notin Q^{**}$. Because $T$ can compare any two elements of $S$, $(y, x) \in T$ holds, which implies $(y, x) \in Q^{**}$ by virtue of (2.8). $R$ being an ordering extension of $Q^{**}$, we then obtain $(y, x) \in R$ and $(x, y) \notin R$. This contradiction completes the proof.  ■

## 2.4  Filters and Ultrafilters

We conclude this chapter with a discussion of filters and ultrafilters, which are indispensable tools in our discussion of the structure of decisive coalitions in Chapter 10. Let $N$ be a finite or infinite set with at least two elements. A *filter* on $N$ is a collection $\mathcal{F}$ of subsets of $N$ such that

$f$.1.  $\emptyset \notin \mathcal{F}$.
$f$.2.  $N \in \mathcal{F}$.
$f$.3.  For all $M, M' \in \mathcal{F}, M \cap M' \in \mathcal{F}$.
$f$.4.  For all $M, M' \subseteq N, [[M \in \mathcal{F} \text{ and } M \subseteq M'] \Rightarrow M' \in \mathcal{F}]$.

An *ultrafilter* on $N$ is a collection $\mathcal{U}$ of subsets of $N$ such that

$u$.1.  $\emptyset \notin \mathcal{U}$.
$u$.2.  For all $M \subseteq N, [M \in \mathcal{U} \text{ or } N \setminus M \in \mathcal{U}]$.
$u$.3.  For all $M, M' \in \mathcal{U}, M \cap M' \in \mathcal{U}$.

The following theorem summarizes some basic properties of ultrafilters. See, for instance, Kelley (1955), Dunford and Schwartz (1957), and Berge (1963) for more detailed discussions of filters and ultrafilters.

**Theorem 2.10** *Let $\mathcal{U}$ be an ultrafilter on $N$.*

   *(i) $N \in \mathcal{U}$.*

   *(ii) For all $M \subseteq N$, $[M \in \mathcal{U} \Rightarrow N \setminus M \notin \mathcal{U}]$.*

   *(iii) For all $M \in \mathcal{U}$ and for all $M' \subseteq M$, $[M' \in \mathcal{U}$ or $M \setminus M' \in \mathcal{U}]$.*

   *(iv) For all $M, M' \subseteq N$, $[[M \in \mathcal{U}$ and $M \subseteq M'] \Rightarrow M' \in \mathcal{U}]$.*

**Proof** (i) By $u.1$, $\emptyset \notin \mathcal{U}$. Thus, by $u.2$, $N = N \setminus \emptyset \in \mathcal{U}$.

(ii) Let $M \subseteq N$ and suppose that, by way of contradiction, $M \in \mathcal{U}$ and $N \setminus M \in \mathcal{U}$. By $u.3$, $\emptyset = M \cap (N \setminus M) \in \mathcal{U}$, contradicting $u.1$.

(iii) Suppose that $M \in \mathcal{U}$ and $M' \subseteq M$. If $M' \in \mathcal{U}$, we are done. If not, $u.2$ implies $N \setminus M' = (N \setminus M) \cup (M \setminus M') \in \mathcal{U}$. By $u.3$, it follows that $M \cap [(N \setminus M) \cup (M \setminus M')] = M \setminus M' \in \mathcal{U}$.

(iv) Suppose $M \in \mathcal{U}$ and $M \subseteq M' \subseteq N$. If $N \setminus M' \in \mathcal{U}$, $u.3$ implies $\emptyset = (N \setminus M') \cap M \in \mathcal{U}$, contradicting $u.1$. By $u.2$, $M' \in \mathcal{U}$. ∎

An ultrafilter $\mathcal{U}$ on $N$ is *principal* if there exists an $i \in N$ such that, for all $M \subseteq N$, $M \in \mathcal{U}$ if and only if $i \in M$. Otherwise, $\mathcal{U}$ is a *free* ultrafilter. If $N$ is a finite set, then *all* ultrafilters are principal, as stated in the following theorem.

**Theorem 2.11** *Let $\mathcal{U}$ be an ultrafilter on $N$. If $N$ is finite, then $\mathcal{U}$ is principal.*

**Proof** Suppose $\mathcal{U}$ is an ultrafilter on $N$ and $N$ is finite. By part (i) of Theorem 2.10, $N \in \mathcal{U}$. Now we can apply part (iii) of Theorem 2.10 repeatedly until, by the finiteness of $N$, we reach an $i \in N$ such that $\{i\} \in \mathcal{U}$. By part (iv) of Theorem 2.10, this immediately implies that $\mathcal{U}$ is principal. ∎

If $N$ is infinite, there also exist free ultrafilters but they cannot be defined explicitly; the available proofs of their existence are non-constructive.

# — II —

## Rationalizability on General Domains

# — 3 —

# Definitions of Rationalizability

## 3.1 Preliminaries

In this chapter, we introduce and discuss the versions of rationalizability that are relevant for our analysis. In addition to rationalizability by Suzumura-consistent relations, we discuss rationalizability by relations with other (or no) coherence properties as well in order to provide a comprehensive treatment of all definitions that involve our basic properties. In addition, this allows us to make comparisons and illustrate that Suzumura-consistent rationalizability indeed is an attractive and plausible alternative to rationalizability involving other coherence properties such as quasi-transitivity or acyclicity. It turns out that there are parallels between transitive rationalizability and Suzumura-consistent rationalizability that do not exist when considering the remaining two forms of coherence. This, in addition to the arguments presented in the previous part of the monograph, points toward Suzumura consistency as the most natural weakening of transitivity in the absence of completeness. The results of this chapter as well as those of the following combine observations made in Bossert, Sprumont, and Suzumura (2005a,b; 2006) and Bossert and Suzumura (2009a).

There are two basic types of rationality requirements that are commonly considered in the literature. The first is *greatest-element rationalizability*, which requires the existence of a relation such that, for any feasible set, every chosen alternative is at least as good as every alternative in the set. Thus, this notion of rationalizability is based on the view that chosen alternatives should weakly dominate all feasible alternatives. *Maximal-element rationalizability*, on the other hand, demands the existence of a relation such that, for each feasible set, there exists no alternative in this set that is strictly preferred to any one of the chosen alternatives. Hence, this version of rationality does not require chosen alternatives to dominate all alternatives in the set but, rather, requires them to be undominated in the strict sense.

In addition to one or the other of these two concepts of rationalizability, we have a choice regarding the properties that we require a rationalizing relation to possess. We consider the standard richness requirements of reflexivity and completeness and, in addition, the coherence properties of transitivity, quasi-transitivity, Suzumura consistency, and acyclicity. By combining each version of rationalizability with one or both (or none) of the richness conditions and with one (or none) of the coherence properties, various definitions of rationalizability are obtained. Some of these definitions turn out to be equivalent, others are independent, and some are implied by others. To get an understanding of what each of these definitions entails, we provide a full analysis of all logical relationships between them in this chapter.

Recall that $\mathcal{X}$ is the set of all non-empty subsets of our non-empty universal set $X$. A *choice function* is a mapping that assigns, to each feasible set in its domain, a non-empty subset of this feasible set. This subset is interpreted as the set of chosen alternatives. The domain of the choice function depends on the choice situation to be analyzed, but it is always a set of subsets of $X$, that is, a subset of $\mathcal{X}$. We assume this subset of $\mathcal{X}$ to be non-empty to avoid degenerate situations. Thus, letting $\Sigma \subseteq \mathcal{X}$ be a non-empty domain, a choice function defined on that domain is a mapping $C \colon \Sigma \to \mathcal{X}$ such that, for all $S \in \Sigma$, $C(S) \subseteq S$. The *image of $\Sigma$ under $C$* is given by $C(\Sigma) = \cup_{S \in \Sigma} C(S)$.

The *direct revealed preference relation $R_C$* of a choice function $C$ with domain $\Sigma$ is defined as

$$R_C = \{(x, y) \mid \exists S \in \Sigma \text{ such that } [x \in C(S) \text{ and } y \in S]\}.$$

The *(indirect) revealed preference relation* of a choice function $C$ is the transitive closure $tc(R_C)$ of the direct revealed preference relation $R_C$.

A choice function $C$ is *greatest-element rationalizable*, *G-rationalizable* for short, if and only if there exists a relation $R$ on $X$, to be called a *G-rationalization* of $C$, such that

$$C(S) = G(S, R) \text{ for all } S \in \Sigma.$$

Analogously, a choice function $C$ is *maximal-element rationalizable*, *M-rationalizable* for short, if and only if there exists a relation $R$ on $X$, to be called an *M-rationalization* of $C$, such that

$$C(S) = M(S, R) \text{ for all } S \in \Sigma.$$

If a rationalization $R$ is required to be reflexive and complete, the notion of greatest-element rationalizability coincides with that of maximal-element rationalizability because, in this case, $G(S, R) = M(S, R)$ for all $S \in \mathcal{X}$; see part (ii) of Theorem 2.5. Without these properties, however, this is not necessarily the case. Greatest-element rationalizability is based on the idea of chosen alternatives weakly dominating all alternatives in the feasible set under consideration, whereas maximal-element rationalizability requires chosen elements not to be strictly dominated by any other feasible alternative. Specific examples illustrating the differences between those two concepts are discussed later.

The following theorem presents a fundamental relationship between the direct revealed preference relation and a G-rationalization of a choice function. This observation, which is due to Samuelson (1938a, 1948), states that any G-rationalization of a G-rationalizable choice function must respect the direct revealed preference relation of this choice function.

**Theorem 3.1** *Suppose $C \colon \Sigma \to \mathcal{X}$ is a choice function with an arbitrary non-empty domain $\Sigma \subseteq \mathcal{X}$ and $R$ is a relation on $X$. If $R$ is a G-rationalization of $C$, then $R_C \subseteq R$.*

**Proof**  Suppose that $R$ is a G-rationalization of $C$ and $x, y \in X$ are such that $(x, y) \in R_C$. By definition of $R_C$, there exists $S \in \Sigma$ such that $x \in C(S)$ and $y \in S$. Because $R$ is a G-rationalization of $C$, this implies $(x, y) \in R$.  ∎

Note that an analogous result is not valid for M-rationalizability. An M-rationalization does not necessarily have to respect the direct revealed preference relation because chosen alternatives merely have to be undominated within the feasible set from which they are chosen. The only restriction that is imposed is that the union of an M-rationalization and its non-comparable factor must respect the revealed preference relation. This is a straightforward observation because a strict preference of any feasible alternative over a chosen one immediately contradicts the definition of M-rationalizability.

Depending on the additional properties that we might want to impose on a rationalization (if any), different notions of rationalizability can be defined. For simplicity of presentation, we use the following convention when identifying a rationalizability axiom. We distinguish three groups of properties of a rationalizing relation, namely, *rationalization* properties, *richness* properties, and *coherence* properties. The first group consists of the two rationalizability properties of G-rationalizability and M-rationalizability, the second of the two requirements of reflexivity and completeness and, finally, the third of the axioms of transitivity, quasi-transitivity, Suzumura consistency, and acyclicity. Greatest-element rationalizability is abbreviated by G, M is short for maximal-element rationalizability, R stands for reflexivity, and C is completeness. Transitivity, quasi-transitivity, Suzumura consistency, and acyclicity are denoted by T, Q, S, and A, respectively. We identify the property or properties to be satisfied within each of the three groups and separate the groups with hyphens. If none of the properties within a group is required, this is denoted by using the symbol ∅. Either greatest-element rationalizability or maximal-element rationalizability may be required. In addition to imposing one of the two richness properties only, reflexivity and completeness may be required simultaneously and we may require rationalizability properties without either of the two. We only consider notions of rationalizability involving at most one of the coherence properties at a time. As is the case for the richness properties, imposing none of the coherence properties is a possibility. Formally, a rationalizability property is identified by an expression of the form $\alpha$-$\beta$-$\gamma$, where $\alpha \in \{G, M\}$, $\beta \in \{RC, R, C, \emptyset\}$, and $\gamma \in \{T, Q, S, A, \emptyset\}$. For example, greatest-element rationalizability by a reflexive, complete, and transitive relation is denoted by G-RC-T, maximal-element rationalizability by a complete relation is M-C-∅, greatest-element rationalizability by a reflexive and Suzumura-consistent relation is G-R-S, and maximal-element rationalizability without any further properties of a rationalizing relation is M-∅-∅. Clearly, according to this classification, there are $2 \times 4 \times 5 = 40$ versions of rationalizability.

In the remainder of this chapter, we provide a full description of the logical relationships between these different notions of rationalizability. These observations synthesize the contributions of Bossert, Sprumont, and Suzumura (2005a,b; 2006) and Bossert and Suzumura (2009a). Because of the complexities involved, we proceed in three steps. First, we state all logical relationships involving greatest-element rationalizability, followed by the corresponding result for all notions of maximal-element rationalizability. In the third and final step, we merge the two earlier results to obtain the complete list of implications among the forty versions of rationalizability identified earlier. Again, we employ a diagrammatic representation as in Theorem 2.2. In addition to the convention spelled out there, we depict axioms that are equivalent in the same box.

## 3.2   Greatest-Element Rationalizability

The following theorem clarifies the relationships between all our notions of greatest-element rationalizability.

**Theorem 3.2**   *Suppose $C: \Sigma \to \mathcal{X}$ is a choice function with an arbitrary non-empty domain $\Sigma \subseteq \mathcal{X}$. Then*

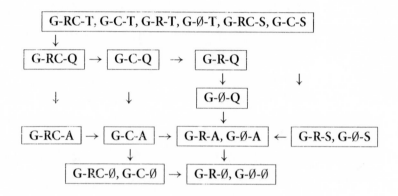

**Proof**   We proceed as follows. First, we show that, for each box, all axioms that appear in the box are equivalent. Next, we establish that G-C-Q implies G-R-Q (all other implications are immediate). Finally, we prove that no further implications are true other than those resulting from those depicted.

(a) We first prove the equivalence of the six axioms in the top box. First, note that Suzumura consistency and transitivity are equivalent in the presence of reflexivity and completeness (see Theorem 2.3) and, thus, G-RC-T and G-RC-S are equivalent. Clearly, it is now sufficient to establish that G-∅-T implies G-RC-T and that G-C-S implies G-RC-S.

Suppose $C$ satisfies G-∅-T, and let $R$ be a transitive G-rationalization of $C$. Clearly, the relation $R \cup \Delta$ is reflexive and transitive. By Theorem 2.7, there exists an ordering extension of $R \cup \Delta$, that is, a reflexive, complete, and transitive relation $R'$ such that $(R \cup \Delta) \subseteq R'$ and $P(R \cup \Delta) \subseteq P(R')$.

Following Richter (1966), we prove that any such $R'$ is a G-rationalization of $C$, which establishes **G-RC-T**. Let $S \in \Sigma$ and $x \in S$.

Suppose first that $x \in C(S)$. Because $R$ is a G-rationalization of $C$, this implies $(x, y) \in R$ for all $y \in S$. Because $R \subseteq R'$, we obtain $(x, y) \in R'$ for all $y \in S$ and, thus, $x \in G(S, R')$.

Now suppose that $x \in G(S, R')$. Because $C(S)$ is non-empty, there exists $z \in C(S)$. If $x = z$, we are done. Now suppose $x \neq z$. Because $R$ is a G-rationalization of $C$, it follows that $(z, y) \in R$ for all $y \in S$ and, in particular, $(z, x) \in R$. Because $z \in S$, we have $(x, z) \in R'$ by hypothesis. If $(x, z) \notin R$, it follows, because $x \neq z$ and hence $(x, z) \notin \Delta$, that $(z, x) \in P(R \cup \Delta)$ and hence $(z, x) \in P(R')$ because $P(R \cup \Delta) \subseteq P(R')$, a contradiction. Therefore, we must have $(x, z) \in R$. Because $(z, y) \in R$ for all $y \in S$, the transitivity of $R$ implies $x \in G(S, R)$ and, because $R$ is a G-rationalization of $C$, it follows that $x \in C(S)$.

To prove the second implication required to complete part (a), suppose $C$ satisfies **G-C-S** and let $R$ be a complete and Suzumura-consistent G-rationalization of $C$. Let

$$R' = [R \cup \Delta \cup \{(y, x) \mid x \notin C(\Sigma) \text{ and } y \in C(\Sigma)\}] \setminus$$
$$\{(x, y) \mid x \notin C(\Sigma) \text{ and } y \in C(\Sigma)\}.$$

Clearly, $R'$ is reflexive by definition.

To show that $R'$ is complete, let $x, y \in X$ be such that $x \neq y$ and $(x, y) \notin R'$. By definition of $R'$, this implies

$$(x, y) \notin R \text{ and } [x \notin C(\Sigma) \text{ or } y \in C(\Sigma)]$$

or

$$x \notin C(\Sigma) \text{ and } y \in C(\Sigma).$$

If the former applies, the completeness of $R$ implies $(y, x) \in R$ and, by definition of $R'$, we obtain $(y, x) \in R'$. If the latter is true, $(y, x) \in R'$ follows immediately from the definition of $R'$.

Next, we show that $R'$ is Suzumura consistent. Suppose $(x, y) \in tc(R')$ for some $x, y \in X$, that is, there exist $K \in \mathbb{N}$ and $x^0, \ldots, x^K \in X$ such that

$$x = x^0 \text{ and } (x^{k-1}, x^k) \in R' \text{ for all } k \in \{1, \ldots, K\} \text{ and } x^K = y.$$

Clearly, we can, without loss of generality, assume that $x^{k-1} \neq x^k$ for all $k \in \{1, \ldots, K\}$. We distinguish two cases.

In the first of these two cases, $x = x^0 \notin C(\Sigma)$. Then it follows that $x^1 \notin C(\Sigma)$; otherwise we would have $(x^1, x^0) \in P(R')$ by the definition of $R'$, contradicting our hypothesis. Successively applying this argument to all $k \in \{1, \ldots, K\}$, we obtain $x^k \notin C(\Sigma)$ for all $k \in \{1, \ldots, K\}$. By the definition of $R'$, this implies $(x^{k-1}, x^k) \in R$ for all $k \in \{1, \ldots, K\}$. By the Suzumura consistency of $R$, we must have $(y, x) = (x^K, x^0) \notin P(R)$. Because $y = x^K \notin C(\Sigma)$, this implies, according to the definition of $R'$, $(y, x) = (x^K, x^0) \notin P(R')$.

In the second case, $x = x^0 \in C(\Sigma)$. If $y = x^K \notin C(\Sigma)$, $(y, x) = (x^K, x^0) \notin P(R')$ follows immediately from the definition of $R'$. If $y = x^K \in C(\Sigma)$, it follows that $x^{K-1} \in C(\Sigma)$; otherwise we would have $(x^{K-1}, x^K) \notin R'$ by the definition of $R'$, contradicting our hypothesis. Successively applying this argument to all $k \in \{1, \ldots, K\}$, we obtain $x^k \in C(\Sigma)$ for all $k \in \{1, \ldots, K\}$. By the definition of $R'$, this implies $(x^{k-1}, x^k) \in R$ for all $k \in \{1, \ldots, K\}$. By the Suzumura consistency of $R$, we must have $(y, x) = (x^K, x^0) \notin P(R)$. Because $x = x^0 \in C(\Sigma)$, this implies, according to the definition of $R'$, $(y, x) = (x^K, x^0) \notin P(R')$.

Finally, we show that $R'$ is a G-rationalization of $C$. Let $S \in \Sigma$ and $x \in S$.

Suppose first that $x \in C(S)$. Because $R$ is a G-rationalization of $C$, we have $(x, y) \in R$ for all $y \in S$. In particular, this implies $(x, x) \in R$ and, according to the definition of $R'$, we obtain $x \in G(S, R')$.

To prove the converse implication, suppose $x \in G(S, R')$ for all $y \in S$. If $|S| = 1$, $x \in C(S)$ follows immediately because $C(S)$ is non-empty. If $|S| \geq 2$, we obtain $x \in C(\Sigma)$. Because $R$ is a G-rationalization of $C$, this implies $(x, x) \in R$. By the definition of $R'$, $(x, z) \in R$ for all $z \in C(S)$. Therefore, $(x, z) \in R$ for all $z \in C(S) \cup \{x\}$. Suppose, by way of contradiction, that $x \notin C(S)$. Because $R$ is a G-rationalization of $C$, it follows that there exists $y \in S \setminus (C(S) \cup \{x\})$ such that $(x, y) \notin R$. The completeness of $R$ implies $(y, x) \in P(R)$. Let $z \in C(S)$. It follows that $(z, y) \in R$ because $R$ is a G-rationalization of $C$ and, as established earlier, $(x, z) \in R$. This contradicts the Suzumura consistency of $R$ and, therefore, we must have $x \in C(S)$.

(b) Next, we prove that G-Ø-S implies G-R-S, which immediately establishes the equivalence of the two axioms. Suppose $R$ is a Suzumura-consistent G-rationalization of $C$. Let

$$R' = (R \cup \Delta) \setminus \{(x, y) \mid x \notin C(\Sigma) \text{ and } x \neq y\}.$$

Clearly, $R'$ is reflexive.

Now we prove that $R'$ is Suzumura consistent. Let $x, y \in X$, $K \in \mathbb{N}$, and $x^0, \ldots, x^K \in X$ be such that

$$x = x^0 \text{ and } (x^{k-1}, x^k) \in R' \text{ for all } k \in \{1, \ldots, K\} \text{ and } x^K = y.$$

Again, we can assume that $x^{k-1} \neq x^k$ for all $k \in \{1, \ldots, K\}$. By the definition of $R'$, $x = x^0 \in C(\Sigma)$. If $y = x^K \notin C(\Sigma)$, $(y, x) = (x^K, x^0) \notin P(R')$ follows immediately from the definition of $R'$. If $y = x^K \in C(\Sigma)$, it follows that $x^{K-1} \in C(\Sigma)$; otherwise we would have $(x^{K-1}, x^K) \notin R'$ by the definition of $R'$, contradicting our hypothesis. Successively applying this argument to all $k \in \{1, \ldots, K\}$, we obtain $x^k \in C(\Sigma)$ for all $k \in \{1, \ldots, K\}$. By the definition of $R'$, this implies $(x^{k-1}, x^k) \in R$ for all $k \in \{1, \ldots, K\}$. By the Suzumura consistency of $R$, we must have $(y, x) = (x^K, x^0) \notin P(R)$. Because $x = x^0 \in C(\Sigma)$, this implies, according to the definition of $R'$, $(y, x) = (x^K, x^0) \notin P(R')$.

It remains to be shown that $R'$ is a G-rationalization of $C$. Let $S \in \Sigma$ and $x \in S$.

First, suppose $x \in C(S)$. This implies $(x, y) \in R$ for all $y \in S$ because $R$ is a G-rationalization of $C$. Furthermore, because $C(S) \subseteq C(\Sigma)$, we have $x \in C(\Sigma)$. By the definition of $R'$, this implies $x \in G(S, R')$.

Finally, suppose $x \in G(S, R')$. If $S = \{x\}$, $x \in C(S)$ follows from the non-emptiness of $C(S)$. If $S \neq \{x\}$, we must have $(x, y) \in R$ for all $y \in S \setminus \{x\}$ by the definition of $R'$. Furthermore, $(x, y) \in R'$ for all $y \in S$ and, together with the definition of $R'$, we obtain $x \in C(\Sigma)$. Because $R$ is a G-rationalization of $C$, this implies $(x, x) \in R$. Thus, it follows that $(x, y) \in R$ for all $y \in S$ and, because $R$ is a G-rationalization of $C$, we must have $x \in C(S)$.

(c) Because the reverse implication is immediate, the equivalence of the two axioms G-R-A and G-∅-A is established by proving that G-∅-A implies G-R-A. Suppose $R$ is an acyclical G-rationalization of $C$. Define

$$R' = (R \cup \Delta) \setminus \{(x, y) \mid (x, x) \notin R \text{ and } x \neq y\}. \tag{3.1}$$

Clearly, $R'$ is reflexive. Furthermore, by definition of $R'$, we have

$$(x, x) \notin R \Rightarrow (x, y) \notin R' \tag{3.2}$$

for all $x \in X$ and for all $y \in X \setminus \{x\}$.

Now suppose $R'$ is not acyclical. Then there exist $x, y \in X$, $K \in \mathbb{N}$, and $x^0, \ldots, x^K \in X$ such that

$$x = x^0 \text{ and } (x^{k-1}, x^k) \in P(R') \text{ for all } k \in \{1, \ldots, K\} \text{ and } x^K = y$$

and $(y, x) = (x^K, x^0) \in P(R')$. Clearly, we can, without loss of generality, assume that the $x^k$ are pairwise distinct. By (3.2), $(x^k, x^k) \in R$ for all $k \in \{0, \dots, K\}$. But this implies that we have $(x^{k-1}, x^k) \in P(R)$ for all $k \in \{1, \dots, K\}$ and $(y, x) = (x^K, x^0) \in P(R)$ by the definition of $R'$, contradicting the acyclicity of $R$.

We now prove that $R'$ is a G-rationalization of $C$. Let $S \in \Sigma$ and $x \in S$.

Suppose $x \in C(S)$. Because $R$ is a G-rationalization of $C$, we have $(x, y) \in R$ for all $y \in S$, which, in particular, implies $(x, x) \in R$. Therefore, by (3.1), $(x, y) \in R'$ for all $y \in S$ and hence $x \in G(S, R')$.

Now suppose $x \in G(S, R')$. Therefore, $(x, y) \in R'$ for all $y \in S$. If $S = \{x\}$, $x \in C(S)$ follows from the non-emptiness of $C(S)$. If there exists $y \in S$ such that $x \neq y$, (3.2) implies $(x, x) \in R$. Therefore, because $(x, y) \in R'$ implies $(x, y) \in R$ for all $y \in S$ and $R$ is a G-rationalization of $C$, we immediately obtain $x \in C(S)$.

(d) We need to show that G-C-Ø implies G-RC-Ø in order to establish the equivalence of the two properties. Suppose $R$ is a complete G-rationalization of $C$. Define

$$R' = [R \cap \{(x, y) \mid (x, y) \in R_C \text{ or } (y, x) \notin R_C\}] \cup \Delta.$$

Clearly, $R'$ is reflexive because $\Delta \subseteq R'$. To show that $R'$ is complete, suppose $x, y \in X$ are such that $x \neq y$ and $(x, y) \notin R'$. By the definition of $R'$ and because $(x, y) \notin \Delta$ by assumption, this implies

$$(x, y) \notin R \text{ or } [(x, y) \notin R_C \text{ and } (y, x) \in R_C].$$

Because $R$ is complete and because $R_C \subseteq R$ by Theorem 3.1, this implies

$$(y, x) \in R \text{ or } [(x, y) \notin R_C \text{ and } (y, x) \in R].$$

This is equivalent to

$$(y, x) \in R \text{ and } (x, y) \notin R_C,$$

which, in turn, implies

$$(y, x) \in R \text{ and } [(y, x) \in R_C \text{ or } (x, y) \notin R_C]$$

and hence $(y, x) \in R'$ by the definition of $R'$. Thus, $R'$ is complete. It remains to show that $R'$ is a G-rationalization of $C$. To this end, let $S \in \Sigma$ and $x \in S$.

First, suppose $x \in C(S)$. This implies $(x, y) \in R_C$ and, by Theorem 3.1, $(x, y) \in R$ for all $y \in S$. By definition of $R'$, this implies $(x, y) \in R'$ for all $y \in S$ and hence $x \in G(S, R')$.

Now suppose $x \in G(S, R')$. By the definition of $R'$, this implies $(x, y) \in R$ for all $y \in S \setminus \{x\}$. By way of contradiction, suppose $x \notin C(S)$. Because $R$ is a G-rationalization of $C$ and $(x, y) \in R$ for all $y \in S \setminus \{x\}$, this implies $(x, x) \notin R$. Because $C(S)$ is non-empty, there exists $z \in C(S)$ and, because $x \notin C(S)$, we must have $x \neq z$. If $(x, z) \in R_C$, it follows that $(x, x) \in R_C$ and thus $(x, x) \in R$ by Theorem 3.1, a contradiction. If $(x, z) \notin R_C$, the definition of $R'$, together with $x \neq z$, implies $(x, z) \notin R'$. Because $z \in S$, this contradicts our assumption that $x \in G(S, R')$.

(e) The remaining equivalence is established by showing that G-Ø-Ø implies G-R-Ø. Suppose $R$ is a G-rationalization of $C$. Define

$$R' = R_C \cup \Delta.$$

Clearly, $R'$ is reflexive because $\Delta \subseteq R'$. To show that $R'$ is a G-rationalization of $C$, let $S \in \Sigma$ and $x \in S$.

First, suppose $x \in C(S)$. This implies $(x, y) \in R_C$ and, by definition, $(x, y) \in R'$ for all $y \in S$. Hence $x \in G(S, R')$.

Now suppose $x \in G(S, R')$. By the definition of $R'$, this implies

$$(x, y) \in R_C \text{ or } x = y$$

for all $y \in S$. If $S = \{x\}$, the non-emptiness of $C(S)$ implies $x \in C(S)$ and we are done. If there exists $z \in S$ such that $x \neq z$, it follows that $(x, z) \in R_C$ and, by the definition of $R_C$, there exists $T \in \Sigma$ such that $x \in C(T)$ and $z \in T$. Again using the definition of $R_C$, this implies $(x, x) \in R_C$. Thus, $(x, y) \in R_C$ for all $y \in S$. By Theorem 3.1, $(x, y) \in R$ for all $y \in S$, and $x \in C(S)$ follows because $R$ is a G-rationalization of $C$.

(f) Now we show that G-C-Q implies G-R-Q. Suppose $R$ is a complete and quasi-transitive G-rationalization of $C$. Define $R'$ as in (3.1). Clearly, $R'$ is reflexive. To prove that $R'$ is quasi-transitive, suppose $(x, y) \in P(R')$ and $(y, z) \in P(R')$. By (3.2), $(x, x) \in R$ and $(y, y) \in R$. Suppose $(x, y) \notin P(R)$. Because $R$ is complete, we have $(y, x) \in R$. Because $(y, y) \in R$, it follows that $(y, x) \in R'$ by the definition of $R'$, contradicting $(x, y) \in P(R')$. Therefore, $(x, y) \in P(R)$.

If $(z, z) \in R$, an argument parallel to that employed above to conclude $(x, y) \in P(R)$ yields $(y, z) \in P(R)$. Because $R$ is quasi-transitive, it follows that $(x, z) \in P(R)$. Because $(x, x) \in R$ and $(x, z) \in P(R)$, we must have $(x, z) \in R'$ by the definition of $R'$. Furthermore, $(z, x) \notin R$ implies $(z, x) \notin R'$ by the definition of $R'$ and, consequently, we obtain $(x, z) \in P(R')$.

If $(z, z) \notin R$, we use (3.2) to obtain $(z, x) \notin R'$. Suppose $(x, z) \notin R'$. Because $(x, x) \in R$, this implies $(x, z) \notin R$ by the definition of $R'$ and hence $(z, x) \in P(R)$ by the completeness of $R$. Because $R$ is quasi-transitive, we obtain $(z, y) \in P(R)$ and hence $(y, z) \notin R$. Because $(z, z) \notin R$, the definition of $R'$ implies $(y, z) \notin R'$, contradicting $(y, z) \in P(R')$. Therefore, $(x, z) \in R'$ and, because $(z, x) \notin R'$, it follows that $(x, z) \in P(R')$.

To prove that $R'$ is a G-rationalization of $C$, let $S \in \Sigma$ and $x \in S$.

Suppose $x \in C(S)$. Because $R$ is a G-rationalization of $C$, we have $(x, y) \in R$ for all $y \in S$, which, in particular, implies $(x, x) \in R$. Therefore, by the definition of $R'$, $(x, y) \in R'$ for all $y \in S$ and hence $x \in G(S, R')$.

Now suppose $x \in G(S, R')$. Therefore, $(x, y) \in R'$ for all $y \in S$. If $S = \{x\}$, $x \in C(S)$ follows from the non-emptiness of $C(S)$. If there exists $y \in S$ such that $x \neq y$, (3.2) implies $(x, x) \in R$. Therefore, because $(x, y) \in R'$ implies $(x, y) \in R$ for all $y \in S$ and $R$ is a G-rationalization of $C$, we immediately obtain $x \in C(S)$.

To prove that no further implications other than those resulting from the arrows depicted in the theorem statement are valid, it is sufficient to provide examples showing that (g) G-RC-Q does not imply G-Ø-S; (h) G-Ø-S does not imply G-Ø-Q; (i) G-Ø-S does not imply G-C-Ø; (j) G-RC-A does not imply G-Ø-Q; (k) G-C-Q does not imply G-RC-A; (l) G-R-Q does not imply G-C-Ø; (m) G-Ø-Q does not imply G-R-Q; and (n) G-C-O does not imply G-Ø-A. Some of these examples may appear to be more elaborate than required to prove the desired result. This is indeed the case. The reason for not employing simpler examples is that we return to some of them when discussing specific domains in Part III of this book.

(g) To show that G-RC-Q does not imply G-Ø-S, consider the following example. Let $X = \{x, y, z\}$ and $\Sigma = \mathcal{X}$. Define the choice function $C$ by letting $C(\{x\}) = \{x\}$, $C(\{x, y\}) = \{x\}$, $C(X) = \{x, z\}$, $C(\{x, z\}) = \{x, z\}$, $C(\{y\}) = \{y\}$, $C(\{y, z\}) = \{y, z\}$, and $C(\{z\}) = \{z\}$. This choice function is G-rationalizable by the reflexive, complete, and quasi-transitive relation

$$R = \{(x, x), (x, y), (x, z), (y, y), (y, z), (z, x), (z, y), (z, z)\}.$$

Suppose $R'$ is a G-rationalization of $C$. Because $y \in C(\{y\})$, we have $(y, y) \in R'$. Therefore, $y \notin C(\{x, y\})$ and $x \in C(\{x, y\})$ together imply $(x, y) \in P(R')$. Because $y \in C(\{y, z\})$, we have $(y, z) \in R'$ and, analogously, because $z \in C(\{x, z\})$, we have $(z, x) \in R'$. This implies that $R'$ cannot be Suzumura consistent.

**(h)** We now prove that **G-Ø-S** does not imply **G-Ø-Q**. Let $X = \{x, y, z, v\}$ and $\Sigma = \{\{x\}, \{x, y\}, X, \{x, v\}, \{y\}, \{y, z\}, \{z\}\}$. Define the choice function $C$ by letting $C(\{x\}) = \{x\}$, $C(\{x, y\}) = \{x\}$, $C(X) = \{v\}$, $C(\{x, v\}) = \{x, v\}$, $C(\{y\}) = \{y\}$, $C(\{y, z\}) = \{y\}$, and $C(\{z\}) = \{z\}$. This choice function is G-rationalizable by the Suzumura-consistent relation

$$R = \{(x, x), (x, y), (x, v), (y, y), (y, z),$$
$$(z, z), (v, x), (v, y), (v, z), (v, v)\}.$$

Suppose $C$ is G-rationalizable by a quasi-transitive relation $R'$. Because $y \in C(\{y\})$, we have $(y, y) \in R'$. Therefore, $y \notin C(\{x, y\})$ and $x \in C(\{x, y\})$ together imply $(x, y) \in P(R') \subseteq R'$. Analogously, $z \in C(\{z\})$ implies $(z, z) \in R'$ and, consequently, $z \notin C(\{y, z\})$ and $y \in C(\{y, z\})$ together imply $(y, z) \in P(R')$. Because $R'$ is quasi-transitive, it follows that $(x, z) \in P(R')$ and hence $(x, z) \in R'$. Furthermore, because $R'$ is a G-rationalization of $C$ and $x \in C(\{x, v\})$, we must have $(x, x) \in R'$ and $(x, v) \in R'$. Thus, $x \in G(X, R')$ and, because $R'$ is a G-rationalization of $C$, it follows that $x \in C(X)$, contradicting the definition of $C$.

**(i)** Next, we prove that **G-Ø-S** does not imply **G-C-Ø**. Let $X = \{x, y, z\}$ and $\Sigma = \{\{x\}, \{x, y\}, X, \{x, z\}\}$. Define the choice function $C$ by letting $C(\{x\}) = \{x\}$, $C(\{x, y\}) = \{x, y\}$, $C(X) = \{x\}$, and $C(\{x, z\}) = \{x, z\}$. $C$ is G-rationalizable by the Suzumura-consistent relation

$$R = \{(x, x), (x, y), (x, z), (y, x), (y, y), (z, x), (z, z)\},$$

but it does not have a complete G-rationalization. By way of contradiction, suppose $R'$ is such a relation. By completeness, we must have $(y, z) \in R'$ or $(z, y) \in R'$. Suppose first that $(y, z) \in R'$. Because $R'$ is a G-rationalization of $C$ and $y \in C(\{x, y\})$, it follows that $(y, x) \in R'$ and $(y, y) \in R'$. Together with $(y, z) \in R'$ and the assumption that $R'$ is a G-rationalization of $C$, we obtain $y \in C(X)$, contradicting the definition of $C$. Now suppose $(z, y) \in R'$. Because $R'$ is a G-rationalization of $C$ and $z \in C(\{x, z\})$, it follows that $(z, x) \in R'$ and $(z, z) \in R'$. Together with $(z, y) \in R'$ and the assumption that $R'$ is a G-rationalization of $C$, we obtain $z \in C(X)$, again contradicting the definition of $C$.

**(j)** To prove that **G-RC-A** does not imply **G-Ø-Q**, let $X = \{x, y, z\}$ and $\Sigma = \mathcal{X}$. Define the choice function $C$ by $C(\{x\}) = \{x\}$, $C(\{x, y\}) = \{x\}$, $C(X) = \{x\}$, $C(\{x, z\}) = \{x, z\}$, $C(\{y\}) = \{y\}$, $C(\{y, z\}) = \{y\}$, and

$C(\{z\}) = \{z\}$. $C$ is G-rationalizable by the reflexive, complete, and acyclical relation

$$R = \{(x,x),(x,y),(x,z),(y,y),(y,z),(z,x),(z,z)\}.$$

By way of contradiction, suppose $R'$ is a quasi-transitive G-rationalization of $C$. Because $y \in C(\{y,z\})$, $z \in C(\{z\})$, and $z \notin C(\{y,z\})$, the assumption that $R'$ is a G-rationalization of $C$ implies $(y,z) \in P(R')$. Furthermore, because $x \in C(\{x,y\})$ and $y \notin C(\{x,y\})$, we obtain $(x,y) \in P(R')$. Because $R'$ is quasi-transitive, it follows that $(x,z) \in P(R')$. This, in turn, implies $(z,x) \notin R'$ and, because $R'$ is a G-rationalization of $C$, $z \notin C(\{x,z\})$, contradicting the definition of $C$.

(k) We now show that **G-C-Q** does not imply **G-RC-A**. Let $X = \{x,y,$ $z,v\}$ and $\Sigma = \{\{x,y,v\},\{x,v\},\{y\},\{y,z\},\{y,z,v\},\{y,v\},\{v\}\}$, and define $C(\{x,y,v\}) = \{v\}$, $C(\{x,v\}) = \{v\}$, $C(\{y\}) = \{y\}$, $C(\{y,z\}) = \{y\}$, $C(\{y,$ $z,v\}) = \{y\}$, $C(\{y,v\}) = \{y,v\}$, and $C(\{v\}) = \{v\}$. This choice function is G-rationalizable by the complete and quasi-transitive relation

$$R = \{(x,y),(x,z),(x,v),(y,y),(y,z),(y,v),$$
$$(z,x),(z,y),(z,v),(v,x),(v,y),(v,v)\}.$$

Suppose $R'$ is a reflexive, complete, and acyclical G-rationalization of $C$. Because $R'$ is reflexive and $C(\{y,z\}) = \{y\}$, we obtain $(y,z) \in P(R')$. Analogously, because $C(\{x,v\}) = \{v\}$ and $R'$ is reflexive, we must have $(v,x) \in P(R')$. Because $y \in C(\{y,v\})$ and $y \notin C(\{x,y,v\})$, we must have $(y,x) \notin R'$ and, because $R'$ is complete, it follows that $(x,y) \in P(R')$. Analogously, because $v \in C(\{y,v\})$ and $v \notin C(\{y,z,v\})$, we must have $(v,z) \notin R'$ and, because $R'$ is complete, it follows that $(z,v) \in P(R')$. Therefore, we have established that $(x,y) \in P(R')$, $(y,z) \in P(R')$, $(z,v) \in P(R')$, and $(v,x) \in P(R')$, contradicting the acyclicity of $R'$.

(l) To see that **G-R-Q** does not imply **G-C-∅**, consider the following example. Let $X = \{x,y,z\}$, $\Sigma = \{\{x\},\{x,y\},X,\{x,z\}\}$, $C(\{x\}) = \{x\}$, $C(\{x,y\}) = \{x,y\}$, $C(X) = \{x\}$, and $C(\{x,z\}) = \{x,z\}$. $C$ is G-rationalizable by the reflexive and quasi-transitive relation

$$R = \{(x,x),(x,y),(x,z),(y,x),(y,y),(z,x),(z,z)\},$$

but it does not have a complete G-rationalization. By way of contradiction, suppose $R'$ is a complete G-rationalization of $C$. Completeness implies that we must have $(y,z) \in R'$ or $(z,y) \in R'$. Suppose first that $(y,z) \in R'$ is true. Because $R'$ is a G-rationalization of $C$ and $y \in C(\{x, y\})$, it follows that $(y, x) \in R'$ and $(y, y) \in R'$. Together with $(y, z) \in R'$ and the definition of G-rationalizability, we obtain $y \in C(X)$, contradicting the definition of $C$. Now suppose $(z, y) \in R'$. Because $R'$ is a G-rationalization of $C$ and $z \in C(\{x, z\})$, it follows that $(z, x) \in R'$ and $(z, z) \in R'$. Together with $(z, y) \in R'$ and the definition of G-rationalizability, we obtain $z \in C(X)$, again contradicting the definition of $C$.

(m) To show that **G-∅-Q** does not imply **G-R-Q**, consider the following example. Let $X = \{x, y, z, v\}$ and $\Sigma = \{\{x, y\}, X, \{x, y, v\}, \{y\}, \{y, z, v\}, \{y, v\}\}$, and define the choice function $C$ by letting $C(\{x, y\}) = \{y\}$, $C(X) = \{v\}$, $C(\{x, y, v\}) = \{y, v\}$, $C(\{y\}) = \{y\}$, $C(\{y, z, v\}) = \{z, v\}$, and $C(\{y, v\}) = \{y, v\}$. This choice function is G-rationalizable by the quasi-transitive relation

$$R = \{(x, y), (x, v), (y, x), (y, y), (y, v), (z, y),$$
$$(z, z), (z, v), (v, x), (v, y), (v, z), (v, v)\}.$$

Suppose $R'$ is a reflexive and quasi-transitive G-rationalization of $C$. By reflexivity, $(x, x) \in R'$ and, because $x \notin C(\{x, y\})$ and $y \in C(\{x, y\})$, we must have $(y, x) \in P(R')$ and $(y, y) \in R'$. Because $y \in C(\{x, y, v\})$, we have $(y, v) \in R'$. Hence, $y \notin C(\{y, z, v\})$ implies $(y, z) \notin R'$ because $R'$ is a G-rationalization of $C$. Because $z \in C(\{y, z, v\})$, the assumption that $R'$ is a G-rationalization of $C$ implies $(z, y) \in R'$ and, thus, $(z, y) \in P(R')$. $R'$ being quasi-transitive, we obtain $(z, x) \in P(R')$. Because $z \in C(\{y, z, v\})$, it follows that $(z, y) \in R', (z, z) \in R'$, and $(z, v) \in R'$. Together with $(z, x) \in P(R') \subseteq R'$ and the assumption that $R'$ is a G-rationalization of $C$, we obtain $z \in C(X)$, which contradicts the definition of $C$.

(n) We complete the proof by showing that **G-C-∅** does not imply **G-∅-A**. Let $X = \{x, y, z, v\}$ and $\Sigma = \{X, \{x, y, v\}, \{x, z, v\}, \{x, v\}, \{y, z, v\}, \{y, v\}, \{z, v\}, \{v\}\}$. Define the choice function $C$ by letting $C(X) = \{v\}$, $C(\{x, y, v\}) = \{x, v\}$, $C(\{x, z, v\}) = \{z, v\}$, $C(\{x, v\}) = \{x, v\}$, $C(\{y, z, v\}) = \{y, v\}$, $C(\{y, v\}) = \{y, v\}$, $C(\{z, v\}) = \{z, v\}$, and $C(\{v\}) = \{v\}$. $C$ is G-rationalizable by the complete relation $R$ given by

$$\{(x, x), (x, y), (x, v), (y, y), (y, z), (y, v), (z, x),$$
$$(z, z), (z, v), (v, x), (v, y), (v, z), (v, v)\},$$

but it does not have an acyclical G-rationalization. Suppose $R'$ is a G-rationalization of $C$. Because $C(\Sigma) = X$ and $R'$ G-rationalizes $C$, it follows that $\Delta \subseteq R'$. Because $y \notin C(\{x, y, v\})$ and $y \in C(\{y, z, v\})$, the assumption that $R'$ is a G-rationalization of $C$ implies that we must have $(x, y) \in P(R')$. Analogously, the conjunction

$$x \notin C(\{x, z, v\}) \text{ and } x \in C(\{x, y, v\})$$

implies $(z, x) \in P(R')$, and

$$z \notin C(\{y, z, v\}) \text{ and } z \in C(\{x, z, v\})$$

implies $(y, z) \in P(R')$. Therefore, $R'$ cannot be acyclical.   ∎

Although the equivalences established in the above theorem reduce the number of distinct notions of G-rationalizability from a possible twenty to eleven, there remains a relatively rich set of possible definitions. In particular, note that none of the coherence properties of transitivity, quasi-transitivity, Suzumura consistency, and acyclicity is redundant: eliminating any one of them reduces the number of distinct rationalizability properties, and so does the elimination of the versions not involving any coherence property.

Furthermore, it is worth pointing out an important and remarkable difference between G-rationalizability by a transitive or a Suzumura-consistent relation on the one hand and G-rationalizability by a quasi-transitive or an acyclical relation on the other. In the case of G-rationalizability with transitivity or Suzumura consistency, the reflexivity requirement is redundant in all cases. That is, irrespective of whether completeness is imposed as a richness condition, any version of G-rationalizability with transitivity or Suzumura consistency and without reflexivity is equivalent to the definition that is obtained if reflexivity is added. This observation applies to the case where no coherence property is imposed as well. In contrast, G-rationalizability by a complete and quasi-transitive relation is not equivalent to G-rationalizability by a reflexive, complete, and quasi-transitive relation, and the same is true for the relationship between G-rationalizability by a complete and acyclical relation and G-rationalizability by a reflexive, complete, and acyclical relation. In addition, while G-rationalizability by an acyclical relation and G-rationalizability by a reflexive and acyclical relation are equivalent, there is yet another discrepancy in the quasi-transitive case: G-rationalizability by a quasi-transitive relation is not the same as G-rationalizability by a reflexive and quasi-transitive relation.

## 3.3   Maximal-Element Rationalizability

Next, we examine the logical relationships between all our notions of maximal-element rationalizability.

**Theorem 3.3**   *Suppose* $C\colon \Sigma \to \mathcal{X}$ *is a choice function with an arbitrary non-empty domain* $\Sigma \subseteq \mathcal{X}$. *Then*

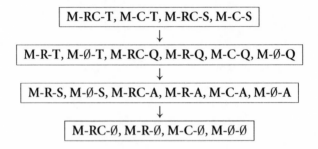

**Proof**   The implications depicted in the theorem statement are straight-forward and, therefore, it is sufficient to establish, for each box, the equiv-alence of all axioms in the box and to provide examples showing that no further implications other than those following from the diagram are valid.

(a) To prove the equivalence of all axioms in the top box, it clearly is suf-ficient to show that **M-C-S** implies **M-RC-T**. Suppose $R$ is a complete and Suzumura-consistent M-rationalization of $C$. Let

$$R' = R \cup \Delta.$$

Clearly, $R'$ is reflexive by definition and complete because $R$ is. Because Suzumura consistency is equivalent to transitivity for a reflexive and com-plete relation, $R'$ is transitive. That $R'$ is an M-rationalization of $C$ follows immediately from the assumption that $R$ is.

(b) The equivalence of the axioms in the second box is established by showing that **M-∅-Q** implies **M-RC-Q** and that **M-∅-Q** implies **M-R-T**.

To establish the first implication, suppose that $R$ is a quasi-transitive M-rationalization of $C$. Define

$$R' = \{(x, y) \in X \times X \mid (y, x) \notin P(R)\}.$$

Clearly, $R'$ is reflexive and complete and, furthermore, $P(R') = P(R)$. Thus, because $R$ is quasi-transitive, $R'$ is quasi-transitive as well. Moreover,

$P(R') = P(R)$ implies $M(S, R') = M(S, R)$ for all $S \in \Sigma$ and, together with the assumption that $R$ M-rationalizes $C$, it follows that $R'$ M-rationalizes $C$ as well.

To complete this part of the proof, we show that M-∅-Q implies M-R-T. Suppose $R$ is a quasi-transitive M-rationalization of $C$. Define

$$R' = P(R) \cup \Delta.$$

Clearly, $R'$ is reflexive and $R'$ is transitive because $R$ is quasi-transitive. Furthermore, we have $P(R') = P(R)$ and hence $M(S, R') = M(S, R)$ for all $S \in \Sigma$, which, together with the assumption that $R$ is an M-rationalization of $C$, implies that $R'$ M-rationalizes $C$.

(c) Now consider the third box. Clearly, it is sufficient to prove that M-∅-S implies M-RC-A and that M-∅-A implies M-R-S.

To prove the first implication, suppose $R$ is a Suzumura-consistent M-rationalization of $C$. As is straightforward to verify, the relation

$$R' = R \cup NC(R)$$

is reflexive and complete. That $R'$ is acyclical follows from the Suzumura consistency of $R$ and the observation that, by definition, $P(R') = P(R)$. Together with the assumption that $R$ is an M-rationalization of $C$, this equality of the asymmetric factor of $R'$ and that of $R$ implies that $R'$ is an M-rationalization of $C$ as well.

Now suppose $R$ is an acyclical M-rationalization of $C$. Defining

$$R' = (R \setminus I(R)) \cup \Delta,$$

it follows immediately that $R'$ is a reflexive and Suzumura-consistent M-rationalization of $C$.

(d) The equivalence of the properties in the fourth box is established by showing that M-∅-∅ implies M-RC-∅. Suppose $R$ is an M-rationalization of $C$. Let

$$R' = R \cup NC(R).$$

As in part (c), in view of $P(R') = P(R)$, it follows immediately that $R'$ is a reflexive and complete M-rationalization of $C$.

Given the equivalences established above, the examples defined in parts (e) through (g) are sufficient to complete the proof of the theorem.

(e) That M-∅-Q does not imply M-C-S is established as follows. Let $X = \{x, y, z\}$ and $\Sigma = \{\{x, y\}, \{x, z\}, \{y, z\}\}$. Define the choice function $C$

by letting $C(\{x, y\}) = \{x, y\}$, $C(\{x, z\}) = \{z\}$, and $C(\{y, z\}) = \{y, z\}$. This choice function is M-rationalizable by the quasi-transitive relation

$$R = \{(z, x)\}.$$

Suppose $R'$ is a complete M-rationalization of $C$. By the definition of M-rationalizability, we must have $(z, x) \in P(R')$ because $x \notin C(\{x, z\})$. The completeness of $R'$ implies, together with the definition of M-rationalizability, that we must have $(x, y) \in I(R')$ and $(y, z) \in I(R')$. This implies that $R'$ cannot be Suzumura consistent.

(f) To show that **M-∅-A** does not imply **M-∅-Q**, consider the set $X = \{x, y, z\}$ and the domain $\Sigma = \{\{x, y\}, \{x, z\}, \{y, z\}\}$, and define the choice function $C$ by letting $C(\{x, y\}) = \{x\}$, $C(\{x, z\}) = \{x, z\}$, and $C(\{y, z\}) = \{y\}$. This choice function is M-rationalizable by the acyclical relation

$$R = \{(x, y), (y, z)\}.$$

Suppose $R'$ is an M-rationalization of $C$. Because $z \in C(\{x, z\})$, the definition of M-rationalizability implies $(x, z) \notin P(R')$. Again using the definition of M-rationalizability, we must have $(x, y) \in P(R')$ because $y \notin C(\{x, y\})$, and $(y, z) \in P(R')$ because $z \notin C(\{y, z\})$. This implies that $R'$ cannot be quasi-transitive.

(g) It remains to be shown that **M-∅-∅** does not imply **M-∅-A**. Let $X = \{x, y, z\}$ and $\Sigma = \{\{x, y\}, \{x, z\}, \{y, z\}\}$, and define $C(\{x, y\}) = \{x\}$, $C(\{x, z\}) = \{z\}$, and $C(\{y, z\}) = \{y\}$. Clearly, $C$ is M-rationalizable by the relation

$$R = \{(x, y), (y, z), (z, x)\}.$$

Suppose $R'$ is an M-rationalization of $C$. Because $y \notin C(\{x, y\})$, the definition of M-rationalizability implies $(x, y) \in P(R')$. Analogously, $x \notin C(\{x, z\})$ implies $(z, x) \in P(R')$, and $z \notin C(\{y, z\})$ implies $(y, z) \in P(R')$. This implies that $R'$ is not acyclical.  ∎

As opposed to the case of greatest-element rationalizability, reflexivity is redundant in all cases now, irrespective of the coherence property imposed (if any), including quasi-transitivity and acyclicity: any version of M-rationalizability without reflexivity is equivalent to the version obtained by adding this richness property.

There is an interesting feature that distinguishes the notions of transitive or Suzumura-consistent M-rationalizability from those involving quasi-transitivity, acyclicity, or none of the coherence properties. All four M-rationalizability properties involving quasi-transitivity are equivalent, and so are all four notions involving acyclicity as well as the four versions without any coherence property. In contrast, there are two distinct notions of transitive M-rationalizability and two distinct notions of Suzumura-consistent M-rationalizability.

## 3.4   A Synthesis

It is worthwhile contrasting Theorem 3.3 with Theorem 3.2. In the case of M-rationalizability, only four distinct notions of rationalizability exist although, in principle, there are twenty versions, as in the case of G-rationalizability. This means that there is a dramatic reduction of possible definitions due to the equivalences established in the theorem. Note that now there is a substantial degree of redundancy. In particular, it is possible to generate all possible versions of M-rationalizability with merely two coherence properties: any of the combinations of transitivity and Suzumura consistency, transitivity and acyclicity, and quasi-transitivity and Suzumura consistency is sufficient to obtain all four notions of M-rationalizability (provided, of course, that the option of not imposing any coherence property is retained).

Finally, we combine Theorems 3.2 and 3.3 to obtain the logical relationships among all forty versions of rationalizability introduced in this chapter. Due to the equivalence of G-rationalizability and M-rationalizability in the case of reflexive and complete rationalizations, the number of distinct definitions remains at eleven—the number of distinct G-rationalizability properties. Because the result follows immediately from Theorems 3.2 and 3.3, together with the observation that greatest-element rationalizability and maximal-element rationalizability coincide in the presence of reflexivity and completeness, no separate proof is required. As is apparent from the statement of the following theorem, M-rationalizability does not add any new versions of rationalizability, provided that all definitions of G-rationalizability with all of the four coherence properties are present. Therefore, the characterization results stated in Chapter 4 can be proved without explicitly having to work with M-rationalizability.

**Theorem 3.4**  *Suppose* $C\colon \Sigma \to \mathcal{X}$ *is a choice function with an arbitrary non-empty domain* $\Sigma \subseteq \mathcal{X}$. *Then*

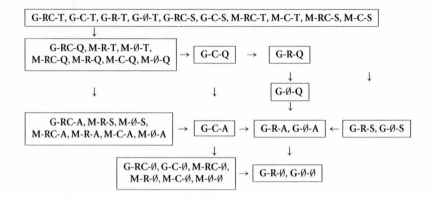

# — 4 —

# Characterizations

## 4.1 A Preliminary Result

The purpose of this chapter is to provide necessary and sufficient conditions for the different versions of rationalizability identified in the previous chapter. We begin with a review of three well-known characterizations in the following section. They involve G-rationalizability without any richness or coherence properties, G-rationalizability by a Suzumura-consistent relation, and G-rationalizability by a transitive relation. The reason why these three forms of rationalizability are singled out will become clear in our discussion following the three corresponding theorems. Again, Suzumura consistency is shown to occupy a special position as compared to the other two weakenings of transitivity.

The following preliminary observation extends Theorem 3.1 to transitive and to Suzumura-consistent G-rationalizations.

**Theorem 4.1** *Suppose* $C : \Sigma \to \mathcal{X}$ *is a choice function with an arbitrary non-empty domain* $\Sigma \subseteq \mathcal{X}$ *and R is a relation on X.*

*(i) If R is a transitive G-rationalization of C, then* $tc(R_C) \subseteq R$.
*(ii) If R is a Suzumura-consistent G-rationalization of C, then* $sc(R_C) \subseteq R$.

**Proof** (i) Suppose that $R$ is a transitive G-rationalization of $C$ and $(x, y) \in tc(R_C)$. By definition, there exist $K \in \mathbb{N}$ and $x^0, \ldots, x^K \in X$ such that

$$x = x^0 \text{ and } (x^{k-1}, x^k) \in R_C \text{ for all } k \in \{1, \ldots, K\} \text{ and } x^K = y.$$

By Theorem 3.1, $(x^{k-1}, x^k) \in R$ for all $k \in \{1, \ldots, K\}$ and the transitivity of $R$ implies $(x, y) = (x^0, x^K) \in R$.

(ii) Now suppose that $R$ is a Suzumura-consistent G-rationalization of $C$ and $(x, y) \in sc(R_C)$. By definition,

$$(x, y) \in R_C \text{ or } [(x, y) \in tc(R_C) \text{ and } (y, x) \in R_C].$$

If $(x, y) \in R_C$, Theorem 3.1 implies $(x, y) \in R$. If $(x, y) \in tc(R_C)$ and $(y, x) \in R_C$, there exist $K \in \mathbb{N}$ and $x^0, \ldots, x^K \in X$ such that

$$x = x^0 \text{ and } (x^{k-1}, x^k) \in R_C \text{ for all } k \in \{1, \ldots, K\} \text{ and } x^K = y.$$

By Theorem 3.1, $(x^{k-1}, x^k) \in R$ for all $k \in \{1, \ldots, K\}$ and, thus, $(x, y) \in tc(R)$. Moreover, $(y, x) \in R$ by Theorem 3.1 because $(y, x) \in R_C$. If $(x, y) \notin R$, it follows that $(y, x) \in P(R)$ because $(y, x) \in R$. Because $(x, y) \in tc(R)$, this contradicts the Suzumura consistency of $R$. Therefore, $(x, y) \in R$. ∎

## 4.2 Three Special Cases

Our first characterization of greatest-element rationalizability without any further requirements or, equivalently, greatest-element rationalizability by a reflexive relation, is due to Richter (1971). Richter (1971) shows that the following axiom, introduced as the V-axiom in his paper, is necessary and sufficient for G-rationalizability without further restrictions on a G-rationalization.

**Direct revelation coherence**  For all $S \in \Sigma$ and for all $x \in S$,

$$(x, y) \in R_C \text{ for all } y \in S \Rightarrow x \in C(S).$$

As established in Theorem 3.1, the direct revealed preference relation of a choice function $C$ must be respected by any G-rationalization and, therefore, direct revelation coherence is a necessary condition for the G-rationalizability of $C$. Richter (1971) shows that this property is sufficient as well. Thus, we obtain the following characterization.

**Theorem 4.2**  *Suppose $C: \Sigma \to \mathcal{X}$ is a choice function with an arbitrary non-empty domain $\Sigma \subseteq \mathcal{X}$. $C$ satisfies any of **G-R-∅**, **G-∅-∅** if and only if $C$ satisfies direct revelation coherence.*

**Proof**  By Theorem 3.4, it is sufficient to establish the equivalence of G-∅-∅ and direct revelation coherence.

To prove the only if part of the theorem, suppose $R$ is a G-rationalization of $C$ and let $S \in \Sigma$ and $x \in S$ be such that $(x, y) \in R_C$ for all $y \in S$. By Theorem 3.1, $(x, y) \in R$ for all $y \in S$ and, because $R$ is a G-rationalization of $C$, it follows that $x \in C(S)$.

Now suppose $C$ satisfies direct revelation coherence. We complete the proof by showing that, under this assumption, $R = R_C$ is a G-rationalization of $C$. Let $S \in \Sigma$ and $x \in S$.

If $x \in C(S)$, we obtain $(x, y) \in R_C$ for all $y \in S$ and therefore $x \in G(S, R_C) = G(S, R)$ by definition.

If $x \in G(S, R) = G(S, R_C)$, we have $(x, y) \in R_C$ for all $y \in S$ and direct revelation coherence immediately implies $x \in C(S)$.   ∎

Next, we present a characterization of **G-R-S** and **G-∅-S** by employing a strengthening of direct revelation coherence that replaces the direct revealed preference relation $R_C$ with its Suzumura-consistent closure $sc(R_C)$. That is, we show that **G-∅-S** (and, thus, **G-R-S**) is equivalent to the following property.

**Suzumura-consistent closure coherence**    For all $S \in \Sigma$ and for all $x \in S$,

$$(x, y) \in sc(R_C) \text{ for all } y \in S \Rightarrow x \in C(S).$$

This axiom demands that the observed choice behavior cannot go against the implications of the observations revealed through $R_C$ in the presence of Suzumura consistency. We already know from part (ii) of Theorem 4.1 that any Suzumura-consistent G-rationalization of a choice function $C$ must respect the Suzumura-consistent closure of the direct revealed preference relation of $C$ and, in analogy to the direct revelation coherence axiom discussed in the context of G-rationalizability without completeness or any coherence conditions, the axiom is necessary and sufficient for **G-∅-S**. Thus, we obtain the following characterization result that is due to Bossert, Sprumont, and Suzumura (2005a).

**Theorem 4.3**   *Suppose $C: \Sigma \to \mathcal{X}$ is a choice function with an arbitrary non-empty domain $\Sigma \subseteq \mathcal{X}$. $C$ satisfies any of* **G-R-S**, **G-∅-S** *if and only if $C$ satisfies Suzumura-consistent closure coherence.*

**Proof**   By Theorem 3.4, it is sufficient to establish the equivalence of **G-∅-S** and Suzumura-consistent closure coherence.

To prove the only if part of the theorem, suppose $R$ is a Suzumura-consistent G-rationalization of $C$ and let $S \in \Sigma$ and $x \in S$ be such that $(x, y) \in sc(R_C)$ for all $y \in S$. By part (ii) of Theorem 4.1, $(x, y) \in R$ for all $y \in S$. Thus, because $R$ is a G-rationalization of $C$, $x \in C(S)$.

Now suppose $C$ satisfies Suzumura-consistent closure coherence. We complete the proof by showing that $R = sc(R_C)$ is a Suzumura-consistent G-rationalization of $C$. That $R$ is Suzumura consistent follows from Theorem 2.4. To prove that $R$ is a G-rationalization of $C$, let $S \in \Sigma$ and $x \in S$.

Suppose first that $x \in C(S)$. By definition, this implies $(x, y) \in R_C$ for all $y \in S$ and, because $R_C \subseteq sc(R_C)$ as an immediate consequence of the definition of the Suzumura-consistent closure, we obtain $(x, y) \in sc(R_C)$ for all $y \in S$. Hence $x \in G(S, R)$.

Conversely, suppose $x \in G(S, R)$ and therefore $(x, y) \in R_C \subseteq sc(R_C)$ for all $y \in S$. Suzumura-consistent closure coherence immediately implies $x \in C(S)$.  ∎

As shown by Richter (1966), the *congruence* axiom is necessary and sufficient for G-RC-T. An equivalent condition is the following axiom of *transitive closure coherence*, introduced by Richter (1971) as the W-axiom. This condition requires that if an alternative $x$ in a feasible set $S$ is indirectly revealed preferred to all alternatives in $S$, then $x$ must be chosen in $S$.

**Transitive closure coherence**    For all $S \in \Sigma$ and for all $x \in S$,

$$(x, y) \in tc(R_C) \text{ for all } y \in S \Rightarrow x \in C(S).$$

This axiom strengthens Suzumura-consistent closure coherence and, thus, direct revelation coherence. It requires that the observed choice behavior cannot go against the implications of the observations revealed through $tc(R_C)$, provided that transitivity is required as a coherence property of a G-rationalization. By part (i) of Theorem 4.1, any transitive G-rationalization of a choice function $C$ must respect the transitive closure of the direct revealed preference relation of $C$ and it is, therefore, not surprising that the axiom is necessary for G-∅-T. In addition, it turns out to be sufficient as well.

In view of Theorem 3.4, the result characterizing the strongest version of rationalizability can be proven by establishing the equivalence of transitive closure coherence and G-∅-T. The following theorem, due to Richter (1971), identifies transitive closure coherence as a necessary and sufficient condition for the strongest notion of rationalizability among those considered here.

**Theorem 4.4**  *Suppose* $C \colon \Sigma \to \mathcal{X}$ *is a choice function with an arbitrary non-empty domain* $\Sigma \subseteq \mathcal{X}$. *C satisfies any of* **G-RC-T, G-C-T, G-R-T, G-Ø-T, G-RC-S, G-C-S, M-RC-T, M-C-T, M-RC-S, M-C-S** *if and only if C satisfies transitive closure coherence.*

**Proof**  By Theorem 3.4, it is sufficient to establish the equivalence of **G-Ø-T** and transitive closure coherence.

Suppose first $C$ satisfies **G-Ø-T** and let $R$ be a transitive G-rationalization of $C$. Let $S \in \Sigma$ and $x \in S$ be such that $(x, y) \in tc(R_C)$ for all $y \in S$. By part (i) of Theorem 4.1, it follows that $(x, y) \in R$ for all $y \in S$. Because $R$ is a G-rationalization of $C$, it follows that $x \in C(S)$.

Now suppose $C$ satisfies transitive closure coherence. We complete the proof by showing that the (by definition, transitive) indirect revealed preference relation $R = tc(R_C)$ is a G-rationalization of $C$. Let $S \in \Sigma$ and $x \in S$.

Suppose $x \in C(S)$. By definition, this implies $(x, y) \in R_C$ and thus $(x, y) \in tc(R_C)$ for all $y \in S$. Hence, $x \in G(S, tc(R_C)) = G(S, R)$.

To complete the proof, suppose $x \in G(S, R)$. By definition, $(x, y) \in R = tc(R_C)$ for all $y \in S$ and transitive closure coherence immediately implies $x \in C(S)$.  ∎

## 4.3  A Unified Approach

We now use a unified framework to provide characterizations of all eleven distinct notions of rationalizability. These axiomatizations follow a format that differs substantially from that of the previous three theorems. The necessary and sufficient conditions of Theorems 4.2, 4.3, and 4.4 are based on respecting the direct revealed preference relation, its Suzumura-consistent closure, and its transitive closure, respectively. For the remaining eight forms of rationalizability, this approach cannot be followed. The reason is that there is no such thing as a *smallest* quasi-transitive relation or a *smallest* acyclical relation containing a given arbitrary relation. Moreover, in the absence of coherence properties when completeness is imposed, an analogous problem arises. Suppose we have found an arbitrary G-rationalization of a choice function. There may or may not exist a complete extension of this relation that is also a G-rationalization of $C$, but even if such a complete G-rationalization exists, not all complete extensions may be such G-rationalizations. Again, there is no *unique* extension of an incomplete relation. In contrast, any relation $R$ has a well-defined *transitive closure* and a well-defined *Suzumura-consistent closure*, which are, respectively, the smallest transitive relation containing $R$ and the smallest Suzumura-consistent relation containing $R$. Intuitively, when moving from $R$ to its transitive or Suzumura-consistent closure, pairs are added that are *necessarily* in any transitive or Suzumura-consistent relation containing $R$. As soon as there exist alternatives $x^0, \ldots, x^K$ connecting two alternatives $x$ and $y$ via a chain of weak preferences, transitivity demands that the pair $(x, y)$ is included in any transitive relation that contains $R$. Analogously, a chain of that nature implies that if, in addition, the pair $(y, x)$ is in $R$, $(x, y)$ must be added if the resulting relation is to be Suzumura consistent. In contrast, there are no necessary additions to a relation in order to transform it into a quasi-transitive relation by augmenting it. For instance, suppose we have $(x, y) \in P(R)$, $(y, z) \in P(R)$, and $(z, x) \in P(R)$. In order to define a quasi-transitive relation that contains $R$, at least two of the three strict preferences must be converted into indifferences but *any two* will do. Thus, there is no unique smallest quasi-transitive relation containing $R$. Similarly, if we have a strict preference cycle, an acyclical relation containing $R$ merely has to have the property that at least *one* of the pairs along the cycle, representing a strict preference, must be converted into an indifference. But, without further information, there is nothing that forces this indifference on a specific pair along the cycle. As a consequence, there is, in general, no smallest acyclical relation containing an arbitrary relation $R$. The same difficulty arises when G-rationalizability involving completeness without any coherence conditions is considered. For that reason, we introduce some further concepts in order to be able to formulate necessary and sufficient conditions for all definitions of rationalizability.

Let $C \colon \Sigma \to \mathcal{X}$ be a choice function with an arbitrary non-empty domain $\Sigma \subseteq \mathcal{X}$, and define

$$\mathcal{A}_C = \{(S, y) \mid S \in \Sigma \text{ and } y \in S \setminus C(S)\}.$$

For a choice function $C$ such that $\mathcal{A}_C \neq \emptyset$, let

$$\mathcal{F}_C = \{f \colon \mathcal{A}_C \to X \mid f(S, y) \in S \text{ for all } (S, y) \in \mathcal{A}_C\}.$$

The set $\mathcal{A}_C$ consists of all pairs of a feasible set and an element that belongs to the set but is not chosen by $C$. If $C(S) = S$ for all $S \in \Sigma$, the set $\mathcal{A}_C$ is empty; in all other cases, $\mathcal{A}_C \neq \emptyset$. The functions in $\mathcal{F}_C$ have an intuitive interpretation. They assign a feasible element to each pair of a feasible set $S$ and an alternative $y$ that is in $S$ but not chosen from $S$. Within the framework of G-rationalizability, the intended interpretation is that $f(S, y)$

is an alternative in $S$ that can be used to prevent $y$ from being chosen in the sense that $y$ is not at least as good as $f(S, y)$ according to a G-rationalization. Clearly, the existence of such an alternative for each $(S, y)$ in $\mathcal{A}_C$ is a necessary condition for G-rationalizability.

In addition to the eight forms of rationalizability that are not covered by Theorems 4.2, 4.3, and 4.4, we provide alternative characterizations of the three notions identified in these results. This is done in order to provide a comprehensive treatment and to illustrate that our method can be applied to all forms of rationalizability.

We begin again with the rationalizability property G-R-Ø (and, of course, its equivalent G-Ø-Ø). To do so, we introduce a crucial property of a function $f \in \mathcal{F}_C$ that proves instrumental in our subsequent axiomatization. It imposes a restriction on the relationship between a choice function $C$ and a function $f \in \mathcal{F}_C$.

**Direct exclusion (DRE)**   For all $(S, y) \in \mathcal{A}_C$, for all $T \in \Sigma$, and for all $x \in T$,

$$f(S, y) = x \Rightarrow y \notin C(T).$$

The interpretation of this condition is very intuitive, given the purpose of a function $f$ as mentioned above. According to the definition of G-rationalizability, if $x = f(S, y) \in S$ is responsible for $y$ being prevented from being chosen in $S$, then $y$ is not at least as good as $x$ according to a G-rationalization of $C$. This being the case, $y$ cannot possibly be chosen from any set containing $x$ because, according to G-rationalizability, such a choice would require that $y$ be at least as good as $x$, which we have just ruled out. Thus, provided that $\mathcal{A}_C$ is non-empty, the existence of a function $f$ satisfying **DRE** clearly is necessary for G-rationalizability even if no richness or coherence properties are imposed on a rationalization. Conversely, this requirement is also sufficient for G-R-Ø and G-Ø-Ø so that we obtain the following theorem, due to Bossert and Suzumura (2009a).

**Theorem 4.5**  *Suppose $C: \Sigma \to \mathcal{X}$ is a choice function with an arbitrary non-empty domain $\Sigma \subseteq \mathcal{X}$. $C$ satisfies any of G-R-Ø, G-Ø-Ø if and only if, whenever $\mathcal{A}_C \neq \emptyset$, there exists $f \in \mathcal{F}_C$ satisfying DRE.*

**Proof**  By Theorem 3.4, it is sufficient to consider G-Ø-Ø.

To prove the only if part of the theorem, let $R$ be a G-rationalization of $C$, and suppose $\mathcal{A}_C \neq \emptyset$. We define a function $f \in \mathcal{F}_C$ as follows. Consider any $(S, y) \in \mathcal{A}_C$. The assumption that $R$ is a G-rationalization of $C$ implies the existence of an alternative $x \in S$ such that $(y, x) \notin R$. Let $f(S, y) = x$. We show that the function $f$ satisfies **DRE**. Suppose $(S, y) \in \mathcal{A}_C$, $T \in \Sigma$, and $x \in T$ are such that $f(S, y) = x$. By the definition of $f$, we obtain $(y, x) \notin R$. Because $R$ is a G-rationalization of $C$, it follows that $y \notin C(T)$.

We now prove the if part of the theorem. If $\mathcal{A}_C = \emptyset$, $R = X \times X$ clearly is a G-rationalization of $C$. If $\mathcal{A}_C \neq \emptyset$, there exists a function $f \in \mathcal{F}_C$ satisfying **DRE**. Define

$$R = \{(x, y) \in X \times X \mid \nexists S \in \Sigma \text{ such that } [(S, x) \in \mathcal{A}_C$$
$$\text{and } f(S, x) = y]\}.$$

To prove that $R$ is a G-rationalization of $C$, let $S \in \Sigma$ and $x \in S$.

Suppose $x \in C(S)$. If there exists $y \in S$ such that $(x, y) \notin R$, it follows from the definition of $R$ that there exists $T \in \Sigma$ such that $(T, x) \in \mathcal{A}_C$ and $f(T, x) = y$. But this contradicts the property **DRE** and, therefore, $x \in G(S, R)$.

Now suppose $x \notin C(S)$. Let $y = f(S, x)$. By definition of $R$, we obtain $(x, y) \notin R$ and thus $x \notin G(S, R)$.   ∎

The intuition underlying the definition of $R$ in the above proof is quite transparent. If $x = f(S, y)$, it follows that $y$ cannot be at least as good as $x$. That $R$ is indeed a G-rationalization of $C$ follows because $f$ satisfies **DRE**.

Next, we examine the consequences of adding completeness as a property of a G-rationalization. The following condition prevents a function $f \in \mathcal{F}_C$ itself from exhibiting incoherent behavior, without reference to its relationship with a choice function.

**Direct irreversibility (DRI)**   For all $(S, y), (T, x) \in \mathcal{A}_C$,

$$\left[ f(S, y) = x \text{ and } x \neq y \right] \Rightarrow f(T, x) \neq y.$$

The existence of a function $f$ with this property is a consequence of requiring a G-rationalization to be complete, given the interpretation of $f$ alluded to above. Suppose $f(S, y) = x$ and $f(T, x) = y$ with distinct $x, y \in X$. According to the interpretation of $f$, this means that $x$ is responsible for keeping $y$ out of $C(S)$ and $y$ is responsible for keeping $x$ out of $C(T)$. By definition of G-rationalizability, this means that, according to a G-rationalization,

$x$ fails to be at least as good as $y$ and, at the same time, $y$ is not at least as good as $x$. But this is in conflict with the completeness requirement.

Conversely, the existence of a function $f$ with the two properties DRE and DRI is sufficient for G-C-Ø and its equivalents. The resulting characterization is a variant of a theorem due to Bossert, Sprumont, and Suzumura (2005b).

**Theorem 4.6** *Suppose* $C \colon \Sigma \to \mathcal{X}$ *is a choice function with an arbitrary non-empty domain* $\Sigma \subseteq \mathcal{X}$. *$C$ satisfies any of* G-RC-Ø, G-C-Ø, M-RC-Ø, M-R-Ø, M-C-Ø, M-Ø-Ø *if and only if, whenever* $\mathcal{A}_C \neq \emptyset$, *there exists* $f \in \mathcal{F}_C$ *satisfying* DRE *and* DRI.

**Proof** Using Theorem 3.4, it is sufficient to treat the case of G-C-Ø.

To prove the only if part of the theorem, let $R$ be a complete G-rationalization of $C$, and suppose $\mathcal{A}_C \neq \emptyset$. We define a function $f \in \mathcal{F}_C$ as follows. Consider any $(S, y) \in \mathcal{A}_C$. The assumption that $R$ is a G-rationalization of $C$ implies the existence of an alternative $x \in S$ such that $(y, x) \notin R$. Let $f(S, y) = x$. We show that the function $f$ has the required properties.

To show that DRE is satisfied, suppose $(S, y) \in \mathcal{A}_C$, $T \in \Sigma$, and $x \in T$ are such that $f(S, y) = x$. By the definition of $f$, we obtain $(y, x) \notin R$. Because $R$ is a G-rationalization of $C$, it follows that $y \notin C(T)$.

To establish the property DRI, let $(S, y), (T, x) \in \mathcal{A}_C$ and suppose $f(S, y) = x$ and $x \neq y$. The definition of $f$ again implies $(y, x) \notin R$. If $f(T, x) = y$, we obtain $(x, y) \notin R$, a contradiction to the completeness of $R$. Thus, $f(T, x) \neq y$.

We now prove the if part of the theorem. If $\mathcal{A}_C = \emptyset$, $R = X \times X$ clearly is a complete G-rationalization of $C$. If $\mathcal{A}_C \neq \emptyset$, there exists a function $f \in \mathcal{F}_C$ satisfying DRE and DRI. Define

$$R = \{(x, y) \in X \times X \mid \not\exists S \in \Sigma \text{ such that } [(S, x) \in \mathcal{A}_C$$
$$\text{and } f(S, x) = y]\}.$$

To prove that $R$ is complete, suppose $x, y \in X$ are such that $x \neq y$, $(x, y) \notin R$ and $(y, x) \notin R$. By definition, there exist $S, T \in \Sigma$ such that $(S, x), (T, y) \in \mathcal{A}_C$, $f(S, x) = y$, and $f(T, y) = x$, contradicting the property DRI.

It remains to be shown that $R$ is a G-rationalization of $C$. Let $S \in \Sigma$ and $x \in S$.

Suppose $x \in C(S)$. If there exists $y \in S$ such that $(x, y) \notin R$, it follows from the definition of $R$ that there exists $T \in \Sigma$ such that $(T, x) \in \mathcal{A}_C$ and $f(T, x) = y$. But this contradicts the property DRE and, therefore, $x \in G(S, R)$.

Now suppose $x \notin C(S)$. Let $y = f(S, x)$. By definition of $R$, we obtain $(x, y) \notin R$ and thus $x \notin G(S, R)$. ∎

The intuition underlying the definition of $R$ in this result is quite straightforward. If $x = f(S, y)$ for distinct $x, y \in X$, it follows that $y$ cannot be at least as good as $x$ and, because of the completeness requirement, this means that $x$ must be better than $y$. The completeness of the resulting relation $R$ is a consequence of the assumption that $f$ possesses the property DRI and, moreover, $R$ is a G-rationalization of $C$ because $f$ satisfies DRE.

Next, we characterize the rationalizability properties that are equivalent to G-∅-A. As a consequence of adding acyclicity as a requirement on a rationalization and removing the completeness condition, the property of direct irreversibility has to be replaced by the following revelation irreversibility axiom.

**Revelation irreversibility (RI)**   For all $K \in \mathbb{N}$ and for all $(S^0, x^0), \ldots,$ $(S^K, x^K) \in \mathcal{A}_C$,

$$[f(S^k, x^k) = x^{k-1} \text{ and } (x^{k-1}, x^k) \in R_C \text{ for all } k \in \{1, \ldots, K\}$$
$$\text{and } (x^K, x^0) \in R_C]$$
$$\Rightarrow f(S^0, x^0) \neq x^K.$$

Revelation irreversibility differs from direct irreversibility in two ways. First, its conclusion applies to chains of relationships between alternatives via $f$ and not only to direct instances thereof. Moreover, the axiom is conditional on any two consecutive elements in the chain being related not only through $f$ but also by means of a direct revealed preference according to $C$. As is straightforward to verify, DRI and RI are independent.

RI is a consequence of the acyclicity of a G-rationalization. To see that this is the case, note first that, according to the interpretation of $f$, $f(S^k, x^k) = x^{k-1}$ means that $x^k$ cannot be at least as good as $x^{k-1}$ according to a G-rationalization. Furthermore, because the direct revealed preference relation has to be respected by any G-rationalization, $x^{k-1}$ must be at least as good as $x^k$, thus leading to a strict preference of $x^{k-1}$ over $x^k$.

Thus, a violation of **RI** immediately yields a violation of the acyclicity of a G-rationalization. Again, the existence of a function $f$ with the requisite properties not only is necessary but also sufficient for the rationalizability definitions under consideration. This result is due to Bossert and Suzumura (2009a).

**Theorem 4.7**  *Suppose $C: \Sigma \to \mathcal{X}$ is a choice function with an arbitrary non-empty domain $\Sigma \subseteq \mathcal{X}$. $C$ satisfies any of* **G-R-A, G-∅-A** *if and only if, whenever $\mathcal{A}_C \neq \emptyset$, there exists $f \in \mathcal{F}_C$ satisfying* **DRE** *and* **RI***.*

**Proof**   By Theorem 3.4, it is sufficient to treat the case of **G-∅-A**.

Suppose $C$ satisfies **G-∅-A** and let $R$ be an acyclical G-rationalization of $C$. Suppose $\mathcal{A}_C \neq \emptyset$. The assumption that $R$ G-rationalizes $C$ implies that, for any pair $(S, y) \in \mathcal{A}_C$, there exists $x \in S$ such that $(y, x) \notin R$. Define $f(S, y) = x$. That $f$ satisfies **DRE** follows as in the previous theorem.

To establish the property **RI**, suppose $K \in \mathbb{N}$ and $(S^0, x^0), \ldots,$ $(S^K, x^K) \in \mathcal{A}_C$ are such that $f(S^k, x^k) = x^{k-1}$ and $(x^{k-1}, x^k) \in R_C$ for all $k \in \{1, \ldots, K\}$ and, moreover, $(x^K, x^0) \in R_C$. By the definition of $f$, we obtain $(x^k, x^{k-1}) \notin R$ for all $k \in \{1, \ldots, K\}$. By Theorem 3.1, $(x^{k-1}, x^k) \in R$ for all $k \in \{1, \ldots, K\}$ and, thus, $(x^{k-1}, x^k) \in P(R)$ for all $k \in \{1, \ldots, K\}$. If $f(S^0, x^0) = x^K$, it follows that $(x^0, x^K) \notin R$ by definition. Because $(x^K, x^0) \in R_C$ implies $(x^K, x^0) \in R$ by Theorem 3.1, we obtain $(x^K, x^0) \in P(R)$. If $K = 1$, this contradicts the observation that $(x^K, x^0) \notin R$, which follows from the hypothesis $f(S^1, x^1) = x^0$ and the definition of $f$. If $K > 1$, we obtain a contradiction to the acyclicity of $R$. Therefore, $f(S^0, x^0) \neq x^K$ and **RI** is satisfied.

We now prove the if part of the theorem. If $\mathcal{A}_C = \emptyset$, $R = X \times X$ is an acyclical G-rationalization of $C$. If $\mathcal{A}_C \neq \emptyset$, there exists a function $f \in \mathcal{F}_C$ satisfying **DRE** and **RI**. Define

$$R = R_C \cup \{(x, y) \mid (y, x) \in R_C \text{ and } \not\exists S \in \Sigma \text{ such that}$$
$$[(S, x) \in \mathcal{A}_C \text{ and } f(S, x) = y]\}.$$

To demonstrate that $R$ is acyclical, suppose $K \in \mathbb{N}$ and $x^0, \ldots, x^K \in X$ are such that $(x^{k-1}, x^k) \in P(R)$ for all $k \in \{1, \ldots, K\}$. Consider any $k \in \{1, \ldots, K\}$. By definition,

$$[(x^{k-1}, x^k) \in R_C \text{ or } [(x^k, x^{k-1}) \in R_C \text{ and } \not\exists T^k \in \Sigma \text{ such that}$$
$$[(T^k, x^{k-1}) \in \mathcal{A}_C \text{ and } f(T^k, x^{k-1}) = x^k]]]$$

and

$$[(x^k, x^{k-1}) \notin R_C \text{ and } [(x^{k-1}, x^k) \notin R_C \text{ or } \exists S^k \in \Sigma \text{ such that}$$
$$[(S^k, x^k) \in \mathcal{A}_C \text{ and } f(S^k, x^k) = x^{k-1}]]].$$

Because $(x^k, x^{k-1}) \notin R_C$ must be true,

$$(x^k, x^{k-1}) \in R_C \text{ and } \nexists T^k \in \Sigma \text{ such that}$$
$$[(T^k, x^{k-1}) \in \mathcal{A}_C \text{ and } f(T^k, x^{k-1}) = x^k]$$

cannot be true. Therefore, $(x^{k-1}, x^k) \in R_C$ must be true, which, in turn, implies that $(x^{k-1}, x^k) \notin R_C$ cannot be true. Therefore, it follows that

$$(x^{k-1}, x^k) \in R_C \text{ and } \exists S^k \in \Sigma \text{ such that}$$
$$[(S^k, x^k) \in \mathcal{A}_C \text{ and } f(S^k, x^k) = x^{k-1}].$$

Using the same argument, it follows that $(x^K, x^0) \in P(R)$ implies $(x^K, x^0) \in R_C$ and there exists $S^0 \in \Sigma$ such that $(S^0, x^0) \in \mathcal{A}_C$ and $f(S^0, x^0) = x^K$. This contradicts the property **RI** and, thus, $(x^K, x^0) \notin P(R)$ and $R$ is acyclical.

We complete the proof by showing that $R$ is a G-rationalization of $C$. Let $S \in \Sigma$ and $x \in S$.

Suppose $x \in C(S)$. This implies $(x, y) \in R_C$ and, by Theorem 3.1, $(x, y) \in R$ for all $y \in S$. Hence, $x \in G(S, R)$.

Now suppose $x \notin C(S)$. Thus, $(S, x) \in \mathcal{A}_C$. Let $y = f(S, x)$. If $(x, y) \in R_C$, there exists $T \in \Sigma$ such that $y \in T$ and $x \in C(T)$. Because $y \in S$, this contradicts the property **DRE**. Therefore, $(x, y) \notin R_C$ and, together with the observations $(S, x) \in \mathcal{A}_C$ and $y = f(S, x)$, it follows that $(x, y) \notin R$ and hence $x \notin G(S, R)$.  ∎

As usual, any G-rationalization $R$ has to respect the direct revealed preference relation $R_C$. Furthermore, the construction of $R$ employed in the above theorem converts all strict direct revealed preferences into indifferences whenever this is possible without conflicting with the interpretation of the function $f$. This is done to reduce the potential for conflicts with acyclicity as much as possible. That the resulting relation satisfies the required properties follows from the properties of $f$.

In order to accommodate completeness as well as acyclicity, we replace **RI** with the following property of distinctness irreversibility.

**Distinctness irreversibility (DSI)**   For all $K \in \mathbb{N}$ and for all $(S^0, x^0), \ldots,$ $(S^K, x^K) \in \mathcal{A}_C$,

$$\left[ f(S^k, x^k) = x^{k-1} \text{ and } x^{k-1} \neq x^k \text{ for all } k \in \{1, \ldots, K\} \right.$$
$$\left. \text{and } x^K \neq x^0 \right] \Rightarrow f(S^0, x^0) \neq x^K.$$

Clearly, distinctness irreversibility implies direct irreversibility (set $K = 1$ to verify this claim). Although **RI** and **DSI** by themselves are independent, **DSI** implies **RI** in the presence of direct exclusion. To see that this is the case, suppose $f$ violates **RI**. Then there exist $K \in \mathbb{N}$ and $(S^0, x^0), \ldots,$ $(S^K, x^K) \in \mathcal{A}_C$ such that $f(S^k, x^k) = x^{k-1}$ and $(x^{k-1}, x^k) \in R_C$ for all $k \in \{1, \ldots, K\}$, $(x^K, x^0) \in R_C$, and $f(S^0, x^0) = x^K$. If any two consecutive elements in this cycle are distinct, we immediately obtain a contradiction to **DSI**. If $x^{k-1} = x^k$ for all $k \in \{1, \ldots, K\}$, it follows that $f(S^0, x^0) = x^0$ and $(x^0, x^0) \in R_C$. By definition of $R_C$, there exists $T \in \Sigma$ such that $x^0 \in C(T) \subseteq T$, contradicting **DRE**.

The property of **DSI** rather than that of **RI** must be added to **DRE** if a rationalization is to be complete in addition to being acyclical. If **DSI** is violated, the completeness of a G-rationalization and the interpretation of $f$ together imply that a G-rationalization must have a strict preference cycle, which immediately yields a contradiction to the acyclicity requirement. The following theorem establishes that the existence of a function $f$ satisfying **DRE** and **DSI** is necessary and sufficient for the rationalizability properties that are equivalent to **G-C-A**. Again, the result is taken from Bossert and Suzumura (2009a).

**Theorem 4.8**   *Suppose $C: \Sigma \to \mathcal{X}$ is a choice function with an arbitrary non-empty domain $\Sigma \subseteq \mathcal{X}$. $C$ satisfies **G-C-A** if and only if, whenever $\mathcal{A}_C \neq \emptyset$, there exists $f \in \mathcal{F}_C$ satisfying **DRE** and **DSI**.*

**Proof**   First, suppose $C$ satisfies **G-C-A** and let $R$ be a complete and acyclical G-rationalization of $C$. Suppose $\mathcal{A}_C \neq \emptyset$. The assumption that $R$ G-rationalizes $C$ implies that, for any pair $(S, y) \in \mathcal{A}_C$, there exists $x \in S$ such that $(y, x) \notin R$. Define $f(S, y) = x$.

To prove that $f$ satisfies **DRE**, suppose $(S, y) \in \mathcal{A}_C$, $T \in \Sigma$, and $x \in T$ are such that $f(S, y) = x$. By the definition of $f$, we obtain $(y, x) \notin R$. Because $R$ is a G-rationalization of $C$, it follows that $y \notin C(T)$.

To establish the property **DSI**, suppose $K \in \mathbb{N}$ and $(S^0, x^0), \ldots, (S^K, x^K) \in \mathcal{A}_C$ are such that $f(S^k, x^k) = x^{k-1}$ and $x^{k-1} \neq x^k$ for all $k \in \{1, \ldots, K\}$ and, furthermore, $x^K \neq x^0$. By the definition of $f$, it follows that $(x^k, x^{k-1}) \notin R$ for all $k \in \{1, \ldots, K\}$. Because $R$ is complete and $x^{k-1} \neq x^k$ for all $k \in \{1, \ldots, K\}$ by assumption, it follows that $(x^{k-1}, x^k) \in P(R)$ for all $k \in \{1, \ldots, K\}$. If $f(S^0, x^0) = x^K$, it follows that $(x^0, x^K) \notin R$ by definition and, by the assumption $x^K \neq x^0$ and the completeness of $R$, we obtain $(x^K, x^0) \in P(R)$. If $K = 1$, this contradicts the observation that $(x^K, x^0) \notin R$, which follows from the hypothesis $f(S^1, x^1) = x^0$ and the definition of $f$. If $K > 1$, we obtain a contradiction to the acyclicity of $R$. Therefore, $f(S^0, x^0) \neq x^K$.

We now prove the if part of the theorem. If $\mathcal{A}_C = \emptyset$, $R = X \times X$ is a complete acyclical G-rationalization of $C$. If $\mathcal{A}_C \neq \emptyset$, there exists a function $f \in \mathcal{F}_C$ satisfying DRE and DSI. Define

$$R = \{(x, y) \in X \times X \mid \not\exists S \in \Sigma \text{ such that}$$
$$[(S, x) \in \mathcal{A}_C \text{ and } f(S, x) = y]\}.$$

We prove that $R$ is complete. By way of contradiction, suppose $x, y \in X$ are such that $x \neq y$, $(x, y) \notin R$, and $(y, x) \notin R$. By the definition of $R$, this implies that there exist $S, T \in \Sigma$ such that $(S, x), (T, y) \in \mathcal{A}_C, f(S, x) = y$, and $f(T, y) = x$. Because $x \neq y$, this contradicts the property DSI. Thus, $R$ is complete.

To show that $R$ is acyclical, suppose $K \in \mathbb{N}$ and $x^0, \ldots, x^K \in X$ are such that $(x^{k-1}, x^k) \in P(R)$ for all $k \in \{1, \ldots, K\}$. By the definition of $R$, this implies that there exist $S^1, \ldots, S^K \in \Sigma$ such that $(S^k, x^k) \in \mathcal{A}_C$ and $x^{k-1} = f(S^k, x^k)$ for all $k \in \{1, \ldots, K\}$. Moreover, for all $k \in \{1, \ldots, K\}$, there exists no $T^k \in \Sigma$ such that $(T^k, x^{k-1}) \in \mathcal{A}_C$ and $x^k = f(T^k, x^{k-1})$. This implies $x^{k-1} \neq x^k$ for all $k \in \{1, \ldots, K\}$. If $(x^K, x^0) \in P(R)$, there exists $S^0 \in \Sigma$ such that $(S^0, x^0) \in \mathcal{A}_C$ and $x^K = f(S^0, x^0)$. Furthermore, there exists no $T^0 \in \Sigma$ such that $(T^0, x^K) \in \mathcal{A}_C$ and $x^0 = f(T^0, x^K)$. This implies $x^0 \neq x^K$ and we obtain a contradiction to the property DSI and, thus, $(x^K, x^0) \notin P(R)$ and $R$ is acyclical.

It remains to be shown that $R$ is a G-rationalization of $C$. Let $S \in \Sigma$ and $x \in S$.

Suppose $x \in C(S)$. If there exist $y \in S$ and $T \in \Sigma$ such that $(T, x) \in \mathcal{A}_C$ and $f(T, x) = y$, we obtain a contradiction to the property DRE. Thus, by definition, $(x, y) \in R$ for all $y \in S$ and hence $x \in G(S, R)$.

Now suppose $x \notin C(S)$. Let $y = f(S, x)$. By the definition of $R$, this implies $(x, y) \notin R$ and, therefore, $x \notin G(S, R)$.  ∎

The intuition underlying the definition of $R$ in this result is quite straightforward. If $x = f(S, y)$, it follows that $y$ cannot be at least as good as $x$ and, because of the completeness assumption, this means that $x$ must be better than $y$ whenever $x \neq y$. The resulting relation has all the required properties as a consequence of the properties of $f$.

Our last set of rationalizability properties involving acyclical G-rationalizations is that containing **G-RC-A**. Because reflexivity is added as a requirement, an unconditional version of irreversibility is called for.

**Indirect irreversibility (II)**   For all $K \in \mathbb{N}$ and for all $(S^0, x^0), \dots,$ $(S^K, x^K) \in \mathcal{A}_C$,

$$f(S^k, x^k) = x^{k-1} \text{ for all } k \in \{1, \dots, K\} \Rightarrow f(S^0, x^0) \neq x^K.$$

Clearly, indirect irreversibility implies all of the irreversibility conditions introduced earlier. The full force of the axiom is needed because, as opposed to the G-rationalizability property **G-C-A**, its conclusion must hold not only for chains of distinct alternatives but, due to the added reflexivity assumption, for any chain. We obtain the following characterization, which, with a slightly different proof, can be found in Bossert, Sprumont, and Suzumura (2005b).

**Theorem 4.9**   *Suppose $C \colon \Sigma \to \mathcal{X}$ is a choice function with an arbitrary non-empty domain $\Sigma \subseteq \mathcal{X}$. $C$ satisfies any of* **G-RC-A, M-R-S, M-Ø-S, M-RC-A, M-R-A, M-C-A, M-Ø-A** *if and only if, whenever $\mathcal{A}_C \neq \emptyset$, there exists $f \in \mathcal{F}_C$ satisfying* **DRE** *and* **II**.

**Proof**   Invoking Theorem 3.4 again, it is sufficient to consider **G-RC-A**.

We first prove the only if part of the theorem. Let $R$ be a reflexive, complete, and acyclical G-rationalization of $C$. Suppose $\mathcal{A}_C \neq \emptyset$ and consider an arbitrary pair $(S, y) \in \mathcal{A}_C$. By definition, $S \in \Sigma$ and $y \in S \setminus C(S)$. The assumption that $R$ is a G-rationalization of $C$ implies the existence of $x \in S$ such that $(y, x) \notin R$. Define $f(S, y) = x$.

To prove that $f$ satisfies **DRE**, suppose $(S, y) \in \mathcal{A}_C, T \in \Sigma$, and $x \in T$ are such that $f(S, y) = x$. By the definition of $f$, we obtain $(y, x) \notin R$. Because $R$ is a G-rationalization of $C$, it follows that $y \notin C(T)$.

To establish the property **II**, suppose $K \in \mathbb{N}$ and $(S^0, x^0), \dots, (S^K, x^K) \in \mathcal{A}_C$ are such that $f(S^k, x^k) = x^{k-1}$ for all $k \in \{1, \dots, K\}$. By definition, $(x^k, x^{k-1}) \notin R$ for all $k \in \{1, \dots, K\}$. Because $R$ is reflexive, we have $x^{k-1} \neq x^k$ for all $k \in \{1, \dots, K\}$ and, thus, the completeness of $R$ implies $(x^{k-1}, x^k) \in P(R)$ for all $k \in \{1, \dots, K\}$. If $f(S^0, x^0) = x^K$, it follows analogously that $(x^K, x^0) \in P(R)$. If $K = 1$, this contradicts the hypothesis

$(x^K, x^0) \notin R$, and if $K > 1$, we obtain a contradiction to the acyclicity of $R$. Therefore, $f(S^0, x^0) \neq x^K$.

Next, we prove the if part of the theorem. If $\mathcal{A}_C = \emptyset$, $R = X \times X$ clearly is a reflexive, complete, and acyclical G-rationalization of $C$. If $\mathcal{A}_C \neq \emptyset$, there exists a function $f \in \mathcal{F}_C$ satisfying **DRE** and **II**. Define

$$R = \{(x, y) \in X \times X \mid \not\exists S \in \Sigma \text{ such that}$$
$$[(S, x) \in \mathcal{A}_C \text{ and } f(S, x) = y]\}.$$

To prove that $R$ is reflexive, suppose, by way of contradiction, that there exists $x \in X$ such that $(x, x) \notin R$. By definition, there exists $S \in \Sigma$ such that $(S, x) \in \mathcal{A}_C$ and $f(S, x) = x$. Letting $K = 1$, $S^0 = S^K = S$, and $x^0 = x^K = x$, we obtain a contradiction to the property **II**.

Next, we establish the completeness of $R$. Suppose $x, y \in X$ are such that $x \neq y$, $(x, y) \notin R$, and $(y, x) \notin R$. By definition, there exist $S, T \in \Sigma$ such that $(S, x), (T, y) \in \mathcal{A}_C$, $f(S, x) = y$, and $f(T, y) = x$, contradicting the property **II** for $K = 1$, $(S^0, x^0) = (S, x)$, and $(S^K, x^K) = (T, y)$.

To show that $R$ is acyclical, suppose $K \in \mathbb{N}$ and $x^0, \ldots, x^K \in X$ are such that $(x^{k-1}, x^k) \in P(R)$ for all $k \in \{1, \ldots, K\}$. By the definition of $R$, this implies that there exist $S^1, \ldots, S^K \in \Sigma$ such that $(S^k, x^k) \in \mathcal{A}_C$ and $x^{k-1} = f(S^k, x^k)$ for all $k \in \{1, \ldots, K\}$. If $(x^K, x^0) \in P(R)$, there exists $S^0 \in \Sigma$ such that $(S^0, x^0) \in \mathcal{A}_C$ and $x^K = f(S^0, x^0)$. But this contradicts the property **II**. Thus, $(x^K, x^0) \notin P(R)$ and $R$ is acyclical.

It remains to be shown that $R$ is a G-rationalization of $C$. Let $S \in \Sigma$ and $x \in S$.

Suppose $x \in C(S)$. If there exists $y \in S$ such that $(x, y) \notin R$, it follows from the definition of $R$ that there exists $T \in \Sigma$ such that $(T, x) \in \mathcal{A}_C$ and $f(T, x) = y$. But this contradicts the property **DRE** and, therefore, $x \in G(S, R)$.

Now suppose $x \notin C(S)$. Let $y = f(S, x)$. By the definition of $R$, we obtain $(x, y) \notin R$ and thus $x \notin G(S, R)$.   ∎

The intuition underlying the definition of $R$ in this result is as follows. If $x = f(S, y)$, it follows that $y$ cannot be at least as good as $x$ and, because of reflexivity and completeness, this means that $x$ must be better than $y$. As opposed to the previous result, $f$ satisfies **II** rather than merely **DSI** and, as a consequence, $R$ is reflexive in addition to being complete and acyclical.

We now turn to rationalizability properties involving quasi-transitivity as the coherence property to be satisfied by a G-rationalization. We begin with

**G-Ø-Q.** According to Theorem 4.7, the existence of a function $f$ satisfying **DRE** and **RI** is necessary and sufficient for **G-Ø-A**. If acyclicity is strengthened to quasi-transitivity, the following additional property of $f$ is required.

**Revelation exclusion (RE)** For all $K \in \mathbb{N}$, for all $(S^1, x^1), \ldots, (S^K, x^K) \in \mathcal{A}_C$, for all $S^0 \in \Sigma$, and for all $x^0 \in S^0$,

$$\{[f(S^k, x^k) = x^{k-1} \text{ and } (x^{k-1}, x^k) \in R_C] \text{ for all } k \in \{1, \ldots, K\}\}$$
$$\Rightarrow x^K \notin C(S^0).$$

Revelation exclusion is necessary to ensure that a G-rationalization is quasi-transitive as opposed to merely acyclical. As illustrated earlier, the conjunction of $f(S^k, x^k) = x^{k-1}$ and $(x^{k-1}, x^k) \in R_C$ implies, given the interpretation of $f$, that a G-rationalization must exhibit a strict preference. Following the resulting chain of strict preferences, quasi-transitivity demands that $x^0$ is strictly preferred to $x^K$ according to the rationalization. This is incompatible with $(x^K, x^0) \in R_C$ and, thus, **RE** must be satisfied. We obtain the following characterization, which appears in Bossert and Suzumura (2009a).

**Theorem 4.10** *Suppose $C: \Sigma \to \mathcal{X}$ is a choice function with an arbitrary non-empty domain $\Sigma \subseteq \mathcal{X}$. $C$ satisfies* **G-Ø-Q** *if and only if, whenever $\mathcal{A}_C \neq \emptyset$, there exists $f \in \mathcal{F}_C$ satisfying* **DRE, RI,** *and* **RE.**

**Proof** Suppose $C$ satisfies **G-Ø-Q** and let $R$ be a quasi-transitive G-rationalization of $C$. Suppose $\mathcal{A}_C \neq \emptyset$ and consider any $(S, y) \in \mathcal{A}_C$. By definition, $S \in \Sigma$ and $y \in S \setminus C(S)$. The assumption that $R$ is a G-rationalization of $C$ implies the existence of an alternative $x \in S$ such that $(y, x) \notin R$. Define $f(S, y) = x$.

To prove that $f$ satisfies **DRE**, suppose $(S, y) \in \mathcal{A}_C$, $T \in \Sigma$, and $x \in T$ are such that $f(S, y) = x$. By the definition of $f$, we obtain $(y, x) \notin R$. Because $R$ is a G-rationalization of $C$, it follows that $y \notin C(T)$.

To establish the property **RI**, suppose $K \in \mathbb{N}$ and $(S^0, x^0), \ldots, (S^K, x^K) \in \mathcal{A}_C$ are such that $f(S^k, x^k) = x^{k-1}$ and $(x^{k-1}, x^k) \in R_C$ for all $k \in \{1, \ldots, K\}$ and $(x^K, x^0) \in R_C$. By the definition of $f$, $(x^k, x^{k-1}) \notin R$ and by Theorem 3.1, $(x^{k-1}, x^k) \in R$ for all $k \in \{1, \ldots, K\}$. Therefore, $(x^{k-1}, x^k) \in P(R)$ for all $k \in \{1, \ldots, K\}$. $R$ being quasi-transitive, it follows that $(x^0, x^K) \in P(R)$ and thus $(x^0, x^K) \in R$, which, by the definition of $f$, implies $f(S^0, x^0) \neq x^K$.

To show that $f$ satisfies **RE**, suppose $K \in \mathbb{N}$, $(S^1, x^1), \ldots, (S^K, x^K) \in \mathcal{A}_C$, $S^0 \in \Sigma$, and $x^0 \in S^0$ are such that $f(S^k, x^k) = x^{k-1}$ and $(x^{k-1}, x^k) \in R_C$ for all $k \in \{1, \ldots, K\}$. By the definition of $f$, $(x^k, x^{k-1}) \notin R$ and by Theorem 3.1, $(x^{k-1}, x^k) \in R$ for all $k \in \{1, \ldots, K\}$. Thus, $(x^{k-1}, x^k) \in P(R)$ for all $k \in \{1, \ldots, K\}$ and the quasi-transitivity of $R$ implies $(x^0, x^K) \in P(R)$. Therefore, $(x^K, x^0) \notin R$ and, because $R$ is a G-rationalization of $C$, we obtain $x^K \notin C(S^0)$.

Now suppose that there exists $f \in \mathcal{F}_C$ satisfying **DRE**, **RI**, and **RE** whenever $\mathcal{A}_C \neq \emptyset$. If $\mathcal{A}_C = \emptyset$, $R = X \times X$ is a quasi-transitive G-rationalization of $C$ and we are done. If $\mathcal{A}_C \neq \emptyset$, there exists a function $f \in \mathcal{F}_C$ satisfying the properties **DRE**, **RI**, and **RE**. Define

$R = R_C$

$\quad \cup \{(x, y) \mid (y, x) \in R_C \text{ and } \nexists S \in \Sigma \text{ such that } [(S, x) \in \mathcal{A}_C \text{ and}$

$\quad\quad f(S, x) = y] \text{ and } \nexists K \in \mathbb{N}, x^0 \in X, \text{ and } (S^1, x^1), \ldots, (S^K, x^K) \in \mathcal{A}_C$

$\quad\quad \text{such that } [y = x^0 \text{ and } [x^{k-1} = f(S^k, x^k) \text{ and } (x^{k-1}, x^k) \in R_C]$

$\quad\quad \text{for all } k \in \{1, \ldots, K\} \text{ and } x^K = x]\}$

$\quad \cup \{(x, y) \mid \exists K \in \mathbb{N}, x^0 \in X, \text{ and } (S^1, x^1), \ldots, (S^K, x^K) \in \mathcal{A}_C \text{ such that}$

$\quad\quad [x = x^0 \text{ and } [x^{k-1} = f(S^k, x^k) \text{ and } (x^{k-1}, x^k) \in R_C]$

$\quad\quad \text{for all } k \in \{1, \ldots, K\} \text{ and } x^K = y]\}.$

To prove that $R$ is quasi-transitive, suppose $x, y, z \in X$ are such that $(x, y) \in P(R)$ and $(y, z) \in P(R)$. By definition, $(x, y) \in R$ implies

$$(x, y) \in R_C \qquad\qquad (4.1)$$

or

$\quad (y, x) \in R_C \text{ and } \nexists S \in \Sigma \text{ such that } [(S, x) \in \mathcal{A}_C \text{ and } f(S, x) = y]$

$\quad\quad \text{and } \nexists K \in \mathbb{N}, x^0 \in X, \text{ and } (S^1, x^1), \ldots, (S^K, x^K) \in \mathcal{A}_C$

$\quad\quad \text{such that } [y = x^0 \text{ and } [x^{k-1} = f(S^k, x^k) \text{ and } (x^{k-1}, x^k) \in R_C]$

$\quad\quad \text{for all } k \in \{1, \ldots, K\} \text{ and } x^K = x] \qquad\qquad (4.2)$

or

$\quad \exists K \in \mathbb{N}, x^0 \in X, \text{ and } (S^1, x^1), \ldots, (S^K, x^K) \in \mathcal{A}_C \text{ such that}$

$\quad\quad [x = x^0 \text{ and } [x^{k-1} = f(S^k, x^k) \text{ and } (x^{k-1}, x^k) \in R_C]$

$\quad\quad \text{for all } k \in \{1, \ldots, K\} \text{ and } x^K = y]. \qquad\qquad (4.3)$

Analogously, $(y, x) \notin R$ implies

$$(y, x) \notin R_C \tag{4.4}$$

and

$(x, y) \notin R_C$ or $\exists S \in \Sigma$ such that $[(S, y) \in \mathcal{A}_C$ and $f(S, y) = x]$

or $\exists K \in \mathbb{N}, x^0 \in X$, and $(S^1, x^1), \ldots, (S^K, x^K) \in \mathcal{A}_C$ such that

$[x = x^0$ and $[x^{k-1} = f(S^k, x^k)$ and $(x^{k-1}, x^k) \in R_C]$

for all $k \in \{1, \ldots, K\}$ and $x^K = y]$ $\tag{4.5}$

and

$\not\exists K \in \mathbb{N}, x^0 \in X$, and $(S^1, x^1), \ldots, (S^K, x^K) \in \mathcal{A}_C$ such that

$[y = x^0$ and $[x^{k-1} = f(S^k, x^k)$ and $(x^{k-1}, x^k) \in R_C]$

for all $k \in \{1, \ldots, K\}$ and $x^K = x]$.

Because (4.4) must be true, (4.2) must be false. Therefore, it follows that (4.1) or (4.3) is true and that (4.5) is true. Because (4.1) and $(x, y) \notin R_C$ are incompatible, it follows that we must have

$$(4.1) \text{ and } \exists S \in \Sigma \text{ such that } [(S, y) \in \mathcal{A}_C \text{ and } f(S, y) = x] \tag{4.6}$$

or

$$(4.1) \text{ and } (4.3) \tag{4.7}$$

or (4.3). Clearly, (4.6) implies (4.3) and (4.7) implies (4.3) trivially. Thus, (4.3) follows in all possible cases. Analogously, $(y, z) \in P(R)$ implies

$\exists L \in \mathbb{N}, y^0 \in X$, and $(T^1, y^1), \ldots, (T^L, y^L) \in \mathcal{A}_C$ such that

$[y = y^0$ and $[y^{\ell-1} = f(T^\ell, y^\ell)$ and $(y^{\ell-1}, y^\ell) \in R_C]$

for all $\ell \in \{1, \ldots, L\}$ and $y^L = z]$. $\tag{4.8}$

Letting $J = K + L$, $z^0 = x^0$, $(U^j, z^j) = (S^j, x^j)$ for all $j \in \{1, \ldots, K\}$, and $(U^j, z^j) = (T^{j-K}, y^{j-K})$ for all $j \in \{K+1, \ldots, K+L\}$, (4.3) and (4.8) together imply

$x = z^0$ and $[z^{j-1} = f(U^j, z^j)$ and $(z^{j-1}, z^j) \in R_C]$

for all $j \in \{1, \ldots, J\}$ and $z^J = z$. $\tag{4.9}$

Therefore, by the definition of $R$, $(x, z) \in R$. Suppose we also have $(z, x) \in R$. This implies

$$(z, x) \in R_C \tag{4.10}$$

or

$(x, z) \in R_C$ and $\not\exists S \in \Sigma$ such that $[(S, z) \in \mathcal{A}_C$ and $f(S, z) = x]$

and $\not\exists K \in \mathbb{N}, x^0 \in X$, and $(S^1, x^1), \ldots, (S^K, x^K) \in \mathcal{A}_C$ such that

$[x = x^0$ and $[x^{k-1} = f(S^k, x^k)$ and $(x^{k-1}, x^k) \in R_C]$

for all $k \in \{1, \ldots, K\}$ and $x^K = z]$                                    (4.11)

or

$\exists K \in \mathbb{N}, x^0 \in X$, and $(S^1, x^1), \ldots, (S^K, x^K) \in \mathcal{A}_C$ such that

$[z = x^0$ and $[x^{k-1} = f(S^k, x^k)$ and $(x^{k-1}, x^k) \in R_C]$

for all $k \in \{1, \ldots, K\}$ and $x^K = x]$.                                    (4.12)

If (4.10) is true, (4.9) yields a contradiction to the property **RE**. (4.11) immediately contradicts (4.9). Finally, if (4.12) applies, combining it with (4.9), we are led to a contradiction to the property **RI**. Thus, $R$ is quasi-transitive.

To show that $R$ is a G-rationalization of $C$, let $S \in \Sigma$ and $x \in S$.

Suppose $x \in C(S)$. This implies $(x, y) \in R_C \subseteq R$ for all $y \in S$ and, therefore, $x \in G(S, R)$.

Now suppose $x \notin C(S)$. Thus, $(S, x) \in \mathcal{A}_C$. Let $y = f(S, x)$ and suppose $(x, y) \in R$.

If $(x, y) \in R_C$, there exists $T \in \Sigma$ such that $y \in T$ and $x \in C(T)$. This contradicts the property **DRE**. If (4.2) applies, it follows that there exists no $S \in \Sigma$ such that $(S, x) \in \mathcal{A}_C$ and $y = f(S, x)$, an immediate contradiction to our hypothesis. Finally, if (4.3) applies, we obtain a contradiction to the property **RI**. Thus, $(x, y) \notin R$ and hence $x \notin G(S, R)$.  ∎

In the above proof, the components of $R$ are constructed by including all pairs that are necessarily in this relation and then invoking the properties of $f$ to ensure that $R$ satisfies all of the requirements. In particular, as is the case whenever G-rationalizability is considered, the direct revealed preference relation $R_C$ has to be respected. To avoid as many potential conflicts with quasi-transitivity as possible, any strict revealed preference is converted into an indifference whenever possible without contradiction. Finally, any chain of strict preference imposed by the conjunction of relationships imposed by $f$ and by the direct revealed preference criterion has to be respected due to the quasi-transitivity requirement.

If reflexivity is added to quasi-transitivity as a requirement on a G-rationalization, the function $f$ must possess an additional property as well. This is accomplished by imposing the following axiom.

**Self-irreversibility (SI)**   For all $(S, x) \in \mathcal{A}_C$,

$$f(S, x) \neq x.$$

According to the interpretation of $f$, $f(S, x) = x$ means that $x$ is excluded from $C(S)$ because $x$ fails to be considered at least as good as itself by a G-rationalization. Clearly, this is incompatible with the reflexivity of a G-rationalization and, thus, self-irreversibility is an additional necessary requirement to be satisfied by $f$. This leads to the following theorem, again a result established in Bossert and Suzumura (2009a).

**Theorem 4.11**  *Suppose $C\colon \Sigma \to \mathcal{X}$ is a choice function with an arbitrary non-empty domain $\Sigma \subseteq \mathcal{X}$. $C$ satisfies G-R-Q if and only if, whenever $\mathcal{A}_C \neq \emptyset$, there exists $f \in \mathcal{F}_C$ satisfying DRE, RI, RE, and SI.*

**Proof**  Suppose $C$ satisfies **G-R-Q** and let $R$ be a reflexive and quasi-transitive G-rationalization of $C$. Suppose $\mathcal{A}_C \neq \emptyset$ and consider any $(S, y) \in \mathcal{A}_C$. By definition, $S \in \Sigma$ and $y \in S \setminus C(S)$. The assumption that $R$ is a G-rationalization of $C$ implies the existence of $x \in S$ such that $(y, x) \notin R$. Define $f(S, y) = x$.

To prove that $f$ satisfies **DRE**, suppose $(S, y) \in \mathcal{A}_C$, $T \in \Sigma$, and $x \in T$ are such that $f(S, y) = x$. By the definition of $f$, we obtain $(y, x) \notin R$. Because $R$ is a G-rationalization of $C$, it follows that $y \notin C(T)$.

To establish the property **RI**, suppose $K \in \mathbb{N}$ and $(S^0, x^0), \ldots, (S^K, x^K) \in \mathcal{A}_C$ are such that $f(S^k, x^k) = x^{k-1}$ and $(x^{k-1}, x^k) \in R_C$ for all $k \in \{1, \ldots, K\}$ and $(x^K, x^0) \in R_C$. By the definition of $f$, $(x^k, x^{k-1}) \notin R$ and by Theorem 3.1, $(x^{k-1}, x^k) \in R$ for all $k \in \{1, \ldots, K\}$. Therefore, $(x^{k-1}, x^k) \in P(R)$ for all $k \in \{1, \ldots, K\}$. $R$ being quasi-transitive, it follows that $(x^0, x^K) \in P(R)$ and thus $(x^0, x^K) \in R$, which, by the definition of $f$, implies $f(S^0, x^0) \neq x^K$.

To show that $f$ satisfies **RE**, suppose $K \in \mathbb{N}$, $(S^1, x^1), \ldots, (S^K, x^K) \in \mathcal{A}_C$, $S^0 \in \Sigma$, and $x^0 \in S^0$ are such that $f(S^k, x^k) = x^{k-1}$ and $(x^{k-1}, x^k) \in R_C$ for all $k \in \{1, \ldots, K\}$. By the definition of $f$, $(x^k, x^{k-1}) \notin R$ and by Theorem 3.1, $(x^{k-1}, x^k) \in R$ for all $k \in \{1, \ldots, K\}$. Thus, $(x^{k-1}, x^k) \in P(R)$ for all $k \in \{1, \ldots, K\}$ and the quasi-transitivity of $R$ implies $(x^0, x^K) \in P(R)$.

Therefore, $(x^K, x^0) \notin R$ and, because $R$ is a G-rationalization of $C$, we obtain $x^K \notin C(S^0)$.

To prove that **SI** is satisfied, suppose there exists $(S, x) \in \mathcal{A}_C$ such that $f(S, x) = x$. By the definition of $f$, this implies $(x, x) \notin R$, contradicting the reflexivity of $R$.

Suppose that, whenever $\mathcal{A}_C \neq \emptyset$, there exists $f \in \mathcal{F}_C$ satisfying **DRE**, **RI**, **RE**, and **SI**. If $\mathcal{A}_C = \emptyset$, $R = X \times X$ is a reflexive and quasi-transitive G-rationalization of $C$ and we are done. If $\mathcal{A}_C \neq \emptyset$, there exists a function $f \in \mathcal{F}_C$ satisfying **DRE**, **RI**, **RE**, and **SI**. Define

$R = R_C \cup \Delta$

$\quad \cup \{(x, y) \mid (y, x) \in R_C \text{ and } \not\exists S \in \Sigma \text{ such that } [(S, x) \in \mathcal{A}_C \text{ and}$
$\qquad f(S, x) = y] \text{ and } \not\exists K \in \mathbb{N}, x^0 \in X, \text{ and } (S^1, x^1), \dots, (S^K, x^K) \in \mathcal{A}_C$
$\qquad \text{such that } [y = x^0 \text{ and } [x^{k-1} = f(S^k, x^k) \text{ and } (x^{k-1}, x^k) \in R_C]$
$\qquad \text{for all } k \in \{1, \dots, K\} \text{ and } x^K = x]\}$

$\quad \cup \{(x, y) \mid \exists K \in \mathbb{N}, x^0 \in X, \text{ and } (S^1, x^1), \dots, (S^K, x^K) \in \mathcal{A}_C \text{ such that}$
$\qquad [x = x^0 \text{ and } [x^{k-1} = f(S^k, x^k) \text{ and } (x^{k-1}, x^k) \in R_C]$
$\qquad \text{for all } k \in \{1, \dots, K\} \text{ and } x^K = y]\}.$

Clearly, $R$ is reflexive because $\Delta \subseteq R$.

To prove that $R$ is quasi-transitive, suppose $x, y, z \in X$ are such that $(x, y) \in P(R)$ and $(y, z) \in P(R)$. This implies that the alternatives $x, y$, and $z$ are pairwise distinct and, thus, $(x, y) \notin \Delta$, $(y, z) \notin \Delta$, and $(x, z) \notin \Delta$. Therefore, $(x, y) \in R$ implies

$$(x, y) \in R_C \tag{4.13}$$

or

$\quad (y, x) \in R_C \text{ and } \not\exists S \in \Sigma \text{ such that } [(S, x) \in \mathcal{A}_C \text{ and } f(S, x) = y]$
$\quad \text{and } \not\exists K \in \mathbb{N}, x^0 \in X, \text{ and } (S^1, x^1), \dots, (S^K, x^K) \in \mathcal{A}_C$
$\quad \text{such that } [y = x^0 \text{ and } [x^{k-1} = f(S^k, x^k) \text{ and } (x^{k-1}, x^k) \in R_C]$
$\quad \text{for all } k \in \{1, \dots, K\} \text{ and } x^K = x] \tag{4.14}$

or

$\quad \exists K \in \mathbb{N}, x^0 \in X, \text{ and } (S^1, x^1), \dots, (S^K, x^K) \in \mathcal{A}_C \text{ such that}$
$\quad [x = x^0 \text{ and } [x^{k-1} = f(S^k, x^k) \text{ and } (x^{k-1}, x^k) \in R_C]$
$\quad \text{for all } k \in \{1, \dots, K\} \text{ and } x^K = y]. \tag{4.15}$

Analogously, $(y, x) \notin R$ implies

$$(y, x) \notin R_C \tag{4.16}$$

and

$$(x, y) \notin R_C \text{ or } \exists S \in \Sigma \text{ such that } [(S, y) \in \mathcal{A}_C \text{ and } f(S, y) = x]$$
$$\text{or } \exists K \in \mathbb{N}, x^0 \in X, \text{ and } (S^1, x^1), \ldots, (S^K, x^K) \in \mathcal{A}_C$$
$$\text{such that } [x = x^0 \text{ and } [x^{k-1} = f(S^k, x^k) \text{ and } (x^{k-1}, x^k) \in R_C]$$
$$\text{for all } k \in \{1, \ldots, K\} \text{ and } x^K = y] \tag{4.17}$$

and

$$\not\exists K \in \mathbb{N}, x^0 \in X, \text{ and } (S^1, x^1), \ldots, (S^K, x^K) \in \mathcal{A}_C \text{ such that}$$
$$[y = x^0 \text{ and } [x^{k-1} = f(S^k, x^k) \text{ and } (x^{k-1}, x^k) \in R_C]$$
$$\text{for all } k \in \{1, \ldots, K\} \text{ and } x^K = x].$$

Because (4.16) must be true, (4.14) must be false. Therefore, it follows that (4.13) or (4.15) is true and that (4.17) is true. Because (4.13) and $(x, y) \notin R_C$ are incompatible, it follows that we must have

$$(4.13) \text{ and } \exists S \in \Sigma \text{ such that } [(S, y) \in \mathcal{A}_C \text{ and } f(S, y) = x] \tag{4.18}$$

or

$$(4.13) \text{ and } (4.15) \tag{4.19}$$

or (4.15). Clearly, (4.18) implies (4.15) and (4.19) implies (4.15) trivially. Thus, (4.15) follows in all possible cases. Analogously, $(y, z) \in P(R)$ implies

$$\exists L \in \mathbb{N}, y^0 \in X, \text{ and } (T^1, y^1), \ldots, (T^L, y^L) \in \mathcal{A}_C \text{ such that}$$
$$[y = y^0 \text{ and } [y^{\ell-1} = f(T^\ell, y^\ell) \text{ and } (y^{\ell-1}, y^\ell) \in R_C]$$
$$\text{for all } \ell \in \{1, \ldots, L\} \text{ and } y^L = z]. \tag{4.20}$$

Letting $J = K + L$, $z^0 = x^0$, $(U^j, z^j) = (S^j, x^j)$ for all $j \in \{1, \ldots, K\}$, and $(U^j, z^j) = (T^{j-K}, y^{j-K})$ for all $j \in \{K+1, \ldots, K+L\}$, (4.15) and (4.20) together imply

$$x = z^0 \text{ and } [z^{j-1} = f(U^j, z^j) \text{ and } (z^{j-1}, z^j) \in R_C]$$
$$\text{for all } j \in \{1, \ldots, J\} \text{ and } z^J = z. \tag{4.21}$$

Therefore, by the definition of $R$, $(x, z) \in R$. Suppose we also have $(z, x) \in R$. This implies

$$(z, x) \in R_C \tag{4.22}$$

or

$(x, z) \in R_C$ and $\nexists S \in \Sigma$ such that $[(S, z) \in \mathcal{A}_C$ and $f(S, z) = x]$
and $\nexists K \in \mathbb{N}, x^0 \in X$, and $(S^1, x^1), \ldots, (S^K, x^K) \in \mathcal{A}_C$
such that $[x = x^0$ and $[x^{k-1} = f(S^k, x^k)$ and $(x^{k-1}, x^k) \in R_C]$
for all $k \in \{1, \ldots, K\}$ and $x^K = z]$                                           (4.23)

or

$\exists K \in \mathbb{N}, x^0 \in X$, and $(S^1, x^1), \ldots, (S^K, x^K) \in \mathcal{A}_C$ such that
$[z = x^0$ and $[x^{k-1} = f(S^k, x^k)$ and $(x^{k-1}, x^k) \in R_C]$
for all $k \in \{1, \ldots, K\}$ and $x^K = x]$.                                          (4.24)

If (4.22) is true, (4.21) yields a contradiction to the property **RE**. (4.23) immediately contradicts (4.21). Finally, if (4.24) applies, in combination with (4.21), it implies a contradiction to the property **RI**. Thus, $R$ is quasi-transitive.

To show that $R$ is a G-rationalization of $C$, let $S \in \Sigma$ and $x \in S$.

Suppose $x \in C(S)$. This implies $(x, y) \in R_C \subseteq R$ for all $y \in S$ and, therefore, $x \in G(S, R)$.

Now suppose $x \notin C(S)$. Thus, $(S, x) \in \mathcal{A}_C$. Let $y = f(S, x)$ and suppose $(x, y) \in R$.

If $(x, y) \in R_C$, there exists $T \in \Sigma$ such that $y \in T$ and $x \in C(T)$. This contradicts the property **DRE**. If $(x, y) \in \Delta$, we obtain a contradiction to the property **SI**. If (4.14) applies, it follows that there exists no $S \in \Sigma$ such that $(S, x) \in \mathcal{A}_C$ and $y = f(S, x)$, an immediate contradiction to our hypothesis. Finally, if (4.15) applies, we obtain a contradiction to the property **RI**. Thus, $(x, y) \notin R$ and hence $x \notin G(S, R)$.  ∎

The construction of the G-rationalization in this proof is analogous to that of the previous theorem. The only difference is that the diagonal relation $\Delta$ appears in the latter theorem. This is necessitated by the addition of reflexivity as a requirement.

If completeness rather than reflexivity is added to quasi-transitivity, we obtain a stronger rationalizability axiom; see Theorem 3.4. As a consequence, the property **RI** of $f$ in Theorem 4.10 is replaced by **DSI** and, instead of **RE**, the following requirement is imposed.

**Distinctness exclusion (DSE)** For all $K \in \mathbb{N}$, for all $(S^1, x^1), \ldots, (S^K, x^K) \in \mathcal{A}_C$, for all $S^0 \in \Sigma$, and for all $x^0 \in S^0$,

$$[f(S^k, x^k) = x^{k-1} \text{ and } x^{k-1} \neq x^k] \text{ for all}$$
$$k \in \{1, \ldots, K\} \Rightarrow x^K \notin C(S^0).$$

In the presence of DRE, RE is implied by DSE. Suppose $f$ violates RE. If all $x^k$ are identical, we obtain an immediate contradiction to DRE. If there exists a $k \in \{1, \ldots, K\}$ such that $x^k \neq x^0$, we can without loss of generality assume that all elements of the chain are pairwise distinct (otherwise, the chain can be reduced to one involving pairwise distinct elements), which leads to a violation of DSE.

The strengthening of revelation exclusion to distinctness exclusion is necessary as a consequence of adding completeness to quasi-transitivity. If $f(S^k, x^k) = x^{k-1}$ and $x^{k-1} \neq x^k$, the interpretation of $f$ and the completeness of a G-rationalization together imply that $x^{k-1}$ is strictly preferred to $x^k$. Following this chain of strict preferences, quasi-transitivity demands that $x^0$ is strictly preferred to $x^K$, which is not compatible with $(x^K, x^0) \in R_C$. The corresponding characterization result (due to Bossert and Suzumura, 2009a) is stated in the following theorem.

**Theorem 4.12** *Suppose $C: \Sigma \to \mathcal{X}$ is a choice function with an arbitrary non-empty domain $\Sigma \subseteq \mathcal{X}$. $C$ satisfies G-C-Q if and only if, whenever $\mathcal{A}_C \neq \emptyset$, there exists $f \in \mathcal{F}_C$ satisfying DRE, DSI, and DSE.*

**Proof** We first prove that G-C-Q implies the existence of a function $f \in \mathcal{F}_C$ that satisfies DRE, DSI, and DSE whenever $\mathcal{A}_C \neq \emptyset$. Let $R$ be a complete and quasi-transitive G-rationalization of $C$. Consider any $(S, y) \in \mathcal{A}_C$. By definition, $S \in \Sigma$ and $y \in S \setminus C(S)$. The assumption that $R$ is a G-rationalization of $C$ implies the existence of $x \in S$ such that $(y, x) \notin R$. Define $f(S, y) = x$.

To show that $f$ satisfies DRE, suppose $(S, y) \in \mathcal{A}_C, T \in \Sigma$, and $x \in T$ are such that $f(S, y) = x$. By the definition of $f$, we have $(y, x) \notin R$. Because $R$ is a G-rationalization of $C$, it follows that $y \notin C(T)$.

Next, we establish DSI. Suppose $K \in \mathbb{N}$ and $(S^0, x^0), \ldots, (S^K, x^K) \in \mathcal{A}_C$ are such that $f(S^k, x^k) = x^{k-1}$ and $x^{k-1} \neq x^k$ for all $k \in \{1, \ldots, K\}$. By definition, $(x^k, x^{k-1}) \notin R$ for all $k \in \{1, \ldots, K\}$ and, because $R$ is complete, $(x^{k-1}, x^k) \in P(R)$ for all $k \in \{1, \ldots, K\}$. $R$ being quasi-transitive, it follows that $(x^0, x^K) \in P(R)$ and hence $(x^0, x^K) \in R$. By the definition of $f$, this implies $f(S^0, x^0) \neq x^K$.

To prove that $f$ satisfies **DSE**, let $K \in \mathbb{N}$, $(S^1, x^1), \ldots, (S^K, x^K) \in \mathcal{A}_C$, $S^0 \in \Sigma$, and $x^0 \in S^0$ be such that $f(S^k, x^k) = x^{k-1}$ and $x^{k-1} \neq x^k$ for all $k \in \{1, \ldots, K\}$. By definition, $(x^k, x^{k-1}) \notin R$ for all $k \in \{1, \ldots, K\}$ and the completeness of $R$ implies $(x^{k-1}, x^k) \in P(R)$ for all $k \in \{1, \ldots, K\}$. $R$ being quasi-transitive, it follows that $(x^0, x^K) \in P(R)$ and, thus, $(x^K, x^0) \notin R$. Because $R$ is a G-rationalization of $C$, we obtain $x^K \notin C(S^0)$.

Now suppose that, whenever $\mathcal{A}_C \neq \emptyset$, there exists $f \in \mathcal{F}_C$ satisfying **DRE**, **DSI**, and **DSE**. If $\mathcal{A}_C = \emptyset$, $R = X \times X$ is a complete and quasi-transitive G-rationalization of $C$ and we are done. If $\mathcal{A}_C \neq \emptyset$, there exists a function $f \in \mathcal{F}_C$ satisfying **DRE**, **DSI**, and **DSE**. Define

$$R = \{(x, y) \in X \times X \mid \exists K \in \mathbb{N}, x^0 \in X, \text{ and } (S^1, x^1), \ldots, (S^K, x^K) \in \mathcal{A}_C$$
$$\text{such that } [y = x^0 \text{ and } [x^{k-1} = f(S^k, x^k) \text{ and } x^{k-1} \neq x^k]$$
$$\text{for all } k \in \{1, \ldots, K\} \text{ and } x^K = x]\}$$
$$\setminus \{(x, x) \mid \exists S \in \Sigma \text{ such that } [(S, x) \in \mathcal{A}_C \text{ and } f(S, x) = x]\}.$$

To prove that $R$ is complete, suppose, by way of contradiction, that there exist $x, y \in X$ such that $x \neq y$, $(x, y) \notin R$, and $(y, x) \notin R$. By definition, this implies that there exist $K, L \in \mathbb{N}$, $x^0, y^0 \in X$, and $(S^1, x^1), \ldots,$ $(S^K, x^K), (T^1, y^1), \ldots, (T^L, y^L) \in \mathcal{A}_C$ such that

$$y = x^0 \text{ and } [x^{k-1} = f(S^k, x^k) \text{ and } x^{k-1} \neq x^k]$$
$$\text{for all } k \in \{1, \ldots, K\} \text{ and } x^K = x$$

and

$$x = y^0 \text{ and } [y^{\ell-1} = f(T^\ell, y^\ell) \text{ and } y^{\ell-1} \neq y^\ell]$$
$$\text{for all } \ell \in \{1, \ldots, L\} \text{ and } y^L = y.$$

Letting $J = K + L - 1$, $(U^0, z^0) = (T^L, y^L)$, $(U^j, z^j) = (S^j, x^j)$ for all $j \in \{1, \ldots, K\}$, and $(U^j, z^j) = (T^{j-K}, y^{j-K})$ for all $j \in \{K+1, \ldots, K+L\} \setminus \{K+L\}$, it follows that $z^{j-1} = f(U^j, z^j)$ and $z^{j-1} \neq z^j$ for all $j \in \{1, \ldots, J\}$ and $z^J = f(U^0, z^0)$, contradicting the property **DSI**.

Next, we show that $R$ is quasi-transitive. Suppose $x, y, z \in X$ are such that $(x, y) \in P(R)$ and $(y, z) \in P(R)$. This implies that $x \neq y$ and $y \neq z$ and, by the definition of $R$, there exist $K, L \in \mathbb{N}$, $x^0, y^0 \in X$, and $(S^1, x^1), \ldots,$ $(S^K, x^K), (T^1, y^1), \ldots, (T^L, y^L) \in \mathcal{A}_C$ such that

$$x = x^0 \text{ and } [x^{k-1} = f(S^k, x^k) \text{ and } x^{k-1} \neq x^k]$$
$$\text{for all } k \in \{1, \ldots, K\} \text{ and } x^K = y$$

and

$$y = y^0 \text{ and } [y^{\ell-1} = f(T^\ell, y^\ell) \text{ and } y^{\ell-1} \neq y^\ell]$$
$$\text{for all } \ell \in \{1, \ldots, L\} \text{ and } y^L = z.$$

Letting $J = K + L$, $z^0 = x^0$, $(U^j, z^j) = (S^j, x^j)$ for all $j \in \{1, \ldots, K\}$, and $(U^j, z^j) = (T^{j-K}, y^{j-K})$ for all $j \in \{K+1, \ldots, K+L\}$, it follows that $(z, x) \notin R$. Because $R$ is complete, we obtain $(x, z) \in P(R)$.

Finally, we prove that $R$ is a G-rationalization of $C$. Let $S \in \Sigma$ and $x \in S$.

Suppose first that $x \in C(S)$ and, by way of contradiction, that there exists $y \in S$ such that $(x, y) \notin R$. If $x = y$ and there exists $S \in \Sigma$ such that $(S, x) \in \mathcal{A}_C$ and $f(S, x) = x$, we obtain a contradiction to the property DRE. If there exist $K \in \mathbb{N}$, $x^0 \in X$, and $(S^1, x^1), \ldots, (S^K, x^K) \in \mathcal{A}_C$ such that

$$y = x^0 \text{ and } [x^{k-1} = f(S^k, x^k) \text{ and } x^{k-1} \neq x^k]$$
$$\text{for all } k \in \{1, \ldots, K\} \text{ and } x^K = x,$$

letting $S^0 = S$ yields a contradiction to the property DSE. Therefore, $x \in G(S, R)$.

Now suppose $x \notin C(S)$. Let $y = f(S, x)$. By definition, this implies $(x, y) \notin R$ and hence $x \notin G(S, R)$. ∎

The G-rationalization $R$ employed in this proof is less complex because of the completeness assumption—an absence of a weak preference for one of two distinct alternatives implies a strict preference for the other. In addition, whenever an element $x$ is not chosen in a set $S$ because, according to $f$, $x$ is not at least as good as itself, the pair $(x, x)$ cannot be in $R$. Because $R$ is also required to be quasi-transitive, chains of strict preference have to be respected as well. In order to arrive at a complete and quasi-transitive G-rationalization of $C$, we define $R$ to be composed of all pairs $(x, y)$ such that $y$ does not have to be strictly preferred to $x$ according to the above-described criterion. The properties of $f$ ensure that $R$ is indeed a complete and quasi-transitive G-rationalization of $C$.

Now we consider the rationalizability property G-RC-Q. Because reflexivity *and* completeness are required, both the exclusion axiom and the irreversibility condition to be employed are unconditional—whenever it is the case that $f(S^k, x^k) = x^{k-1}$, the conjunction of reflexivity and completeness, together with the interpretation of $f$, implies that $x^{k-1}$ must be strictly preferred to $x^k$ by a G-rationalization. Quasi-transitivity demands that any chain of strict preferences from $x^0$ to $x^K$ be respected and, thus, $x^0$ must be strictly preferred to $x^K$. This immediately rules out $(x^K, x^0) \in R_C$ (as required by the axiom **IE** introduced below) and $f(S^0, x^0) = x^K$ (see **II**).

**Indirect exclusion (IE)** For all $K \in \mathbb{N}$, for all $(S^1, x^1), \ldots, (S^K, x^K)$ $\in \mathcal{A}_C$, for all $S^0 \in \Sigma$, and for all $x^0 \in S^0$,

$$f(S^k, x^k) = x^{k-1} \text{ for all } k \in \{1, \ldots, K\} \Rightarrow x^K \notin C(S^0).$$

Clearly, indirect exclusion implies all of the exclusion properties introduced earlier. We can now state the following result, which, with an alternative proof, has been established in Bossert, Sprumont, and Suzumura (2005b).

**Theorem 4.13** *Suppose $C \colon \Sigma \to \mathcal{X}$ is a choice function with an arbitrary non-empty domain $\Sigma \subseteq \mathcal{X}$. $C$ satisfies any of* **G-RC-Q, M-R-T, M-Ø-T, M-RC-Q, M-R-Q, M-C-Q, M-Ø-Q** *if and only if, whenever $\mathcal{A}_C \neq \emptyset$, there exists $f \in \mathcal{F}_C$ satisfying* **II** *and* **IE**.

**Proof** In view of Theorem 3.4, it is sufficient to treat the case of **G-RC-Q**.

We first prove that **G-RC-Q** implies the existence of an $f \in \mathcal{F}_C$ that satisfies **II** and **IE** provided that $\mathcal{A}_C \neq \emptyset$. Let $R$ be a reflexive, complete, and quasi-transitive G-rationalization of $C$. Consider any $(S, y) \in \mathcal{A}_C$. By definition, $S \in \Sigma$ and $y \in S \setminus C(S)$. The assumption that $R$ is a G-rationalization of $C$ implies the existence of $x \in S$ such that $(y, x) \notin R$. Define $f(S, y) = x$.

To prove that **II** is satisfied, suppose $K \in \mathbb{N}$ and $(S^0, x^0), \ldots, (S^K, x^K) \in \mathcal{A}_C$ are such that $f(S^k, x^k) = x^{k-1}$ for all $k \in \{1, \ldots, K\}$. By definition, $(x^k, x^{k-1}) \notin R$ for all $k \in \{1, \ldots, K\}$. Because $R$ is reflexive, we have $x^{k-1} \neq x^k$ for all $k \in \{1, \ldots, K\}$ and, because $R$ is complete, $(x^{k-1}, x^k) \in P(R)$ for all $k \in \{1, \ldots, K\}$. $R$ being quasi-transitive, it follows that $(x^0, x^K) \in P(R)$ and hence $(x^0, x^K) \in R$. By definition of $f$, this implies $f(S^0, x^0) \neq x^K$.

To show that any such function $f$ satisfies **IE**, suppose $K \in \mathbb{N}$, $(S^1, x^1), \ldots, (S^K, x^K) \in \mathcal{A}_C$, $S^0 \in \Sigma$, and $x^0 \in S^0$ are such that $f(S^k, x^k) = x^{k-1}$ for all $k \in \{1, \ldots, K\}$. By definition, $(x^k, x^{k-1}) \notin R$ for all $k \in \{1, \ldots, K\}$. Because $R$ is reflexive, it must be the case that $x^{k-1} \neq x^k$ for all $k \in \{1, \ldots, K\}$. Thus, the completeness of $R$ implies $(x^{k-1}, x^k) \in P(R)$ for all $k \in \{1, \ldots, K\}$. $R$ being quasi-transitive, it follows that $(x^0, x^K) \in P(R)$ and, thus, $(x^K, x^0) \notin R$. Because $R$ is a G-rationalization of $C$, we obtain $x^K \notin C(S^0)$.

Now suppose that, provided $\mathcal{A}_C \neq \emptyset$, there exists $f \in \mathcal{F}_C$ satisfying **II** and **IE**. If $\mathcal{A}_C = \emptyset$, $R = X \times X$ is a reflexive, complete, and quasi-transitive G-rationalization of $C$ and we are done. If $\mathcal{A}_C \neq \emptyset$, there exists a function $f \in \mathcal{F}_C$ satisfying **II** and **IE**. Define

$$R = \{(x, y) \in X \times X \mid \nexists K \in \mathbb{N}, x^0 \in X, \text{ and } (S^1, x^1), \ldots, (S^K, x^K) \in \mathcal{A}_C$$

$$\text{such that } [\, y = x^0 \text{ and } x^{k-1} = f(S^k, x^k)$$

$$\text{for all } k \in \{1, \ldots, K\} \text{ and } x^K = x]\}.$$

To see that $R$ is reflexive, let $x \in X$. If $(x, x) \notin R$, there exist $K \in \mathbb{N}$, $x^0 \in X$, and $(S^1, x^1), \ldots, (S^K, x^K) \in \mathcal{A}_C$ such that

$$x = x^0 \text{ and } x^{k-1} = f(S^k, x^k) \text{ for all } k \in \{1, \ldots, K\} \text{ and } x^K = x.$$

Letting $S^0 = S^K$, we obtain a contradiction to **II**. Thus, we must have $(x, x) \in R$.

To establish the completeness of $R$, suppose $x, y \in X$ are two distinct alternatives such that $(x, y) \notin R$ and $(y, x) \notin R$. By definition, this implies that there exist $K, L \in \mathbb{N}$, $x^0, y^0 \in X$, and $(S^1, x^1), \ldots, (S^K, x^K)$, $(T^1, y^1), \ldots, (T^L, y^L) \in \mathcal{A}_C$ such that

$$y = x^0 \text{ and } x^{k-1} = f(S^k, x^k) \text{ for all } k \in \{1, \ldots, K\} \text{ and } x^K = x$$

and

$$x = y^0 \text{ and } y^{\ell-1} = f(T^\ell, y^\ell) \text{ for all } \ell \in \{1, \ldots, L\} \text{ and } y^L = y.$$

Letting $J = K + L - 1$, $(U^0, z^0) = (T^L, y^L)$, $(U^j, z^j) = (S^j, x^j)$ for all $j \in \{1, \ldots, K\}$, and $(U^j, z^j) = (T^{j-K}, y^{j-K})$ for all $j \in \{K+1, \ldots, K+L\} \setminus \{K+L\}$, it follows that $z^{j-1} = f(U^j, z^j)$ for all $j \in \{1, \ldots, J\}$ and $z^J = f(U^0, z^0)$, contradicting **II**.

Next, we show that $R$ is quasi-transitive. Suppose three alternatives $x, y, z \in X$ are such that $(x, y) \in P(R)$ and $(y, z) \in P(R)$. This implies that there exist $K, L \in \mathbb{N}$, $x^0, y^0 \in X$, and $(S^1, x^1), \ldots, (S^K, x^K), (T^1, y^1), \ldots, (T^L, y^L) \in \mathcal{A}_C$ such that

$$x = x^0 \text{ and } x^{k-1} = f(S^k, x^k) \text{ for all } k \in \{1, \ldots, K\} \text{ and } x^K = y$$

and

$$y = y^0 \text{ and } y^{\ell-1} = f(T^\ell, y^\ell) \text{ for all } \ell \in \{1, \ldots, L\} \text{ and } y^L = z.$$

Letting $J = K + L$, $z^0 = x^0$, $(U^j, z^j) = (S^j, x^j)$ for all $j \in \{1, \ldots, K\}$, and $(U^j, z^j) = (T^{j-K}, y^{j-K})$ for all $j \in \{K + 1, \ldots, K + L\}$, it follows that $(z, x) \notin R$. Because $R$ is complete, we obtain $(x, z) \in P(R)$. Thus, $R$ is quasi-transitive.

It remains to show that $R$ is a G-rationalization of $C$. Let $S \in \Sigma$ and $x \in S$.

Suppose first that $x \in C(S)$. If there exists $y \in S$ such that $(x, y) \notin R$, it follows that there exist $K \in \mathbb{N}$, $x^0 \in X$, and $(S^1, x^1), \ldots, (S^K, x^K) \in \mathcal{A}_C$ such that

$$y = x^0 \text{ and } x^{k-1} = f(S^k, x^k) \text{ for all } k \in \{1, \ldots, K\} \text{ and } x^K = x.$$

Letting $S^0 = S$, we obtain a contradiction to IE. Therefore, $x \in G(S, R)$.

Now suppose $x \notin C(S)$. Let $y = f(S, x)$. By definition, this implies $(x, y) \notin R$ and hence $x \notin G(S, R)$. ∎

The definition of the relation $R$ in the above proof is based on the following intuition. Recall that $f$ is intended to identify, for each feasible set $S$ and for each element $y$ of $S$ that is not chosen by $C$, an alternative $x$ in $S$ such that $y$ is not at least as good as $x$. Because G-rationalizability by a reflexive and complete relation is considered in the above theorem, the absence of a weak preference of $y$ over $x$ is equivalent to a strict preference of $x$ over $y$, that is, $(x, y) \in P(R)$. In consequence, we must have a strict preference of an alternative $x$ over an alternative $y$ according to a reflexive and complete G-rationalization whenever $x$ is identified by $f$ to be responsible for keeping $y$ out of the set of chosen alternatives from $S$. Because $R$ is also required to be quasi-transitive, chains of strict preference have to be respected as well. In order to arrive at a reflexive, complete, and quasi-transitive G-rationalization of $C$, we define $R$ to be composed of all pairs $(x, y)$ such that $y$ does not have to be strictly preferred to $x$ according to the above-described criterion. The properties of $f$ ensure that $R$ indeed is a reflexive, complete, and quasi-transitive G-rationalization of $C$.

We conclude this section with characterizations of G-R-S and G-RC-T (and, of course, their equivalents). Their axiomatizations are simpler than those analyzed thus far because there are well-defined Suzumura consistent and transitive closure operations whose existence facilitates the formulation of the requisite properties of $f$.

In the case of Suzumura-consistent G-rationalizability, the following property of $f$ is relevant.

**Suzumura-consistent closure irreversibility (SCI)**   For all $(S, x) \in \mathcal{A}_C$ and for all $y \in S$,

$$(x, y) \in sc(R_C) \Rightarrow f(S, x) \neq y.$$

SCI requires that the Suzumura-consistent closure of the direct revealed preference relation $R_C$ be respected as established in part (ii) of Theorem 4.1: if a pair of alternatives $(x, y)$ is in this Suzumura-consistent closure, then $(x, y)$ must be in any Suzumura-consistent G-rationalization of $C$ and, as a consequence, $y$ cannot be the element that keeps $x$ from being chosen from a set in which both are present. The existence of a function $f$ with this property is also sufficient for G-R-S and G-Ø-S, as demonstrated in the following theorem that is taken from Bossert and Suzumura (2009a).

**Theorem 4.14**  *Suppose* $C \colon \Sigma \to \mathcal{X}$ *is a choice function with an arbitrary non-empty domain* $\Sigma \subseteq \mathcal{X}$. *$C$ satisfies any of* **G-R-S**, **G-Ø-S** *if and only if, whenever* $\mathcal{A}_C \neq \emptyset$, *there exists* $f \in \mathcal{F}_C$ *satisfying* **SCI**.

**Proof**   In view of Theorem 3.4, it is sufficient to treat the case of **G-Ø-S**.

We first prove that **G-Ø-S** implies the existence of a function $f \in \mathcal{F}_C$ that satisfies **SCI** provided that $\mathcal{A}_C \neq \emptyset$. Let $R$ be a Suzumura-consistent G-rationalization of $C$. Consider any $(S, y) \in \mathcal{A}_C$. By definition, $S \in \Sigma$ and $y \in S \setminus C(S)$. The assumption that $R$ is a G-rationalization of $C$ implies the existence of $x \in S$ such that $(y, x) \notin R$. Define $f(S, y) = x$. To show that $f$ satisfies **SCI**, suppose $(S, x) \in \mathcal{A}_C$ and $y \in S$ are such that $(x, y) \in sc(R_C)$. By part (ii) of Theorem 4.1, it follows that $(x, y) \in R$ and, thus, $f(S, x) \neq y$ by definition of $f$.

Now suppose that, provided $\mathcal{A}_C \neq \emptyset$, there exists $f \in \mathcal{F}_C$ satisfying **SCI**. If $\mathcal{A}_C = \emptyset$, $R = X \times X$ is a Suzumura-consistent G-rationalization of $C$ and we are done. If $\mathcal{A}_C \neq \emptyset$, there exists a function $f \in \mathcal{F}_C$ satisfying **SCI**. Define

$$R = sc(R_C).$$

Clearly, $R$ is Suzumura consistent. We complete the proof by showing that it is a G-rationalization of $C$. To that end, suppose $S \in \Sigma$ and $x \in S$.

Suppose first that $x \in C(S)$. This implies $(x, y) \in R_C \subseteq sc(R_C) = R$ for all $y \in S$ and, thus, $x \in G(S, R)$.

Now suppose $x \in G(S, R)$. By definition, $(x, y) \in sc(R_C)$ for all $y \in S$. If $(S, x) \in \mathcal{A}_C$, **SCI** implies $f(S, x) \neq y$ for all $y \in S$, contrary to the existence of $f$. Thus, $(S, x) \notin \mathcal{A}_C$, which implies $x \in C(S)$ by definition.  ∎

Our final result in this chapter provides an analogous characterization of G-RC-T and its equivalents. All that needs to be done is to replace the Suzumura-consistent closure with the transitive closure in the relevant property of $f$.

**Transitive closure irreversibility (TCI)**    For all $(S, x) \in \mathcal{A}_C$ and for all $y \in S$,

$$(x, y) \in tc(R_C) \Rightarrow f(S, x) \neq y.$$

Analogously to **SCI**, **TCI** requires that the transitive closure of the direct revealed preference relation $R_C$ be respected as established in part (i) of Theorem 4.1: if a pair of alternatives $(x, y)$ is in the transitive closure of $R_C$, then $(x, y)$ must be in any transitive G-rationalization of $C$ and, as a consequence, $y$ cannot be the element that keeps $x$ from being chosen from a set in which both are present. The existence of a function $f$ with this property is also sufficient for **G-$\emptyset$-T** and all of its equivalent properties, and we obtain the following result, first established in Bossert and Suzumura (2009a).

**Theorem 4.15**    *Suppose $C: \Sigma \to \mathcal{X}$ is a choice function with an arbitrary non-empty domain $\Sigma \subseteq \mathcal{X}$. $C$ satisfies any of G-RC-T, G-C-T, G-R-T, G-$\emptyset$-T, G-RC-S, G-C-S, M-RC-T, M-C-T, M-RC-S, M-C-S if and only if, whenever $\mathcal{A}_C \neq \emptyset$, there exists $f \in \mathcal{F}_C$ satisfying TCI.*

**Proof**    In view of Theorem 3.4, it is sufficient to treat the case of **G-$\emptyset$-T**.

We begin by proving that **G-$\emptyset$-T** implies the existence of a function $f \in \mathcal{F}_C$ that satisfies **TCI** provided that $\mathcal{A}_C \neq \emptyset$. Let $R$ be a transitive G-rationalization of $C$. Consider any $(S, y) \in \mathcal{A}_C$. By definition, $S \in \Sigma$ and $y \in S \setminus C(S)$. The assumption that $R$ is a G-rationalization of $C$ implies the existence of $x \in S$ such that $(y, x) \notin R$. Define $f(S, y) = x$. To show that $f$ satisfies **TCI**, suppose $(S, x) \in \mathcal{A}_C$ and $y \in S$ are such that $(x, y) \in tc(R_C)$. By part (i) of Theorem 4.1, it follows that $(x, y) \in R$ and, thus, $f(S, x) \neq y$ by definition of $f$.

Now suppose that, provided $\mathcal{A}_C \neq \emptyset$, there exists $f \in \mathcal{F}_C$ satisfying **TCI**. If $\mathcal{A}_C = \emptyset$, $R = X \times X$ is a transitive G-rationalization of $C$ and we are done. If $\mathcal{A}_C \neq \emptyset$, there exists a function $f \in \mathcal{F}_C$ satisfying **TCI**. Define

$$R = tc(R_C).$$

Clearly, $R$ is transitive. We complete the proof by showing that it is a G-rationalization of $C$. To that end, suppose $S \in \Sigma$ and $x \in S$.

Suppose first that $x \in C(S)$. This implies $(x, y) \in R_C \subseteq tc(R_C) = R$ for all $y \in S$ and, thus, $x \in G(S, R)$.

Now suppose $x \in G(S, R)$. By definition, $(x, y) \in tc(R_C)$ for all $y \in S$. If $(S, x) \in \mathcal{A}_C$, **TCI** implies $f(S, x) \neq y$ for all $y \in S$, contrary to the existence of $f$. Thus, $(S, x) \notin \mathcal{A}_C$, which implies $x \in C(S)$ by definition. ∎

## 4.4 Summary

As established in the previous two sections, G-rationalizability by a relation without any further restrictions, by a Suzumura-consistent relation and by an ordering, can be characterized by means of various coherence condition on the direct revealed preference relation and its Suzumura-consistent and transitive closures. When the G-rationalization is required to be acyclical or quasi-transitive, however, the situation becomes more complex and an alternative method is to be employed. For the sake of easy reference, the resulting characterization theorems for all eleven forms of rationalizability are summarized in Table 4.1. Each row corresponds to a rationalizability property and each column except for the last (which identifies the relevant theorem) represents a property of a function $f$ as defined earlier. An asterisk in a cell means that the corresponding property of $f$ is used in the characterization of the corresponding rationalizability requirement.

Unlike the coherence conditions regarding $R_C$, $sc(R_C)$, and $tc(R_C)$, the members of the latter category of conditions formulated in terms of

**Table 4.1.** Rationalizability and Properties of $f$

|  | DRE | DRI | RI | DSI | II | RE | SI | DSE | IE | SCI | TCI | Theorem |
|---|---|---|---|---|---|---|---|---|---|---|---|---|
| G-R-∅ | * | | | | | | | | | | | 4.5 |
| G-RC-∅ | * | * | | | | | | | | | | 4.6 |
| G-R-A | * | | * | | | | | | | | | 4.7 |
| G-C-A | * | | | * | | | | | | | | 4.8 |
| G-RC-A | * | | | | * | | | | | | | 4.9 |
| G-∅-Q | * | | * | | | * | | | | | | 4.10 |
| G-R-Q | * | | * | | | * | * | | | | | 4.11 |
| G-C-Q | * | | | * | | | | * | | | | 4.12 |
| G-RC-Q | * | | | | * | | | | * | | | 4.13 |
| G-R-S | | | | | | | | | | * | | 4.14 |
| G-RC-T | | | | | | | | | | | * | 4.15 |

a function $f$ involve existential clauses. This is sometimes seen as a short-coming, but this objection, by itself, does not stand on solid ground: there is nothing inherently undesirable in an axiom involving existential clauses. If the argument is that existential clauses are difficult to verify in practice, this is easily countered by the observation that universal quantifiers are no easier to check algorithmically. At least, in the case of existential clauses, a search algorithm can terminate once one object with the desired property is found. In this respect, our conditions compare rather favorably with those that are required for many forms of rationalizability where universal quantifiers play a dominant role. On the other hand, establishing that an axiom is violated may prove to be less complex in the case of universal quantifiers. Thus, we do not think that ease of verifiability or falsifiability can be used as an argument against the use of conditions involving existential clauses, just as it cannot be used against axioms based on universal quantifiers.

We suspect that a major reason behind the reluctance to accept existential clauses in the context of rational choice may be that conditions involving existential requirements are seen as being "too close" to the rationalizability property itself, because the desired property is expressed in terms of the existence of a rationalization. This is (except for obvious cases) a matter of judgment, of course. Our view is that the combinations of the axioms employed in the characterization results presented in the last eleven theorems represent an interesting and insightful way of separating the properties that are necessary and sufficient for each class of rationalizability. Moreover, as is apparent from the proofs of our results, there is a substantial amount of work to be done in order to deduce the existence of a rationalization from the mere existence of a function $f$ with the requisite properties. Furthermore, the axioms we use appear to be rather clear and the roles they play in the respective results have very intuitive interpretations. Finally, we observe that the mathematical structures encountered here are similar to those appearing in *dimension theory*, which addresses the question of how many orderings are required to express a quasi-ordering as the intersection of those orderings. Consequently, closely related complexities cannot but arise. In fact, existential clauses appear in many of the characterization results in that area; see, for example, Dushnik and Miller (1941).

In concluding this part of this monograph, some remarks on further problems to be explored are in order. Because we do not impose any restrictions on the domain of a choice function (other than non-emptiness) in this chapter, our results are extremely general. Consequently, our theorems can be of relevance in whatever context of rational choices as purposive behavior we may care to specify, which is an obvious merit of our general approach. Note, however, that this approach may overlook some meaningful further directions to explore by being insensitive to the structural properties of the domain that may make perfect sense in the specific contexts on which we are focusing. Two representative examples may be worthwhile to mention. The first structural property of the domain is *closedness under union* stating that, for any collection of sets in the domain, their set-theoretical union is also a member of the domain. The second structural property of the domain is *coveredness:* for any collection of sets in the domain, there exists a member of the domain that contains the set-theoretical union of that collection. Note that the former structural property of the domain is not satisfied by the Samuelson-Houthakker domain, which consists of the budget sets in a commodity space, whereas the latter structural property of the domain is. Indeed, the second property can be construed as a generalization of the first; it is also a property that is satisfied by the Arrow-Sen domain with a finite universal set. The exploration of the theory of rational choice under one or the other of these domain restrictions (or yet others not mentioned here) is a worthwhile direction of further research. The task of Part III is to explore the implications of some of these domain restrictions.

# — III —

## Rationalizability on Specific Domains

# — 5 —

# Domain Closedness Properties

## 5.1  Additional Choice Coherence Axioms

An important class of domain restrictions that has been explored quite extensively in the literature on rational choice is based on set-theoretic *closedness* properties of the domain $\Sigma$. The two properties that have received the most attention are *closedness under intersection* and *closedness under union*. Closedness under intersection requires that, whenever the members of a collection of sets in $\mathcal{X}$ belong to $\Sigma$ and their intersection is non-empty, then this intersection is an element of $\Sigma$ as well. Analogously, closedness under union demands that, for any collection of sets in $\mathcal{X}$ each of which belongs to $\Sigma$, their union is also a member of $\Sigma$.

These domain restrictions are of importance because they are plausible for several economic choice models. For example, closedness under intersection is satisfied by the domain consisting of all compact, convex, and comprehensive subsets of $\mathbb{R}_+^n$, the non-negative orthant of Euclidean $n$-space for $n \in \mathbb{N} \setminus \{1\}$. This domain is relevant in axiomatic models of bargaining where the elements of $\mathbb{R}_+^n$ are interpreted as possible utility or payoff distributions among $n$ agents that can be achieved through a bargaining process, and the origin represents the outcome that results if the agents fail to reach an agreement—the disagreement outcome. Feasible sets of utility distributions are usually assumed to be compact (closed and bounded), convex (for any two points in a feasible set, any point on the line segment joining the two points is also in the set), and comprehensive (for any point $x$ in a feasible set, any point $y \in \mathbb{R}_+^n$ that is vector dominated by $x$ is in this feasible set as well). Compactness is a standard regularity condition in economic models, convexity accommodates the possibility of considering probability distributions in addition to certain outcomes,

115

and comprehensiveness formalizes the commonly imposed free-disposal assumption.

Rationalizability plays an important role in the literature on axiomatic approaches dealing with the bargaining problem. The most prominent bargaining solution is the Nash (1950) solution. It selects, for each compact, convex, and comprehensive subset of $\mathbb{R}^n_+$, the unique utility distribution that maximizes the product of the agents' utilities. Clearly, by its very definition, this solution is rationalizable: it selects the best elements according to the ordering on $X = \mathbb{R}^n_+$ that ranks utility vectors on the basis of the product of their components. More general rationalizable solutions to the bargaining problem are studied in Lensberg (1987, 1988), Thomson and Lensberg (1989), Peters and Wakker (1991), Bossert (1994), and Sanchez (2000); see also Thomson (forthcoming 2010) for a survey of axiomatic models of bargaining.

Closedness under union is satisfied, for example, by the domain that consists of all compact and comprehensive (but not necessarily convex) subsets of $\mathbb{R}^n_+$ (or subsets of $\mathbb{R}^n$ with suitably modified definitions of comprehensiveness or a weakening of compactness to make the two properties compatible). A prominent example of an application of this domain is analyzed by Donaldson and Weymark (1988) who study rationalizable solutions to social choice problems in economic environments.

Although we appreciate that the specific domain assumptions employed in the above-mentioned applications undoubtedly are of great interest and importance, we concentrate on more general domain restrictions that allow us to capture the implications of what we think of as fundamental *types* of domain assumptions. We do hope, however, that the notion of Suzumura consistency will at some point be examined in these (and other) special cases as well.

Until recently, the application of these types of domain restrictions has been limited to the study of full rationalizability—rationalizability by an ordering (note that in the case of an ordering, it is not necessary to specify whether greatest-element rationalizability or maximal-element rationalizability is considered because the two notions coincide). The usefulness of these domain assumptions lies in the fact that they allow us to work with properties that are weaker (and, thus, easier to justify) than others on arbitrary domains but turn out to be equivalent on suitably specified domains. In particular, the assumption of closedness under union implies that rationalizability by an ordering can be obtained as a consequence of a property that is, on arbitrary domains, considerably weaker than the requisite necessary and sufficient condition for that type of rationalizability. This property is what has become to be known as Arrow's choice axiom; see Arrow (1959). However, as pointed out by Shubik (1982, pp. 420–421 and p. 423, footnote 2), Nash communicated this property as early as 1950 in an informal note. While closedness under intersection is not sufficient to obtain the equivalence of Arrow's choice axiom and full rationalizability, it does imply that Arrow's choice axiom has some additional strength as compared to its power on arbitrary domains.

We extend some known results regarding full rationalizability by integrating some of the properties used in Chapter 4 into the results concerning their logical relationships. This is done because there are some conceptual similarities and it is of interest to contrast the resulting logical relationships under various domain closedness assumptions, in addition to those obtained on arbitrary domains. Furthermore, following Bossert and Suzumura (2007a), we ask whether new logical relationships, in addition to those summarized in Chapter 3, emerge under one or the other of our closedness properties.

It turns out that closedness under intersection does not give us any additional results: the same logical relationships as those of Chapter 3 are valid. In contrast, closedness under union leads to an additional implication, namely, that G-C-Q implies G-RC-A. It is worth mentioning that, unlike most of the earlier literature, we employ a closedness property with respect to set-theoretic unions that is not restricted to *finite* unions. The reason is that the argument employed to establish the above-mentioned new implication does not go through if attention is restricted to finite unions; this will become clear in the proof that relies on the axiom of choice.

We now introduce the formal definitions of our closedness assumptions. A non-empty domain $\Sigma \subseteq \mathcal{X}$ is *closed under intersection* if and only if, for all non-empty collections $\mathcal{V}$ of elements of $\Sigma$, if $(\cap_{S \in \mathcal{V}} S) \neq \emptyset$, then $(\cap_{S \in \mathcal{V}} S) \in \Sigma$. Analogously, $\Sigma$ is *closed under union* if and only if, for all non-empty collections $\mathcal{V}$ of elements of $\Sigma$, $(\cup_{S \in \mathcal{V}} S) \in \Sigma$.

As mentioned in Chapter 4, in addition to transitive closure coherence, an alternative necessary and sufficient condition for full rationalizability on arbitrary domains is Richter's (1966) *congruence* axiom. This property is defined as follows.

**Congruence**   For all $S \in \Sigma$ and for all $x, y \in X$,

$$[(x, y) \in tc(R_C) \text{ and } y \in C(S) \text{ and } x \in S] \Rightarrow x \in C(S).$$

The congruence axiom expresses an alternative way to ensure that the indirect revealed preference relation $tc(R_C)$ be respected. If an alternative $x$ is (indirectly) revealed preferred to an alternative $y$, any transitive G-rationalization must respect this preference. Thus, if $y$ is selected in a choice situation in which $x$ is available, then $x$ must be chosen as well. Congruence and transitive closure coherence are equivalent and, therefore, congruence is necessary and sufficient for G-rationalizability by a transitive relation. This equivalence result, due to Richter (1966, 1971), follows as a consequence of a more comprehensive theorem regarding the logical relationships between these two and other properties; this theorem is stated after introducing the remaining axioms to be considered.

A natural weakening of congruence is obtained if, in the formulation of the axiom, the transitive closure of the revealed preference relation is replaced with its Suzumura-consistent closure. We call the resulting new axiom *intermediate congruence.*

**Intermediate congruence**    For all $S \in \Sigma$ and for all $x, y \in X$,

$$[(x, y) \in sc(R_C) \text{ and } y \in C(S) \text{ and } x \in S] \Rightarrow x \in C(S).$$

Interestingly, intermediate congruence is *not* equivalent to Suzumura-consistent closure coherence; this observation is also included in our general theorem to follow.

Yet another weakening is obtained by using the direct revealed preference relation $R_C$ itself instead of its Suzumura-consistent closure. We call the resulting axiom *weak congruence;* see Sen (1971).

**Weak congruence**    For all $S \in \Sigma$ and for all $x, y \in X$,

$$[(x, y) \in R_C \text{ and } y \in C(S) \text{ and } x \in S] \Rightarrow x \in C(S).$$

Analogously to the corresponding observation for Suzumura-consistent closure coherence and intermediate congruence, weak congruence is *not* equivalent to direct revelation coherence; this result is due to Richter (1971), and it also emerges as a consequence of our general theorem to follow shortly.

Another axiom that plays an important role in the context of choice problems whose domains satisfy one or the other of our closedness properties is *Arrow's choice axiom* (Arrow, 1959).

**Arrow's choice axiom**    For all $S, T \in \Sigma$,

$$[S \subseteq T \text{ and } S \cap C(T) \neq \emptyset] \Rightarrow C(S) = S \cap C(T).$$

In the context of single-valued bargaining problems, Arrow's choice axiom is equivalent to Nash's (1950) *independence of irrelevant alternatives.*

## 5.2   Logical Relationships

We now examine the logical relationships between the four axioms introduced in the previous section on arbitrary domains in order to establish a benchmark for comparison with the corresponding results that emerge if one of the domain closedness properties applies. In addition, we include the properties of transitive closure coherence, Suzumura-consistent closure coherence, and direct revelation coherence because of their close conceptual link to these axioms.

**Theorem 5.1**   *Suppose $C: \Sigma \to \mathcal{X}$ is a choice function with an arbitrary non-empty domain $\Sigma \subseteq \mathcal{X}$. Then*

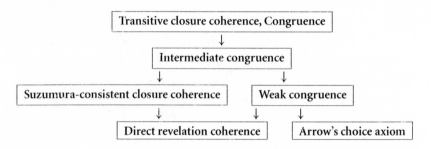

**Proof**   (a) We first show that transitive closure coherence and congruence are equivalent.

Suppose first that $C$ satisfies transitive closure coherence, and let $S \in \Sigma$ and $x, y \in X$ be such that $(x, y) \in tc(R_C)$, $y \in C(S)$, and $x \in S$. By definition of $R_C$, this implies $(y, z) \in R_C$ for all $z \in S$, which, combined with $(x, y) \in tc(R_C)$, implies $(x, z) \in tc(R_C)$ for all $z \in S$. By transitive closure coherence, $x \in C(S)$.

Conversely, suppose that $C$ satisfies congruence, and let $S \in \Sigma$ and $x \in S$ be such that $(x, y) \in tc(R_C)$ for all $y \in S$. Because $C(S) \neq \emptyset$, there exists $z \in C(S)$. If $z = x$, we are done. If $z \neq x$, it follows that $(x, z) \in tc(R_C)$, $z \in C(S)$, and $x \in S$, and congruence implies $x \in C(S)$.

(b) That congruence (and, thus, transitive closure coherence) implies intermediate congruence follows immediately from the observation that $sc(R_C) \subseteq tc(R_C)$ due to part (i) of Theorem 2.4.

(c) Next, we prove that intermediate congruence implies Suzumura-consistent closure coherence. Suppose that $C$ satisfies intermediate congruence, and let $S \in \Sigma$ and $x \in S$ be such that $(x, y) \in sc(R_C)$ for all $y \in S$. Because $C(S) \neq \emptyset$, there exists $z \in C(S)$. If $z = x$, we are done. If $z \neq x$, it follows that $(x, z) \in sc(R_C)$, $z \in C(S)$, and $x \in S$, and intermediate congruence implies $x \in C(S)$.

(d) That intermediate congruence implies weak congruence follows from the observation that $R_C \subseteq sc(R_C)$ by definition of the Suzumura-consistent closure of a relation.

(e) Analogously, that Suzumura-consistent closure coherence implies direct revelation coherence follows immediately from the observation that $R_C \subseteq sc(R_C)$.

(f) To establish that weak congruence implies direct revelation coherence, suppose that $C$ satisfies weak congruence, and let $S \in \Sigma$ and $x \in S$ be such that $(x, y) \in R_C$ for all $y \in S$. Because $C(S) \neq \emptyset$, there exists $z \in C(S)$. If $z = x$, we are done. If $z \neq x$, it follows that $(x, z) \in R_C$, $z \in C(S)$, and $x \in S$, and weak congruence implies $x \in C(S)$.

(g) The last implication to be established is that weak congruence implies Arrow's choice axiom. Suppose $C$ satisfies weak congruence and let $S, T \in \Sigma$ be such that $S \subseteq T$ and $S \cap C(T) \neq \emptyset$.

To prove that $C(S) \subseteq S \cap C(T)$, let $x \in C(S)$. This implies $x \in S$ because $C(S) \subseteq S$ and $x \in T$ because $S \subseteq T$. Furthermore, by definition of $R_C$, $(x, y) \in R_C$ for all $y \in S$ and, thus, $(x, y) \in R_C$ for all $y \in S \cap C(T)$. By assumption, $S \cap C(T) \neq \emptyset$. Let $z \in S \cap C(T)$. This implies $(x, z) \in R_C$, $z \in C(T)$, and $x \in T$. By weak congruence, $x \in C(T)$. Combined with $x \in S$, we obtain $x \in S \cap C(T)$.

Now we prove the reverse set inclusion. Suppose $x \in S \cap C(T)$. This implies $(x, y) \in R_C$ for all $y \in T$ and, thus, for all $y \in S$ because $S \subseteq T$. Let $z \in C(S)$. This implies $(x, z) \in R_C$, $z \in C(S)$, and $x \in S$. By weak congruence, $x \in C(S)$.

To complete the proof of the theorem, it is sufficient to show that (h) Suzumura-consistent closure coherence does not imply Arrow's choice axiom; (i) weak congruence does not imply Suzumura-consistent closure coherence; (j) Arrow's choice axiom does not imply direct revelation coherence; and (k) direct revelation coherence does not imply Suzumura-consistent closure coherence.

(h) Let $X = \{x, y, z, v\}$ and $\Sigma = \{X, \{x, y, v\}, \{y\}, \{y, z\}, \{z\}\}$. Define the choice function $C$ by letting $C(X) = \{v\}$, $C(\{x, y, v\}) = \{x, v\}$, $C(\{y\}) = \{y\}$, $C(\{y, z\}) = \{y\}$, and $C(\{z\}) = \{z\}$. $C$ satisfies Suzumura-consistent closure coherence and violates Arrow's choice axiom because $\{x, y, v\} \subseteq X, \{x, y, v\}$ $\cap C(X) = \{v\} \neq \emptyset$, and $C(\{x, y, v\}) = \{x, v\} \neq \{v\} = \{x, y, v\} \cap C(X)$.

(i) Suppose $X = \{x, y, z\}$ and $\Sigma = \{\{x\}, \{x, y\}, \{x, z\}, \{y\}, \{y, z\}, \{z\}\}$. The choice function defined by $C(\{x\}) = \{x\}, C(\{x, y\}) = \{x\}, C(\{x, z\}) = \{z\}, C(\{y\}) = \{y\}, C(\{y, z\}) = \{y\}$, and $C(\{z\}) = \{z\}$ trivially satisfies weak congruence and violates Suzumura-consistent closure coherence because $(x, x) \in sc(R_C)$ and $(x, z) \in sc(R_C)$ but $x \notin C(\{x, z\})$.

(j) Let $X = \{x, y, z, v\}$ and $\Sigma = \{\{x, y, z\}, \{x, y, v\}, \{x, z, v\}\}$ and define the choice function $C$ by $C(\{x, y, z\}) = \{y, z\}, C(\{x, y, v\}) = \{x\}$, and $C(\{x, z, v\}) = \{x\}$. This choice function trivially satisfies Arrow's choice axiom and violates direct revelation coherence because $(x, x) \in R_C, (x, y) \in R_C$, and $(x, z) \in R_C$ but $x \notin C(\{x, y, z\})$.

(k) To show that direct revelation coherence does not imply Suzumura-consistent closure coherence, let $X = \{x, y, z\}, \Sigma = \{\{x, y\}, X\}, C(\{x, y\}) = \{x, y\}$, and $C(X) = \{y, z\}$. This choice function satisfies direct revelation coherence and violates Suzumura-consistent closure coherence because $(x, x) \in sc(R_C), (x, y) \in sc(R_C)$, and $(x, z) \in sc(R_C)$ but $x \notin C(X)$.  ∎

## 5.3   Closedness under Intersection

For domains that are closed under intersection, the distinction between weak congruence and Arrow's choice axiom disappears. This result, a strengthening of which is due to Hansson (1968), follows from the following theorem. Because the examples used in parts (h), (i), and (k) of the proof of the previous theorem are such that $\Sigma$ is closed under intersection, all other strict implications remain valid.

**Theorem 5.2**   *Suppose* $C \colon \Sigma \to \mathcal{X}$ *is a choice function with a non-empty domain* $\Sigma \subseteq \mathcal{X}$ *that is closed under intersection. Then*

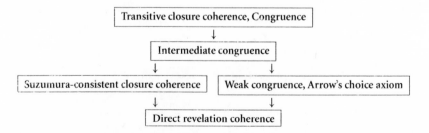

**Proof**   In view of Theorem 5.1 and the observations preceding the theorem statement, it is sufficient to show that Arrow's choice axiom implies weak congruence if $\Sigma$ is closed under intersection. Suppose $C$ satisfies Arrow's choice axiom, and let $S \in \Sigma$ and $x, y \in X$ be such that $(x, y) \in R_C$, $y \in C(S)$, and $x \in S$. By definition of $R_C$, there exists $T \in \Sigma$ such that $x \in C(T)$ and $y \in T$. Because $\Sigma$ is closed under intersection, $S \cap T \in \Sigma$. Clearly, $S \cap T \subseteq S$ and $S \cap T \subseteq T$. Because $y \in S \cap T$ and $y \in C(S)$, $(S \cap T) \cap C(S) \neq \emptyset$. Analogously, because $x \in S \cap T$ and $x \in C(T)$, $(S \cap T) \cap C(T) \neq \emptyset$. By Arrow's choice axiom,

$$C(S \cap T) = (S \cap T) \cap C(S) \text{ and } C(S \cap T) = (S \cap T) \cap C(T).$$

Therefore, $(S \cap T) \cap C(S) = (S \cap T) \cap C(T)$ and, because $x \in (S \cap T) \cap C(T)$, it follows that $x \in (S \cap T) \cap C(S)$ and thus $x \in C(S)$. ∎

As a final remark on the consequences of closedness under intersection, observe that this domain assumption does not change the results of Chapter 3 at all: to see this, we simply have to note that all the implications established in Chapter 3 remain true because they are valid on any domain (and, thus, in particular, on domains that are closed under intersection) and, furthermore, the examples employed in the proof of Theorem 3.2 are all defined on domains that are closed under intersection. Therefore, all results continue to hold under this domain closedness condition.

## 5.4  Closedness under Union

If the domain of a choice function is closed under union, some further equivalences can be established. In particular, Arrow's choice axiom (and, thus, weak congruence) is equivalent to congruence in this setting. Again, Hansson (1968), who established a stronger statement, is to be credited for this result; see also Donaldson and Weymark (1988). Thus, in these circumstances, Arrow's choice axiom is not only necessary but also sufficient for full rationalizability.

**Theorem 5.3** *Suppose* $C \colon \Sigma \to \mathcal{X}$ *is a choice function with a non-empty domain* $\Sigma \subseteq \mathcal{X}$ *that is closed under union. Then*

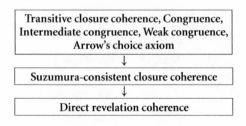

**Proof** In view of Theorems 5.1 and 5.2, together with the observation that the examples employed in parts (h) and (k) of the proof of Theorem 5.1 are such that $\Sigma$ is closed under union, we have only to prove that Arrow's choice axiom implies congruence, provided that $\Sigma$ is closed under union. Suppose $C$ satisfies Arrow's choice axiom, and let $S \in \Sigma$ and $x, y \in X$ be such that $(x, y) \in tc(R_C)$, $y \in C(S)$, and $x \in S$. By definition, there exist $K \in \mathbb{N}, S^0, \ldots, S^{K-1} \in \Sigma$, and $x^0, \ldots, x^K \in X$ such that

$$x = x^0 \text{ and } [x^{k-1} \in C(S^{k-1}) \text{ and } x^k \in S^{k-1}]$$
$$\text{for all } k \in \{1, \ldots, K\} \text{ and } x^K = y.$$

Let $S^K = S$. Because $\Sigma$ is closed under union, it follows that $(S^0 \cup \cdots \cup S^K) \in \Sigma$. We next show that, for all $k \in \{1, \ldots, K\}$,

$$C\left(S^0 \cup \cdots \cup S^K\right) \cap S^k \neq \emptyset \Rightarrow C\left(S^0 \cup \cdots \cup S^K\right) \cap S^{k-1} \neq \emptyset. \tag{5.1}$$

Suppose $C(S^0 \cup \cdots \cup S^K) \cap S^k \neq \emptyset$ for some $k \in \{1, \ldots, K\}$. By Arrow's choice axiom, $C(S^k) = C(S^0 \cup \cdots \cup S^K) \cap S^k$. Thus, because $x^k \in C(S^k)$, it follows that $x^k \in C(S^0 \cup \cdots \cup S^K) \cap S^k$ and thus $x^k \in C(S^0 \cup \cdots \cup S^K)$. By assumption, we also have $x^k \in S^{k-1}$ and, therefore, $x^k \in C(S^0 \cup \cdots \cup S^K) \cap S^{k-1}$, which establishes that $C(S^0 \cup \cdots \cup S^K) \cap S^{k-1} \neq \emptyset$. This completes the proof of (5.1).

Because $C(S^0 \cup \cdots \cup S^K) \neq \emptyset$, it follows that there exists $k \in \{0, \ldots, K\}$ such that $C(S^0 \cup \cdots \cup S^K) \cap S^k \neq \emptyset$. Applying (5.1) as many times as required, it follows that $C(S^0 \cup \cdots \cup S^K) \cap S^0 \neq \emptyset$. By Arrow's choice axiom, we obtain $C(S^0) = C(S^0 \cup \cdots \cup S^K) \cap S^0$ and, because $x = x^0 \in C(S^0)$, $x \in C(S^0 \cup \cdots \cup S^K)$. By assumption, $x \in S^K = S$ and, therefore, $x \in C(S^0 \cup \cdots \cup S^K) \cap S$ and hence $C(S^0 \cup \cdots \cup S^K) \cap S \neq \emptyset$. Using Arrow's choice axiom again, it follows that $C(S) = C(S^0 \cup \cdots \cup S^K) \cap S$, which, in turn, implies $x \in C(S)$. ∎

Requiring $\Sigma$ to be closed under union also produces a new result as far as the notions of rationalizability discussed in Chapter 3 are concerned. In particular, it is now the case that **G-C-Q** implies **G-RC-A** so that we obtain the following theorem, which is due to Bossert and Suzumura (2007a).

**Theorem 5.4** *Suppose $C \colon \Sigma \to \mathcal{X}$ is a choice function with a non-empty domain $\Sigma \subseteq \mathcal{X}$ that is closed under union. If $C$ satisfies **G-C-Q**, then $C$ satisfies **G-RC-A**.*

**Proof**  Suppose $\Sigma$ is closed under union, and let $R$ be a complete and quasi-transitive G-rationalization of $C$. Define

$$\mathcal{M} = \big\{(x, S) \mid (x, x) \notin R \text{ and } S \in \Sigma \text{ and }$$
$$(x, y) \in R \text{ for all } y \in S \setminus \{x\}\big\}.$$

If $\mathcal{M} = \emptyset$, it follows immediately that $R \cup \Delta$ is a reflexive, complete, and quasi-transitive (and thus acyclical) G-rationalization of $C$ and we are done.

Now suppose $\mathcal{M} \neq \emptyset$. Let $\mathcal{Z}$ denote the set of all non-empty subsets of $X \times \Sigma$, and define a function $\tau \colon \Sigma \to \mathcal{Z}$ by $\tau(S) = \{(z, S) \mid z \in C(S)\}$ for all $S \in \Sigma$. Furthermore, let

$$\mathcal{T} = \{\tau(S) \mid S \in \Sigma\}.$$

Let $\Phi$ be the set of all functions $\varphi \colon \mathcal{T} \to \cup_{T \in \mathcal{T}} T$ such that $\varphi(t) \in t$ for all $t \in \mathcal{T}$. By the axiom of choice, $\Phi \neq \emptyset$.

For all $\varphi \in \Phi$, define a function $g_\varphi \colon \mathcal{M} \to X$ by

$$g_\varphi(x, S) = z \Leftrightarrow \varphi(\tau(S)) = (z, S)$$

for all $(x, S) \in \mathcal{M}$. Let

$$\mathcal{G} = \big\{g \colon \mathcal{M} \to X \mid \exists \varphi \in \Phi \text{ such that } g = g_\varphi\big\}.$$

The set $\mathcal{G}$ is non-empty because $\Phi$ is non-empty.

For all $g \in \mathcal{G}$, let

$$R_g = (R \cup \Delta) \setminus \{(x, y) \mid \exists S \in \Sigma \text{ such that }$$
$$[(x, S) \in \mathcal{M} \text{ and } y = g(x, S)]\}.$$

Clearly, $R_g$ is reflexive because $\Delta \subseteq R_g$.

By definition of $\mathcal{M}$ and $\mathcal{G}$, $(x, y) \in I(R)$ for all pairs $(x, y)$ such that there exists $S \in \Sigma$ with $(x, S) \in \mathcal{M}$ and $y = g(x, S)$. Thus, $(y, x) \in P(R_g)$ for all such pairs. This, together with the completeness of $R$, implies that $R_g$ is complete. This argument also establishes that $P(R) \subseteq P(R_g)$.

Next, we show that $R_g$ is a G-rationalization of $C$ for all $g \in \mathcal{G}$. Let $S \in \Sigma$ and $x \in S$.

Suppose first that $x \in C(S)$. Because $R$ is a G-rationalization of $C$, $(x, y) \in R$ for all $y \in S$ and in particular $(x, x) \in R$. By definition of $\mathcal{M}$, this implies $(x, S) \notin \mathcal{M}$, which implies $(x, y) \in R_g$ for all $y \in S$. Thus, $x \in G(R_g, S)$.

Now suppose $x \in G(R_g, S)$. If there exists $y \in S \setminus \{x\}$ such that $(x, y) \notin R$, the completeness of $R$ implies that $(y, x) \in P(R) \subseteq P(R_g)$, contradicting the hypothesis $x \in G(R_g, S)$. If $(x, x) \notin R$, the definition of $R_g$ implies that $\big(x, g(x, S)\big) \notin R_g$, again contradicting the hypothesis $x \in G(R_g, S)$ because, by definition, $g(x, S) \in S$. Thus, $(x, y) \in G(R, S)$ and $x \in C(S)$ follows from the assumption that $R$ G-rationalizes $C$.

We have now established that $R_g$ is a reflexive and complete G-rationalization of $C$ for *all* $g \in \mathcal{G}$. To complete the proof, we show that there must exist *some* $g \in \mathcal{G}$ such that $R_g$ is acyclical.

A strict preference cycle in $R_g$ can be written as a pair $c = (K_c, \{x_c^0, \ldots, x_c^{K_c}\})$ where $K_c \in \mathbb{N} \setminus \{1\}$ and $x_c^k \in X$ for all $k \in \{0, \ldots, K_c\}$ such that $(x_c^{k-1}, x_c^k) \in P(R_g)$ for all $k \in \{1, \ldots, K_c\}$ and $(x_c^{K_c}, x_c^0) \in P(R_g)$. Without loss of generality, we can assume that the $x_c^k$ are pairwise distinct.

Let $\mathcal{C}_g$ be the set of all strict preference cycles in $R_g$. We need to show that there exists $g \in \mathcal{G}$ such that $\mathcal{C}_g = \emptyset$. By way of contradiction, suppose that $\mathcal{C}_g \neq \emptyset$ for all $g \in \mathcal{G}$. Consider any $g \in \mathcal{G}$ and any $c \in \mathcal{C}_g$.

If there exists $k \in \{1, \ldots, K_c - 1\}$ such that $(x_c^{k-1}, x_c^k) \in P(R)$ and $(x_c^k, x_c^{k+1}) \in P(R)$, the quasi-transitivity of $R$ implies $(x_c^{k-1}, x_c^{k+1}) \in P(R)$. The same reasoning implies that if $(x_c^{K_c-1}, x_c^{K_c}) \in P(R)$ and $(x_c^{K_c}, x_c^0) \in P(R)$, we must have $(x_c^{K_c-1}, x_c^0) \in P(R)$. Thus, because $K_c$ is finite, we can without loss of generality assume that, in any strict preference cycle, there are never two consecutive instances of strict preference according to $P(R)$.

If there exists $k \in \{1, \ldots, K_c - 1\}$ such that $(x_c^{k-1}, x_c^k) \in P(R_g) \setminus P(R)$ and $(x_c^k, x_c^{k+1}) \in P(R_g) \setminus P(R)$, the definition of $R_g$ implies that there exist $S, T \in \Sigma$ such that

$$(x_c^k, S) \in \mathcal{M} \text{ and } x_c^{k-1} = g(x_c^k, S)$$
$$\text{and } (x_c^{k+1}, T) \in \mathcal{M} \text{ and } x_c^k = g(x_c^{k+1}, T).$$

By definition of $\mathcal{M}$ and $g$, this implies $(x_c^k, x_c^k) \notin R$ and $x_c^k \in C(T)$, a contradiction to the assumption that $R$ is a G-rationalization of $C$. Thus, there cannot be two consecutive instances of strict preference according to $P(R_g) \setminus P(R)$ either.

Because $R$ is quasi-transitive and therefore acyclical, every strict preference cycle must contain at least one instance of strict preference according to $P(R_g) \setminus P(R)$. Because there cannot be any two consecutive instances of strict preference according to $P(R_g) \setminus P(R)$ and $K_c \geq 2$ for any strict preference cycle $c$ by assumption, it follows that every strict preference cycle must also contain at least one instance of strict preference according to $P(R)$.

Combining the findings of the previous three paragraphs, it follows that we can, without loss of generality, assume that all strict preference cycles alternate between instances of strict preference according to $P(R_g) \setminus P(R)$ and according to $P(R)$. Thus, for all $g \in \mathcal{G}$ and for all strict preference cycles $c = (K_c, \{x_c^0, \ldots, x_c^{K_c}\}) \in C_g$, we assume that $(x_c^{k-1}, x_c^k) \in P(R_g) \setminus P(R)$ for all odd $k \in \{1, \ldots, K_c\}$, $(x_c^{k-1}, x_c^k) \in P(R)$ for all even $k \in \{1, \ldots, K_c\}$, and $(x_c^{K_c}, x_c^0) \in P(R)$. Note that this implies that $K_c$ must be an odd number greater than or equal to three. Furthermore, for all odd $k \in \{1, \ldots, K_c\}$, there exists $S_c^k \in \Sigma$ such that $(x_c^k, S_c^k) \in \mathcal{M}$ and $x_c^{k-1} = g(x_c^k, S_c^k)$.

Let $\Upsilon$ be the set of all alternatives in $C(\Sigma)$ that do not appear in any strict preference cycle. That is, $x \in C(\Sigma)$ is an element of $\Upsilon$ if and only if, for all $g \in \mathcal{G}$, for all $c \in C_g$, and for all odd $k \in \{1, \ldots, K_c\}$, $x_c^{k-1} \neq x$. Now define $\Sigma' = \{S \in \Sigma \mid C(S) \cap \Upsilon = \emptyset\}$; that is, $\Sigma'$ is composed of those sets $S$ in $\Sigma$ such that all elements of $C(S)$ appear in some strict preference cycle. Note that $\Sigma' = \Sigma$ is possible. Let, for all sets $S \in \Sigma \setminus \Sigma'$, $y_S$ be an alternative in $C(S)$ that does not appear in any strict preference cycle. Let $\mathcal{G}'$ be the subset of $\mathcal{G}$ containing all functions $g$ such that, for all $(x, S) \in \mathcal{M}$ with $S \in \Sigma \setminus \Sigma'$, $g(x, S) = y_S$. Clearly, $\mathcal{G}' \neq \emptyset$. If $\Sigma' = \emptyset$, any $g \in \mathcal{G}'$ is such that $C_g = \emptyset$, a contradiction. Therefore, $\Sigma' \neq \emptyset$. Let

$$T = \bigcup_{g \in \mathcal{G}'} \bigcup_{c \in C_g} \bigcup_{k \in \{1, \ldots, K_c\}} S_c^k. \tag{5.2}$$

Because $\mathcal{G}'$ is non-empty and $C_g$ is non-empty for all $g \in \mathcal{G}'$, $T \neq \emptyset$. Because $\Sigma$ is closed under union, $T \in \Sigma$. By definition, all sets $S_c^k$ in (5.2) are elements of $\Sigma'$. Because $C$ is G-rationalizable by $R$, it follows that, for all $y \in S_c^k \setminus C(S_c^k)$, there exists $x \in S_c^k \subseteq T$ such that $(y, x) \notin R$. Again invoking the G-rationalizability of $C$ by $R$, this implies that

$$C(T) \subseteq \bigcup_{g \in \mathcal{G}'} \bigcup_{c \in C_g} \bigcup_{k \in \{1, \ldots, K_c\}} C(S_c^k). \tag{5.3}$$

Consider any $g \in \mathcal{G}'$, $c \in C_g$, and $k \in \{1, \ldots, K_c\}$, and let $x \in C(S_c^k)$. Because $S_c^k \in \Sigma'$, there exists a strict preference cycle containing $x$. Thus, there exist $g' \in \mathcal{G}'$, $c' \in C_g$, and $y \in X$ such that $(x, y) \in P(R_g) \setminus P(R)$. Furthermore, there exist $z, v \in X$ such that $(z, v) \in P(R_g) \setminus P(R)$ and $(v, x) \in P(R)$. By definition, there exists $S \in \Sigma'$ such that $v \in S \subseteq T$ and, because $R$ is a G-rationalization of $C$, $x \notin C(T)$. This argument applies to all elements in the union on the right side of (5.3) and, therefore, $C(T) = \emptyset$, a contradiction. ∎

G-RC-A and its equivalents remain stronger than G-C-A even if $\Sigma$ is closed under union. To see that this is the case, let $X = \{x, y, z, v\}$ and consider the domain

$$\Sigma = \{X, \{x, y, v\}, \{x, v\}, \{y\}, \{y, z\}, \{y, z, v\}, \{y, v\}, \{v\}\}.$$

Clearly, $\Sigma$ is closed under union. Define a choice function $C$ by letting $C(X) = \{v\}$, $C(\{x, y, v\}) = \{x, v\}$, $C(\{x, v\}) = \{x, v\}$, $C(\{y\}) = \{y\}$, $C(\{y, z\}) = \{y\}$, $C(\{y, z, v\}) = \{y, v\}$, $C(\{y, v\}) = \{y, v\}$, and $C(\{v\}) = \{v\}$. This choice function is G-rationalizable by the complete and acyclical relation

$$R = \{(x, x), (x, y), (x, v), (y, y), (y, z), (y, v),$$
$$(z, x), (z, y), (v, x), (v, y), (v, z), (v, v)\}.$$

Suppose $R'$ is a reflexive, complete, and acyclical G-rationalization of $C$. Reflexivity implies that we must have $(z, z) \in R'$. This, in turn, implies $(y, z) \in P(R')$ because $C(\{y, z\}) = \{y\}$. Furthermore, because $C(\{y, v\}) = \{y, v\}$, we must have $(y, y) \in R'$ and $(y, v) \in R'$. Thus, because $y \notin C(\{x, y, v\})$, it must be the case that $(y, x) \notin R'$ and, because $R'$ is complete, $(x, y) \in P(R')$. Because $x \in C(\{x, y, v\})$, it follows that $(x, x) \in R'$, $(x, y) \in R'$, and $(x, v) \in R'$. Thus, $x \notin C(X)$ implies $(x, z) \notin R'$. The completeness of $R'$ implies $(z, x) \in P(R')$, contradicting the acyclicity of $R'$.

# — 6 —

# Cardinality-Complete Domains

## 6.1 Base Domains

A second type of domain assumption that has been used in the literature requires that, at least, the subsets of $X$ with specific cardinalities are included in $\Sigma$. The richest possible domain is obtained if we assume that $\Sigma$ is equal to $\mathcal{X}$. A weaker assumption, used by Arrow (1959) and Sen (1971), for example, requires that $\Sigma$ contain all *finite* subsets of $X$. As pointed out by Sen (1971), however, it is sufficient for many purposes to assume that all subsets of $X$ of cardinality two and three are elements of $\Sigma$.

The domain assumption we consider here dispenses with the requirement that the subsets of cardinality three are present in $\Sigma$ and, instead, demands that the singletons and two-element sets are included in $\Sigma$. This is, we think, a very weak domain assumption that was introduced in Bossert, Sprumont, and Suzumura (2005a, 2006). We say that $\Sigma \subseteq \mathcal{X}$ is a *base domain* if and only if

$$\{S \in \mathcal{X} \mid |S| \in \{1, 2\}\} \subseteq \Sigma.$$

If $\Sigma$ is a base domain, the logical relationships among our notions of rationalizability simplify considerably. This is due to the observation that, in this case, any G-rationalization must be reflexive and complete. We explore this issue in the following section.

## 6.2 Logical Relationships on Base Domains

On base domains, the number of different notions of rationalizability can be reduced considerably. We obtain the following theorem.

**Theorem 6.1**   *Suppose* $C: \Sigma \to \mathcal{X}$ *is a choice function with a base domain* $\Sigma \subseteq \mathcal{X}$. *Then*

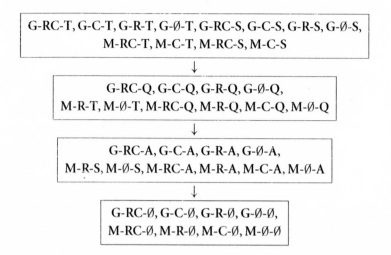

G-RC-T, G-C-T, G-R-T, G-∅-T, G-RC-S, G-C-S, G-R-S, G-∅-S,
M-RC-T, M-C-T, M-RC-S, M-C-S

↓

G-RC-Q, G-C-Q, G-R-Q, G-∅-Q,
M-R-T, M-∅-T, M-RC-Q, M-R-Q, M-C-Q, M-∅-Q

↓

G-RC-A, G-C-A, G-R-A, G-∅-A,
M-R-S, M-∅-S, M-RC-A, M-R-A, M-C-A, M-∅-A

↓

G-RC-∅, G-C-∅, G-R-∅, G-∅-∅,
M-RC-∅, M-R-∅, M-C-∅, M-∅-∅

**Proof**   All implications that are valid for arbitrary domains continue to apply. Thus, it is sufficient to prove the equivalences appearing in Theorem 6.1 that do not hold on arbitrary domains and to provide examples establishing that no further implications other than those following from the arrows depicted in the theorem statement are valid.

(a) Suppose $C$ satisfies G-∅-$\gamma$, where $\gamma \in \{T, Q, S, A, \emptyset\}$. Let $R$ be a G-rationalization of $C$ satisfying the coherence property identified by $\gamma$. Because $\Sigma$ is a base domain, it follows that $\{x\} \in \Sigma$ for all $x \in X$. The non-emptiness of $C(\{x\})$ implies $C(\{x\}) = \{x\}$, which, in turn, yields $(x, x) \in R_C$. By Theorem 3.1, it follows that $(x, x) \in R$ for all $x \in X$ and, therefore, $R$ is reflexive. Analogously, the assumption that $\Sigma$ is a base domain implies that $\{x, y\} \in \Sigma$ for all $x, y \in X$ such that $x \neq y$. By the non-emptiness of $C(\{x, y\})$, we must have $x \in C(\{x, y\})$ or $y \in C(\{x, y\})$. This implies $(x, y) \in R_C$ or $(y, x) \in R_C$ and, again invoking Theorem 3.1, we obtain $(x, y) \in R$ or $(y, x) \in R$ for all $x, y \in X$ such that $x \neq y$. Thus, $R$ is complete. We have therefore established that G-∅-$\gamma$ implies G-RC-$\gamma$, and the equivalences in the theorem statement now follow from this result and Theorem 3.4.

(b) That the first two implications are strict follows immediately from the observation that the examples employed in parts (g) and (j) in the proof of Theorem 3.2 involve base domains. To prove that the properties in the fourth box do not imply those in the third, let $X = \{x, y, z\}$ and $\Sigma = \{\{x\}, \{x, y\}, \{x, z\}, \{y\}, \{y, z\}, \{z\}\}$. Clearly, $\Sigma$ is a base domain. Now define a choice function on $\Sigma$ by letting $C(\{x\}) = \{x\}$, $C(\{x, y\}) = \{x\}$, $C(\{x, z\}) = \{z\}$, $C(\{y\}) = \{y\}$, $C(\{y, z\}) = \{y\}$, and $C(\{z\}) = \{z\}$. This choice function is rationalized by the reflexive and complete relation

$$R = \{(x, x), (x, y), (y, y), (y, z), (z, x), (z, z)\}$$

but it does not have an acyclical G-rationalization. By way of contradiction, suppose $R'$ is an acyclical G-rationalization of $C$. Because $C(\{x, y\}) = \{x\}$, it follows that $(x, x) \in R'$ and $(x, y) \in R'$. Analogously, $C(\{y, z\}) = \{y\}$ implies $(y, y) \in R'$ and $(y, z) \in R'$, and $C(\{x, z\}) = \{z\}$ implies $(z, x) \in R'$ and $(z, z) \in R'$. Therefore, because $y \notin C(\{x, y\})$, we must have $(x, y) \in P(R')$. Analogously, $z \notin C(\{y, z\})$ implies $(y, z) \in P(R')$ and $x \notin C(\{x, z\})$ implies $(z, x) \in P(R')$, contradicting the acyclicity of $R'$.  ∎

## 6.3  Characterizations on Base Domains

We now illustrate the use of the base domain assumption by providing characterizations of all four distinct notions of rationalizability identified in the previous section. As compared to the corresponding characterizations for arbitrary domains, the necessary and sufficient conditions can be simplified considerably. These characterizations are due to Bossert, Sprumont, and Suzumura (2005a, 2006).

We begin with the strongest notion of rationalizability. The twelve properties in the top box of Theorem 6.1 are equivalent to a weakening of congruence the scope of which is restricted to chains of direct revealed preferences involving at most three alternatives.

**T-congruence**  For all $S \in \Sigma$ and for all $x, y, z \in X$,

$$[(x, y) \in R_C \text{ and } (y, z) \in R_C \text{ and } z \in C(S) \text{ and } x \in S] \Rightarrow x \in C(S).$$

On base domains, T-congruence is necessary and sufficient for the notions of rationalizability in the top box of Theorem 6.1; the full force of congruence (or, equivalently, transitive closure coherence) is not required.

**Theorem 6.2**  *Suppose $C: \Sigma \to \mathcal{X}$ is a choice function with a base domain $\Sigma \subseteq \mathcal{X}$. C satisfies any of* G-RC-T, G-C-T, G-R-T, G-Ø-T, G-RC-S, G-C-S,

**G-R-S, G-Ø-S, M-RC-T, M-C-T, M-RC-S, M-C-S** *if and only if C satisfies T-congruence.*

**Proof**  Let $\Sigma$ be a base domain. This implies that $R_C$ is reflexive and complete—see the proof of Theorem 6.1. By Theorem 6.1, it is sufficient to consider the property **G-RC-T**. That **G-RC-T** implies T-congruence follows immediately from Richter's (1966) result and the observation that T-congruence is weaker than congruence. Thus, it remains to be shown that T-congruence implies **G-RC-T**. We prove that $R = R_C$ is an ordering that G-rationalizes $C$. Reflexivity and completeness have already been established. To prove that $R = R_C$ is transitive, suppose $(x, y) \in R_C$ and $(y, z) \in R_C$ for some $x, y, z \in X$. Because $\Sigma$ is a base domain, it follows that $\{x, z\} \in \Sigma$. By T-congruence, $x \in C(\{x, z\})$ and hence $(x, z) \in R_C = R$.

Finally, we show that $R = R_C$ greatest-element rationalizes $C$. Let $S \in \Sigma$ and $x \in S$.

Suppose $x \in C(S)$. This implies $(x, y) \in R_C = R$ for all $y \in S$ and hence $x \in G(S, R)$.

Now suppose $x \in G(S, R)$, that is, $(x, y) \in R = R_C$ for all $y \in S$. If $S = \{x\}$, we have $C(S) = \{x\}$ because $C(S)$ is non-empty and hence $(x, x) \in R_C$. If there exists $y \in S$ such that $y \neq x$, it follows that $(x, y) \in R_C$ and, by definition of $R_C$, $x$ must be chosen for some feasible set in $\Sigma$. Thus, again, $(x, x) \in R_C$. Therefore, $(x, y) \in R_C$ for all $y \in S$. Let $z \in C(S)$. This implies $(z, z) \in R_C$. Because $z \in S$, $(x, z) \in R_C$. Letting $y = z$ in the definition of T-congruence, the axiom implies $x \in C(S)$.  ∎

Next, we consider the rationalizability properties in the second box of Theorem 6.1. To obtain a set of necessary and sufficient conditions for these notions of rationalizability in the case of a base domain, we add the following Q-congruence axiom to direct revelation coherence.

**Q-congruence**   For all $S \in \Sigma$ and for all $x, y, z \in X$,

$$[(x, y) \in P(R_C) \text{ and } (y, z) \in P(R_C) \text{ and } x \in S] \Rightarrow z \notin C(S).$$

Together with direct revelation coherence, Q-congruence guarantees that the direct revealed preference relation $R_C$ is quasi-transitive. Note that, again, we do not need to impose a restriction regarding chains of (strict) revealed preferences of arbitrary length. We obtain

**Theorem 6.3**  *Suppose $C \colon \Sigma \to \mathcal{X}$ is a choice function with a base domain $\Sigma \subseteq \mathcal{X}$. C satisfies any of* **G-RC-Q, G-C-Q, G-R-Q, G-Ø-Q, M-R-T, M-Ø-T, M-RC-Q, M-R-Q, M-C-Q, M-Ø-Q** *if and only if C satisfies direct revelation coherence and Q-congruence.*

**Proof**  Let $\Sigma$ be a base domain. Again, this implies that $R_C$ is reflexive and complete. By Theorem 6.1, we can restrict attention to the property **G-RC-Q**.

(a) We first show that **G-RC-Q** implies Q-congruence (that direct revelation coherence is implied follows immediately because the axiom is necessary for any form of G-rationalizability on any domain; see Theorem 4.2). Suppose $R$ is a reflexive, complete, and quasi-transitive G-rationalization of $C$. Let $S \in \Sigma$ and $x, y, z \in X$ be such that $(x, y) \in P(R_C)$, $(y, z) \in P(R_C)$, and $x \in S$. This implies $(x, y) \in R_C$ and $(y, z) \in R_C$ and, thus, $(x, y) \in R$ and $(y, z) \in R$ by Theorem 3.1. Suppose $(y, x) \in R$. Because $\Sigma$ is a base domain, $\{y\} \in \Sigma$. By the non-emptiness of $C(\{y\})$, $y \in C(\{y\})$. Hence, $(y, y) \in R_C$ and, invoking Theorem 3.1 again, we obtain $(y, y) \in R$. Because $\Sigma$ is a base domain, $\{x, y\} \in \Sigma$. We have $(y, x) \in R$ and $(y, y) \in R$, which, due to the assumption that $R$ is a G-rationalization of $C$, implies $y \in C(\{x, y\})$ and hence $(y, x) \in R_C$. But this contradicts the assumption that $(x, y) \in P(R_C)$. Therefore, we must have $(x, y) \in P(R)$. Analogously, it follows that $(y, z) \in P(R)$. The quasi-transitivity of $R$ now implies $(x, z) \in P(R)$ and, thus, $(z, x) \notin R$. Because $R$ is a G-rationalization of $C$, we obtain $z \notin C(S)$.

(b) We show that direct revelation coherence and Q-congruence together imply **G-RC-Q**. First, we prove that $R_C$ is quasi-transitive. Suppose $(x, y) \in P(R_C)$ and $(y, z) \in P(R_C)$ for some $x, y, z \in X$. Because $\Sigma$ is a base domain, $\{x, z\} \in \Sigma$. By Q-congruence, $z \notin C(\{x, z\})$ and hence $x \in C(\{x, z\})$ because $C(\{x, z\})$ is non-empty. Thus, $(x, z) \in R_C$. Because $R_C$ is reflexive, $(z, z) \in R_C$. If $(z, x) \in R_C$, direct revelation coherence implies $z \in C(\{x, z\})$, a contradiction. Therefore, $(x, z) \in P(R_C)$.

The rest of the proof proceeds as in Richter (1971) by showing that $R = R_C$ is a G-rationalization of $C$, given direct revelation coherence. Let $S \in \Sigma$ and $x \in S$.

Suppose $x \in C(S)$. This implies $(x, y) \in R_C = R$ for all $y \in S$ and hence $x \in G(S, R)$.

Now suppose $x \in G(S, R)$, that is, $(x, y) \in R = R_C$ for all $y \in S$. By direct revelation coherence, $x \in C(S)$.  ∎

Direct revelation coherence and Q-congruence are independent on base domains. The choice function defined in part (b) in the proof of Theorem 6.1 satisfies direct revelation coherence but violates Q-congruence. Now let $X = \{x, y, z\}$ and $\Sigma = \mathcal{X}$, and define $C(\{x\}) = \{x\}$, $C(\{x, y\}) = \{x, y\}$, $C(X) = \{y, z\}$, $C(\{x, z\}) = \{x, z\}$, $C(\{y\}) = \{y\}$, $C(\{y, z\}) = \{y, z\}$, and $C(\{z\}) = \{z\}$. This choice function satisfies Q-congruence but violates direct revelation coherence.

Q-congruence by itself is a weaker axiom than the requirement that $R_C$ be quasi-transitive; only in conjunction with direct revelation coherence does it imply the quasi-transitivity of $R_C$. Strengthening Q-congruence to the quasi-transitivity of $R_C$ does not allow us to drop direct revelation coherence in the above characterization. The choice function $C$ in the above example showing that Q-congruence does not imply direct revelation coherence is such that $R_C$ is quasi-transitive and, because direct revelation coherence is necessary for G-rationalizability on any domain, $C$ cannot be G-rationalizable.

If a G-rationalization is required to be acyclical instead of quasi-transitive, it may seem natural to replace Q-congruence by the following A-congruence axiom in order to obtain a characterization for base domains.

**A-congruence**    For all $S \in \Sigma$ and for all $x, y \in X$,

$$[(x, y) \in tc(P(R_C)) \text{ and } y \in C(S) \text{ and } x \in S] \Rightarrow x \in C(S).$$

Although it is true that direct revelation coherence and A-congruence together are necessary and sufficient for the properties in the third box of Theorem 6.1 on base domains, a stronger result can be obtained. A-congruence by itself is stronger than the acyclicity of $R_C$, which, in conjunction with direct revelation coherence, is all that is required to obtain the desired characterization result.

**Theorem 6.4**  *Suppose $C \colon \Sigma \to \mathcal{X}$ is a choice function with a base domain $\Sigma \subseteq \mathcal{X}$. $C$ satisfies any of* G-RC-A, G-C-A, G-R-A, G-Ø-A, M-R-S, M-Ø-S, M-RC-A, M-R-A, M-C-A, M-Ø-A *if and only if $C$ satisfies direct revelation coherence and $R_C$ is acyclical.*

**Proof**  Let $\Sigma$ be a base domain. Again, it follows that $R_C$ is reflexive and complete. We prove the theorem by considering G-RC-A.

(a) We first show that **G-RC-A** implies that $R_C$ is acyclical (that direct revelation coherence is implied follows from its necessity for all versions of G-rationalizability).

Suppose $R$ is a reflexive, complete, and acyclical G-rationalization of $C$. Let $K \in \mathbb{N}$ and $x^0, \ldots, x^K \in X$ be such that $(x^{k-1}, x^k) \in P(R_C)$ for all $k \in \{1, \ldots, K\}$. Analogously to the proof of Theorem 6.3, this implies $(x^{k-1}, x^k) \in P(R)$ for all $k \in \{1, \ldots, K\}$ (note that the argument employed in that proof does not require quasi-transitivity of a G-rationalization; the assumption that $\Sigma$ is a base domain is sufficient). Because $R$ is acyclical, we have $(x^K, x^0) \notin P(R)$ and, since $R$ is reflexive and complete, $(x^0, x^K) \in R$. Invoking reflexivity again, we obtain $(x^K, x^K) \in R$. Because $\Sigma$ is a base domain, $\{x^0, x^K\} \in \Sigma$. By assumption, $R$ is a G-rationalization of $C$, which implies $x^0 \in C(\{x^0, x^K\})$ and hence $(x^0, x^K) \in R_C$, which implies $(x^K, x^0) \notin P(R_C)$.

(b) Direct revelation coherence and the acyclicity of $R_C$ together imply **G-RC-A** because direct revelation coherence implies that $R_C$ is a G-rationalization of $C$, as shown in the proof of Theorem 6.3.  ∎

That direct revelation coherence and the acyclicity of $R_C$ are independent can be shown by employing the same examples as those used to establish the independence of direct revelation coherence and Q-congruence.

The properties in the last box of Theorem 6.1 are characterized by direct revelation coherence if $\Sigma$ is a base domain. This is an immediate consequence of the observation that direct revelation coherence is necessary and sufficient for G-∅-∅ (see Theorem 4.2) and Theorem 6.1 and, thus, we state the result without a proof.

**Theorem 6.5** *Suppose $C: \Sigma \to \mathcal{X}$ is a choice function with a base domain $\Sigma \subseteq \mathcal{X}$. $C$ satisfies any of* **G-RC-∅, G-C-∅, G-R-∅, G-∅-∅, M-RC-∅, M-R-∅, M-C-∅, M-∅-∅** *if and only if $C$ satisfies direct revelation coherence.*

## 6.4   Base Domains and Closedness under Union

We conclude this chapter by examining the consequences of assuming that $\Sigma$ is closed under union *and* a base domain. While the first two implications of Theorem 6.1 remain irreversible, the properties in the last two boxes of the theorem statement become equivalent if closedness under union is added as a requirement on $\Sigma$.

**Theorem 6.6**   *Suppose* $C: \Sigma \to \mathcal{X}$ *is a choice function with a base domain* $\Sigma \subseteq \mathcal{X}$ *that is closed under union. Then*

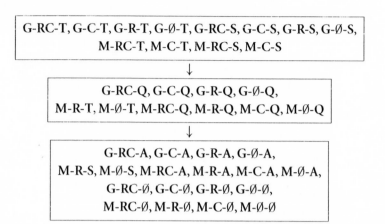

Proof   In view of Theorem 6.1, it is sufficient to show that the first two implications remain strict if closedness under union is added as a requirement and that the properties in the last box appearing in the statement of Theorem 6.1 imply those of the next-to-last box. That the first two implications are strict even if $\Sigma$ is closed under union in addition to being a base domain follows immediately from the observation that the examples in parts (g) and (j) of the proof of Theorem 3.2 are such that $\Sigma$ is a base domain that is closed under union.

To complete the proof, suppose $R$ is a G-rationalization of $C$. By way of contradiction, suppose $R$ is not acyclical. Thus, there exist $K \in \mathbb{N}$ and $x^0, \ldots, x^K \in X$ such that $(x^{k-1}, x^k) \in P(R)$ for all $k \in \{1, \ldots, K\}$ and $(x^K, x^0) \in P(R)$. Because $\Sigma$ is a base domain, it follows that $\{x^{k-1}, x^k\} \in \Sigma$ for all $k \in \{1, \ldots, K\}$. Because $\Sigma$ is closed under union, $\{x^0, \ldots, x^K\} \in \Sigma$. Thus, for all $k \in \{0, \ldots, K\}$, there exists $\ell \in \{0, \ldots, K\}$ such that $(x^\ell, x^k) \in P(R)$. Because $R$ is a G-rationalization of $C$, this implies $C(\{x^0, \ldots, x^K\}) = \emptyset$, a contradiction.   ∎

The assumption that $\Sigma$ is a base domain could be weakened for some of the observations reported in this chapter. For example, T-congruence is necessary and sufficient for G-RC-T even if $\Sigma$ contains all two-element sets but not necessarily all singletons, domains that we refer to as *binary* domains. This is the case because reflexivity does not have to be assumed explicitly when examining G-rationalizability by a transitive relation. Analogously, G-Ø-Ø implies G-Ø-A not only on base domains but on binary domains as well; this is an immediate consequence of the observation that the corresponding part of the proof of Theorem 6.6 uses two-element sets only.

# — IV —

## Alternative Notions of Rationalizability

# — 7 —

# Non-deteriorating Choice

## 7.1 Individual Non-deteriorating Choice

The basic forms of rationalizability we have analyzed thus far (greatest-element rationalizability and maximal-element rationalizability) are sometimes considered too demanding, especially in social choice problems. The requirement that *all* elements of a feasible set should be weakly dominated by a chosen alternative may be rather difficult to satisfy in some circumstances and, thus, we may not necessarily want to declare an agent violating this requirement irrational. Although greatest-element rationalizability and maximal-element rationalizability are based on a sound normative foundation, systematic violations have been observed in several contexts; see, for instance, the surveys by Camerer (1995) and Shafir and Tversky (1995). Thus, it is of interest to examine less ambitious rationality notions. One such possibility is to analyze the requirement of *non-deteriorating choice,* introduced by Bossert and Sprumont (2009). There are other notions of *bounded rationality* in the literature, dating back as far as the contributions by Simon (1955, 1956) but we focus on non-deteriorating choice here because its analysis fits in very well with the issues addressed throughout this monograph. Large parts of this chapter are based on Bossert and Sprumont (2003, 2009) and Bossert and Suzumura (2007b).

The concept of non-deteriorating choice is based on the idea that a chosen alternative need not dominate *all* elements in the feasible set from which it is chosen but, instead, should be at least as good as a *reference alternative.* This requirement is what is often referred to as individual rationality but we prefer to use the term *non-deteriorating choice* to avoid confusion with the notion of rationality discussed in earlier chapters. To incorporate it into a model of choice, we assume that, in each feasible set, there exists a reference alternative, which, along with the set of feasible objects, determines the choice of the agent. There are several natural and plausible interpretations of such a reference alternative. In general, it can be thought of as an alternative representing the status quo. This interpretation is applicable in abstract choice problems (which, as in most of the book, are the ones we focus on here) but also in more specific contexts. For example, in dynamic environments in which consecutive choices have to be made, a plausible reference alternative at a given stage of the process is one that has been selected in the previous stage, provided that it is still feasible in the current stage. In an economic environment, a natural choice of a reference alternative is an initial consumption bundle held by an agent.

The potential role that a status quo option may play is recognized in other contributions as well; see, for instance, Zhou (1997) for an alternative notion of rationality in such a setting. The importance of a reference alternative for choice behavior is also examined in Rubinstein and Zhou (1999), and Masatlioglu and Ok (2005) analyze the notion of a status quo *bias* in a similar framework.

Clearly, in order to formulate a precise definition of the concept of non-deterioration, we need to identify the reference alternative for each feasible set and, therefore, a choice function that maps feasible sets into sets of chosen objects no longer is an adequate description of a choice situation. To accommodate the presence of a reference alternative, we introduce the notion of a *selection function*. Let $\Gamma \subseteq \{(S, y) \mid S \in \mathcal{X} \text{ and } y \in S\}$ be a non-empty domain. The interpretation of the elements in $\Gamma$ is straightforward: they represent all observable choice situations where, for any $(S, y) \in \Gamma$, $S$ is the feasible set of options and $y \in S$ is the reference alternative. A selection function is a mapping $D: \Gamma \to \mathcal{X}$ such that, for all $(S, y) \in \Gamma$, $D(S, y) \subseteq S$.

In line with the intuitive interpretation of non-deteriorating choice given above, we say that a selection function $D$ is *ND-rationalizable* if and only if there exists an antisymmetric relation $R$ on $X$ such that, for all $(S, y) \in \Gamma$ and for all $x \in D(S, y)$,

$$(x, y) \in R.$$

A relation $R$ with this property is said to be an *ND-rationalization* of $D$ or, alternatively, $D$ is *ND-rationalized* by $R$.

The antisymmetry assumption imposed on $R$ is intended to avoid degenerate situations. Without a restriction such as antisymmetry, the concept of non-deterioration becomes vacuous: *any* selection function would be declared to be ND-rationalizable if we were to permit the *universal indiffer-ence* relation—the relation $R = X \times X$—as a potential ND-rationalization. Although representing a rather weak notion of rationality even if antisym-metry is imposed on an ND-rationalization, non-deterioration as defined above is not a vacuous concept. For instance, suppose that $X = \{x, y\}$, $\Gamma = \{(\{x, y\}, x), (\{x, y\}, y)\}$, $D(\{x, y\}, x) = \{y\}$, and $D(\{x, y\}, y) = \{x\}$. ND-rationalizability requires the existence of an antisymmetric relation $R$ such that $(x, y) \in R$ and $(y, x) \in R$, which is an immediate contradiction to the antisymmetry assumption.

We can now define versions of ND-rationalizability analogous to those introduced earlier for G-rationalizability and M-rationalizability. For $\beta \in \{RC, R, C, \emptyset\}$ and $\gamma \in \{T, Q, S, A, \emptyset\}$, N-$\beta$-$\gamma$ denotes ND-rationalizability by a relation satisfying the richness property or properties represented by $\beta$ and the coherence property identified by $\gamma$.

As is the case for G-rationalizability and for M-rationalizability, there are, in principle, twenty versions of ND-rationalizability according to this classification. It turns out, however, that there remain merely two distinct versions because many of them are equivalent, even on arbitrary domains. This is in stark contrast with the results obtained for G-rationalizability and M-rationalizability, where we identified eleven and four distinct ver-sions, respectively. Thus, we can think of this notion as being remarkably robust with respect to the additional properties that are imposed on an ND-rationalization.

Before stating the formal result regarding the logical relationships be-tween all of our notions of ND-rationalizability, we prove a preliminary result that is analogous to the relationship between the direct revealed pre-ference relation of a choice function and any G-rationalization thereof. Analogously to the relation $R_C$ defined for a choice function $C$, we define the relation $R_D$ corresponding to a selection function $D: \Gamma \to \mathcal{X}$ by

$$R_D = \{(x, y) \mid \exists S \in \mathcal{X} \text{ such that } [(S, y) \in \Gamma \text{ and } x \in D(S, y)]\}.$$

As is the case for the direct revealed preference relation of a choice func-tion, any ND-rationalization of a selection function $D$ must respect the relation $R_D$.

**Theorem 7.1**  *Suppose $D: \Gamma \to \mathcal{X}$ is a selection function with an arbitrary non-empty domain $\Gamma \subseteq \{(S, y) \mid S \in \mathcal{X} \text{ and } y \in S\}$ and $R$ is a relation on $X$. If $R$ is an ND-rationalization of $D$, then $R_D \subseteq R$.*

**Proof**   Suppose that $R$ is an ND-rationalization of $D$ and $x, y \in X$ are such that $(x, y) \in R_D$. By definition of $R_D$, there exists $S \in \mathcal{X}$ such that $(S, y) \in \Gamma$ and $x \in D(S, y)$. Because $R$ is an ND-rationalization of $D$, this implies $(x, y) \in R$.  ∎

   The only distinction to be made between our different notions of ND-rationalizability is whether an ND-rationalization possesses any of the coherence properties of transitivity, Suzumura consistency, quasi-transitivity, or acyclicity: as soon as one of these conditions is satisfied, all of them are. Moreover, both reflexivity and completeness are redundant because any notion of ND-rationalizability without these richness properties is equivalent to that obtained by adding both of them. These observations are summarized in the following theorem.

**Theorem 7.2**   *Suppose* $D: \Gamma \to \mathcal{X}$ *is a selection function with an arbitrary non-empty domain* $\Gamma \subseteq \{(S, y) \mid S \in \mathcal{X} \text{ and } y \in S\}$. *Then*

| N-RC-T, N-C-T, N-R-T, N-Ø-T, |
| :---: |
| N-RC-S, N-C-S, N-R-S, N-Ø-S, |
| N-RC-Q, N-C-Q, N-R-Q, N-Ø-Q, |
| N-RC-A, N-C-A, N-R-A, N-Ø-A |

$$\downarrow$$

| N-RC-Ø, N-C-Ø, N-R-Ø, N-Ø-Ø |
| :---: |

**Proof**   To establish the theorem, we need to show that the properties in each of the two boxes are equivalent and, furthermore, that the implication indicated by the arrow in the theorem statement is strict; it is obvious that the implication itself is true.

   (a) We first prove the equivalence of the axioms in the top box. To do so, it clearly is sufficient to show that N-Ø-A implies N-RC-T. Suppose $R$ is an acyclical ND-rationalization of $D$. Let $R'$ be an ordering extension of $tc(R) \cup \Delta$ (the existence of such an ordering extension is guaranteed by Theorem 2.7). It remains to be established that $R'$ is an ND-rationalization of $D$.

   First, we establish that $R'$ is antisymmetric (recall that this property is required by definition of an ND-rationalization). By way of contradiction, suppose $R'$ is not antisymmetric. Then there exist $x, y \in X$ such that $(x, y) \in I(R')$ and $x \neq y$. Because $x \neq y$, $(x, y) \notin \Delta$ and, thus, by definition of $R'$, there exist $K, L \in \mathbb{N}$ and $x^0, \ldots, x^K, y^0, \ldots, y^L \in X$ such that $x = x^0$, $(x^{k-1}, x^k) \in R$ for all $k \in \{1, \ldots, K\}$, $x^K = y = y^0$, $(y^{\ell-1}, y^\ell) \in R$ for all

$\ell \in \{1, \ldots, L\}$, and $y^L = x$. Clearly, we can, without loss of generality, assume that the $x^k$ are pairwise distinct and, analogously, the $y^\ell$ are pairwise distinct. Because $R$ is an ND-rationalization of $D$ and, thus, antisymmetric, it follows that $(x^{k-1}, x^k) \in P(R)$ for all $k \in \{1, \ldots, K\}$ and $(y^{\ell-1}, y^\ell) \in P(R)$ for all $\ell \in \{1, \ldots, L\}$. But this contradicts the acyclicity of $R$. Therefore, $R'$ is antisymmetric.

To complete the proof, suppose that $x \in X$ and $(S, y) \in \Gamma$ are such that $x \in D(S, y)$. By definition of $R_D$, this implies $(x, y) \in R_D$. Using Theorem 7.1, the definition of the transitive closure of a relation and the definition of $R'$, we have $R_D \subseteq R \subseteq tc(R) \subseteq tc(R) \cup \Delta \subseteq R'$. Thus, $(x, y) \in R'$.

(b) To prove the equivalence of the axioms in the second box, it suffices to show that N-Ø-Ø implies N-RC-Ø. Let $R$ be an ND-rationalization of $D$.

If $R$ is complete, the relation $R' = R \cup \Delta$ clearly is a reflexive and complete ND-rationalization of $D$.

Now suppose $R$ is not complete. Let $\mathcal{T} = \{\{x, y\} \mid (x, y) \in NC(R)$ and $x \neq y\}$. Because $R$ is not complete, it follows that $\mathcal{T} \neq \emptyset$. By the axiom of choice, there exists a function $\varphi \colon \mathcal{T} \to \cup_{T \in \mathcal{T}} T$ such that $\varphi(t) \in t$ for all $t \in \mathcal{T}$. Let

$$R' = R \cup \Delta \cup \{(\varphi(\{x, y\}), z) \mid \{x, y\} \in \mathcal{T} \text{ and}$$
$$\{x, y\} \setminus \{\varphi(\{x, y\})\} = \{z\}\}.$$

Clearly, $R'$ is reflexive and complete. To see that $R'$ is antisymmetric, note that the three relations the union of which constitutes $R'$ are antisymmetric and the relation

$$\{(\varphi(\{x, y\}), z) \mid \{x, y\} \in \mathcal{T} \text{ and } \{x, y\} \setminus \{\varphi(\{x, y\})\} = \{z\}\}$$

only contains pairs of distinct elements that are non-comparable according to $R \cup \Delta$. To complete the proof that $R'$ is an ND-rationalization of $D$, suppose $x \in X$ and $(S, y) \in \Gamma$ are such that $x \in D(S, y)$. Because $R$ is an ND-rationalization of $D$, it follows that $(x, y) \in R$ and, because $R \subseteq R'$ by definition, $(x, y) \in R'$.

(c) To see that the implication in the theorem statement is strict, consider the following example. Let $X = \{x, y, z\}$ and $\Gamma = \{(S, v) \mid S \in \mathcal{X}$ and $v \in S\}$, and define a selection function $D \colon \Gamma \to \mathcal{X}$ by $D(\{x, y\}, y) = \{x\}$, $D(\{x, z\}, x) = \{z\}$, $D(\{y, z\}, z) = \{y\}$, and $D(S, v) = \{v\}$ for all $(S, v) \in \Gamma \setminus \{(\{x, y\}, y), (\{x, z\}, x), (\{y, z\}, z)\}$. This selection function is ND-rationalized by the (antisymmetric) relation

$$R = \{(x, x), (x, y), (y, y), (y, z), (z, x), (z, z)\}$$

and, therefore, $D$ satisfies **N-Ø-Ø**. By way of contradiction, suppose that $D$ satisfies **N-Ø-A** and let $R'$ be an acyclical ND-rationalization of $D$. It follows that we must have $(x, y) \in R'$ because $x \in D(\{x, y\}, y)$, $(y, z) \in R'$ because $y \in D(\{y, z\}, z)$, and $(z, x) \in R'$ because $z \in D(\{x, z\}, x)$. Because ND-rationalizability requires that $R'$ is antisymmetric, it follows that $(x, y) \in P(R'), (y, z) \in P(R')$, and $(z, x) \in P(R')$, contradicting the acyclicity of $R'$. ∎

The selection function employed in part (c) of the above proof is defined on the full domain $\{(S, y) \mid S \in \mathcal{X} \text{ and } y \in S\}$. Therefore, the logical relationships displayed in the theorem statement (in particular, the *strict* implication) remain true even if the domain $\Gamma$ is assumed to be extremely rich.

## 7.2  Characterizations of ND-Rationalizability

We now provide characterizations of the two distinct notions of ND-rationalizability identified in the above theorem. We begin with a characterization of the properties in the top box of Theorem 7.2, which is due to Bossert and Sprumont (2009). Analogously to the congruence axiom of Richter (1966), we define a variant that is suitable for selection functions.

**Selection congruence**    For all $S \in \mathcal{X}$ and for all $x, y \in X$,

$$[(x, y) \in tc(R_D) \text{ and } (S, x) \in \Gamma \text{ and } x \neq y] \Rightarrow y \notin D(S, x).$$

Analogously to the congruence axiom for choice functions, selection congruence ensures that chains of preference according to $R_D$ are respected. This axiom is necessary and sufficient for ND-rationalizability on any domain.

**Theorem 7.3**    *Suppose* $D: \Gamma \to \mathcal{X}$ *is a selection function with an arbitrary non-empty domain* $\Gamma \subseteq \{(S, y) \mid S \in \mathcal{X} \text{ and } y \in S\}$. *$D$ satisfies* **N-$\beta$-$\gamma$** *for any* $\beta \in \{\text{RC}, \text{R}, \text{C}, \text{Ø}\}$ *and any* $\gamma \in \{\text{T}, \text{Q}, \text{S}, \text{A}\}$ *if and only if $D$ satisfies selection congruence.*

**Proof**    By Theorem 7.2, it is sufficient to establish the equivalence of **N-Ø-T** and selection congruence.

Suppose first that $D$ satisfies **N-Ø-T** and that $R$ is a transitive ND-rationalization of $D$. By way of contradiction, suppose that selection congruence is violated. Then there exist $S \in \mathcal{X}$ and $x, y \in X$ such that

$(x, y) \in tc(R_D)$, $(S, x) \in \Gamma$, $x \neq y$, and $y \in D(S, x)$. By definition, $(y, x) \in R_D$ and, by Theorem 7.1, $(y, x) \in R$. Because $(x, y) \in tc(R_D)$, there exist $K \in \mathbb{N}$ and $x^0, \ldots, x^K \in X$ such that $x = x^0$, $(x^{k-1}, x^k) \in R_D$ for all $k \in \{1, \ldots, K\}$, and $x^K = y$. Using Theorem 7.1 again, we obtain $(x^{k-1}, x^k) \in R$ for all $k \in \{1, \ldots, K\}$ and, because $R$ is transitive, $(x, y) \in R$. Because $x \neq y$ by assumption, this contradicts the antisymmetry of $R$.

Now suppose $D$ satisfies selection congruence. We complete the proof by establishing that the transitive relation $R = tc(R_D)$ is an ND-rationalization of $D$. To show that $R = tc(R_D)$ is antisymmetric, suppose, to the contrary, that there exist $x, y \in X$ such that $x \neq y$ and $(x, y) \in I(R) = I(tc(R_D))$. Then there exist $K, L \in \mathbb{N}$, $x^0, \ldots, x^K \in X$, and $y^0, \ldots, y^L \in X$ such that $x = x^0$, $(x^{k-1}, x^k) \in R$ for all $k \in \{1, \ldots, K\}$, $x^K = y = y^0$, $(y^{\ell-1}, y^\ell) \in R$ for all $\ell \in \{1, \ldots, L\}$, and $y^L = x$. Clearly, we can, without loss of generality, assume that the $x^k$ are pairwise distinct and that the $y^\ell$ are pairwise distinct. Thus, $y^{L-1} \neq y^L = x$. By definition, $(x, y^{L-1}) \in tc(R_D)$ and there exists $S \in \mathcal{X}$ such that $(S, x) \in \Gamma$ and $y^{L-1} \in D(S, x)$, contradicting selection congruence. To complete the proof, note that $x \in D(S, y)$ for some $x \in X$ and $(S, y) \in \Gamma$ immediately implies $(x, y) \in R_D \subseteq tc(R_D) = R$. ∎

Our next task is the characterization of the remaining four (equivalent) notions of ND-rationalizability. The following axiom of weak selection congruence is obtained from selection congruence by replacing the transitive closure of $R_D$ with $R_D$ itself.

**Weak selection congruence**   For all $S \in \mathcal{X}$ and for all $x, y \in X$,

$$[(x, y) \in R_D \text{ and } (S, x) \in \Gamma \text{ and } x \neq y] \Rightarrow y \notin D(S, x).$$

Interestingly, whereas weak congruence is not a necessary and sufficient condition for the G-rationalizability of a choice function, weak selection congruence can be used to provide a characterization of the ND-rationalizability of a selection function in the absence of any coherence property.

**Theorem 7.4**   *Suppose $D: \Gamma \to \mathcal{X}$ is a selection function with an arbitrary non-empty domain $\Gamma \subseteq \{(S, y) \mid S \in \mathcal{X} \text{ and } y \in S\}$. $D$ satisfies N-$\beta$-$\emptyset$ for any $\beta \in \{RC, R, C, \emptyset\}$ if and only if $D$ satisfies weak selection congruence.*

**Proof**   By Theorem 7.2, it is sufficient to establish the equivalence of N-$\emptyset$-$\emptyset$ and weak selection congruence.

Suppose first that $D$ satisfies **N-∅-∅** and that $R$ is an ND-rationalization of $D$. By way of contradiction, suppose that weak selection congruence is violated. Then there exist $S \in \mathcal{X}$ and $x, y \in X$ such that $(x, y) \in R_D$, $(S, x) \in \Gamma$, $x \neq y$, and $y \in D(S, x)$. By definition, $(y, x) \in R_D$ and, by Theorem 7.1, $(y, x) \in R$. Invoking Theorem 7.1 again, the assumption $(x, y) \in R_D$ implies $(x, y) \in R$ and, because $x \neq y$, we obtain a contradiction to the antisymmetry of $R$.

Now suppose $D$ satisfies weak selection congruence. We prove that $R = R_D$ is an ND-rationalization of $D$. To show that $R = R_D$ is antisymmetric, suppose, to the contrary, that there exist $x, y \in X$ such that $x \neq y$ and $(x, y) \in I(R) = I(R_D)$. Because $(y, x) \in R_D$, there exists $S \in \mathcal{X}$ such that $(S, x) \in \Gamma$ and $y \in D(S, x)$. Thus, we have $(x, y) \in R_D$, $(S, x) \in \Gamma$, $x \neq y$, and $y \in D(S, x)$, contradicting weak selection congruence. To complete the proof, note that $x \in D(S, y)$ for some $x \in X$ and $(S, y) \in \Gamma$ immediately implies $(x, y) \in R_D$.  ∎

## 7.3   The Multi-agent Case

The remainder of this chapter is devoted to a discussion of non-deteriorating choice in a multi-agent environment. In the case of theories of *collective* choice, a test of a particular theory (or a class of theories) involves not only a *single* relation that rationalizes the observed choices according to a particular notion of rationalizability but, instead, an entire *profile* of preference relations, one relation for each member of society.

There have been several revealed-preference approaches to *non-cooperative* theories of collective decision making. For example, Sprumont (2000) examines necessary and sufficient conditions for *Nash rationalizability*. Suppose the observable data set consists of a collection of feasible sets of actions and, for each of these feasible sets, a set of resulting outcomes. These observations are Nash rationalizable if and only if there exists a profile of preference relations defined on combinations of these actions such that, for each game defined by a set of feasible actions and the restrictions of the individual preference relations to the corresponding combinations of feasible actions, the set of observed outcomes coincides with the set of Nash equilibria of the game. An analogous analysis is performed for subgame perfection in Ray and Zhou (2001).

Our approach follows that of Bossert and Sprumont (2003), which focuses on two central features of *cooperative* collective choice. In addition to requiring selections to be non-deteriorating for each agent, the rationalizing profile of individual preferences is required to induce *efficient* selections. Both of these properties are of fundamental importance in many applications. For instance, studying non-deteriorating and efficient behavior is essential in developing testable restrictions of prominent concepts such as the core and the set of Walrasian equilibria in an exchange economy; see Brown and Matzkin (1996) and Bossert and Sprumont (2002). As we do throughout this monograph, however, we focus on abstract choice problems in order to provide the most general treatment.

Suppose there is a set $N = \{1, \ldots, |N|\}$ of $|N| \in \mathbb{N} \setminus \{1\}$ agents. A selection function $D$ on an arbitrary domain is defined as in the single-agent case discussed earlier in this chapter. Analogously, the definition of the relation $R_D$ is unchanged. However, the notion of rationalizability we examine now differs from that of ND-rationalizability: instead of merely considering non-deteriorating choice, we now analyze *efficient and non-deteriorating* choice. We say that a selection function $D$ is *END-rationalizable* if and only if there exists a profile $\langle R_i \rangle_{i \in N}$ of antisymmetric relations on $X$ such that, for all $(S, y) \in \Gamma$, for all $x \in D(S, y)$, and for all $i \in N$,

$$(x, y) \in R_i \tag{7.1}$$

and, for all $(S, y) \in \Gamma$ and for all $x \in D(S, y)$,

$$\{z \in S \setminus \{x\} \mid (z, x) \in R_i \text{ for all } i \in N\} = \emptyset. \tag{7.2}$$

A profile of antisymmetric relations with these properties is said to be an *END-rationalization* of $D$ or, alternatively, $D$ is *END-rationalized* by the profile $\langle R_i \rangle_{i \in N}$.

The efficiency requirement (7.2) by itself does not impose any restrictions. For any selection function $D$, let $R_1$ be an arbitrary antisymmetric relation and define

$$R_i = \{(x, y) \mid (y, x) \in R_1\}$$

for all $i \in N \setminus \{1\}$; that is, each $R_i$ with $i \geq 2$ is given by the *inverse* of $R_1$. Clearly, *all* elements of $X$ are efficient for this profile and, thus, (7.2) is satisfied for any selection function $D$.

Interestingly, when combined with the non-deterioration requirement (7.1), efficiency does impose further restrictions. For example, let $X = \{x, y, z\}$, $\Gamma = \{(X, y), (X, z)\}$, $D(X, y) = \{x\}$, and $D(X, z) = \{y\}$. Clearly, there exists a profile of antisymmetric relations $\langle R_i \rangle_{i \in N}$ such that (7.1) is satisfied (letting, for instance, $R_i = \{(x, y), (y, z)\}$ for all $i \in N$ will do) but any such profile must be such that $(x, y) \in R_i$ for all $i \in N$ because $x \in D(X, y)$. But this contradicts efficiency because $x \in X \setminus \{y\}$ and $y \in D(X, z)$.

We now analyze the possible notions of END-rationalizability that are obtained by adding our combinations of richness and coherence properties. For $\beta \in \{\mathbf{RC}, \mathbf{R}, \mathbf{C}, \emptyset\}$ and $\gamma \in \{\mathbf{T}, \mathbf{Q}, \mathbf{S}, \mathbf{A}, \emptyset\}$, E-$\beta$-$\gamma$ denotes END-rationalizability by a relation satisfying the richness property or properties represented by $\beta$ and the coherence property identified by $\gamma$.

As a preliminary observation, we note that any END-rationalization $\langle R_i \rangle_{i \in N}$ of a selection function $D$ must be such that all relations $R_i$ respect the relation $R_D$; this result is parallel to Theorem 7.1. Efficiency is not required for this implication—it is sufficient to assume that (7.1) is satisfied.

**Theorem 7.5**  *Suppose* $D \colon \Gamma \to \mathcal{X}$ *is a selection function with an arbitrary non-empty domain* $\Gamma \subseteq \{(S, y) \mid S \in \mathcal{X}$ *and* $y \in S\}$ *and* $\langle R_i \rangle_{i \in N}$ *is a profile of antisymmetric relations on $X$. If $D$ and $\langle R_i \rangle_{i \in N}$ are such that (7.1) is satisfied, then* $R_D \subseteq \bigcap_{i \in N} R_i$.

**Proof**  Suppose that $D$ and $\langle R_i \rangle_{i \in N}$ are such that (7.1) is satisfied and $x, y \in X$ are such that $(x, y) \in R_D$. By definition of $R_D$, there exists $S \in \mathcal{X}$ such that $(S, y) \in \Gamma$ and $x \in D(S, y)$. By (7.1), this implies $(x, y) \in R_i$ for all $i \in N$.  ∎

Analogously to our procedure employed for other forms of rationalizability, we now examine the logical relationships between the various notions of END-rationalizability on arbitrary domains. As a preliminary result, we show that the distinction between transitivity and quasi-transitivity disappears in the presence of antisymmetry and, analogously, Suzumura consistency and acyclicity are equivalent for antisymmetric relations.

**Theorem 7.6**  *Suppose $R$ is an antisymmetric relation on $X$.*

   *(i) If $R$ is quasi-transitive, then $R$ is transitive.*
   *(ii) If $R$ is acyclical, then $R$ is Suzumura consistent.*

**Proof**  (i) Suppose $R$ is an antisymmetric and quasi-transitive relation. Let $x, y, z \in X$ be such that $(x, y) \in R$ and $(y, z) \in R$. If $x, y, z$ are not pairwise distinct, $(x, z) \in R$ follows trivially. Now suppose the three alternatives are pairwise distinct. By the antisymmetry of $R$, it follows that

$(x, y) \in P(R)$ and $(y, z) \in P(R)$. Because $R$ is quasi-transitive, we obtain $(x, z) \in P(R) \subseteq R$.

(ii) Suppose $R$ is an antisymmetric and acyclical relation. Let $K \in \mathbb{N}$ and $x^0, \ldots, x^K \in X$ be such that $(x^{k-1}, x^k) \in R$ for all $k \in \{1, \ldots, K\}$. If $x^K = x^0$, $(x^K, x^0) \notin P(R)$ follows trivially. If $x^K \neq x^0$ we can, without loss of generality, assume that the $x^k$ are pairwise distinct (if not, all elements in the chain between two identical ones can be omitted). The antisymmetry of $R$ implies that $(x^{k-1}, x^k) \in P(R)$ for all $k \in \{1, \ldots, K\}$ and, because $R$ is acyclical, we must have $(x^K, x^0) \notin P(R)$. ∎

Using Theorem 7.6, we now prove that, out of a possible twenty, only four distinct versions of END-rationalizability exist.

**Theorem 7.7** *Suppose $D \colon \Gamma \to \mathcal{X}$ is a selection function with an arbitrary non-empty domain $\Gamma \subseteq \{(S, y) \mid S \in \mathcal{X} \text{ and } y \in S\}$. Then*

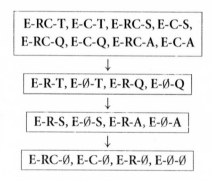

**Proof** The implications in the theorem statement are straightforward. Thus, it remains to establish the equivalences in each of the four boxes and to provide three examples showing that the implications are strict.

(a) By Theorem 7.6, E-RC-A and E-RC-S are equivalent. Furthermore, by Theorem 2.3, E-RC-S and E-RC-T are equivalent. Thus, in order to establish the equivalences in the first box, it is sufficient to prove that E-C-A implies E-RC-A. Let $\langle R_i \rangle_{i \in N}$ be an END-rationalization of $D$ such that the $R_i$ are complete and acyclical. Letting $R_i' = R_i \cup \Delta$ for all $i \in N$, it is immediate that each $R_i'$ is reflexive, complete, and acyclical and $\langle R_i' \rangle_{i \in N}$ is an END-rationalization of $D$.

(b) Given part (i) of Theorem 7.6, the equivalence of the axioms in the second box follows as soon as we establish that E-∅-Q implies E-R-Q.

As in part (a), it is straightforward to see that if $\langle R_i \rangle_{i \in N}$ is an END-rationalization of $D$ and the $R_i$ are quasi-transitive, then $\langle R_i \cup \Delta \rangle_{i \in N}$ is an END-rationalization of $D$ and $R_i \cup \Delta$ is reflexive and quasi-transitive for all $i \in N$.

(c) Analogously, the equivalence of the axioms in the third box follows from part (ii) of Theorem 7.6 and the observation that if $\langle R_i \rangle_{i \in N}$ is an END-rationalization of $D$ with acyclical relations $R_i$, then $\langle R_i \cup \Delta \rangle_{i \in N}$ is an END-rationalization of $D$ such that $R_i \cup \Delta$ is reflexive and acyclical for all $i \in N$.

(d) To show that the axioms in the last box are equivalent, it is sufficient to prove that E-Ø-Ø implies E-RC-Ø. Suppose $\langle R_i \rangle_{i \in N}$ is an END-rationalization of $D$.

If $R_i$ is complete for all $i \in N$, the profile $\langle R'_i \rangle_{i \in N}$ obtained by letting $R'_i = R_i \cup \Delta$ for all $i \in N$ clearly is an END-rationalization of $D$ and the $R'_i$ are reflexive and complete.

Now suppose there exists $i \in N$ such that $R_i$ is not complete. Let $\mathcal{I} \subseteq N$ be the set of individuals $i \in N$ such that $R_i$ is incomplete. Clearly, $\mathcal{I}$ is non-empty by assumption, and it may coincide with the entire set $N$. Let $m = |\mathcal{I}| \in \{1, \ldots, |N|\}$ be the number of elements in $\mathcal{I}$ and suppose, without loss of generality, that $\mathcal{I} = \{1, \ldots, m\}$. Define $R'_j = R_j \cup \Delta$ for all $j \in N \setminus \{1, \ldots, m\}$. Clearly, $R'_j$ is reflexive, complete, and antisymmetric for all $j \in N \setminus \{1, \ldots, m\}$.

Let

$$R_1^0 = R_1 \cup \Delta \cup \{(x,y) \in NC(R_1) \mid (y,x) \in R'_j$$
$$\text{for all } j \in N \setminus \{1, \ldots, m\} \text{ and } x \neq y\}.$$

If $R_1^0$ is complete, let $R'_1 = R_1^0$. It is evident that $R'_1$ is reflexive and complete. To establish that $R'_1$ is antisymmetric, observe first that $R_1$ is antisymmetric by assumption and $\Delta$ is trivially antisymmetric. Furthermore, if $(y,x) \in R'_j$ for all $j \in N \setminus \{1, \ldots, m\}$ for any two distinct alternatives $x$ and $y$, then the antisymmetry of the relations $R'_j$ implies that we cannot have $(x,y) \in R'_j$ for all $j \in N \setminus \{1, \ldots, m\}$ and, thus, the relation

$$\{(x,y) \in NC(R_1) \mid (y,x) \in R'_j \text{ for all } j \in N \setminus \{1, \ldots, m\} \text{ and } x \neq y\}$$

is antisymmetric as well. Finally, note that the latter relation only contains pairs that are non-comparable according to $R_1 \cup \Delta$.

If $R_1^0$ is not complete, define $\mathcal{T}_1 = \{\{x, y\} \mid (x, y) \in NC(R_1^0)\}$. Because $R_1^0$ is not complete, it follows that $\mathcal{T}_1 \neq \emptyset$. By the axiom of choice, there exists a function $\varphi_1 : \mathcal{T}_1 \to \cup_{T \in \mathcal{T}_1} T$ such that $\varphi_1(t) \in t$ for all $t \in \mathcal{T}_1$. Let

$$R_1' = R_1^0 \cup \{(\varphi_1(\{x, y\}), z) \mid \{x, y\} \in \mathcal{T}_1 \text{ and}$$
$$\{x, y\} \setminus \{\varphi_1(\{x, y\})\} = \{z\}\}.$$

Clearly, $R_1'$ is reflexive and complete. To see that $R_1'$ is antisymmetric, note that the two relations the union of which constitutes $R_1'$ are antisymmetric and that the second of these relations contains only pairs of distinct elements that are non-comparable according to $R_1^0$.

If $m = 1$, we have defined a profile $\langle R_i' \rangle_{i \in N}$ of reflexive, complete, and antisymmetric relations. If $m > 1$, we define the relations $R_2', \ldots, R_m'$ iteratively as follows. Let $i \in \{2, \ldots, m\}$, and suppose $R_j'$ has been defined for all $j \in \{1, \ldots, i-1\}$ (note that $R_j'$ is already defined for all $j \in N \setminus \{1, \ldots, m\}$). Define

$$R_i^0 = R_i \cup \Delta \cup \{(x, y) \in NC(R_i) \mid (y, x) \in R_j'$$
$$\text{for all } j \in N \setminus \{i, \ldots, m\} \text{ and } x \neq y\}.$$

If $R_i^0$ is complete, let $R_i' = R_i^0$. The proof that $R_i'$ is reflexive, complete, and antisymmetric is identical to that establishing these properties for $R_1'$.

If $R_i^0$ is not complete, define $\mathcal{T}_i = \{\{x, y\} \mid (x, y) \in NC(R_i^0)\}$. Because $R_i^0$ is not complete, it follows that $\mathcal{T}_i \neq \emptyset$. By the axiom of choice, there exists a function $\varphi_i : \mathcal{T}_i \to \cup_{T \in \mathcal{T}_i} T$ such that $\varphi_i(t) \in t$ for all $t \in \mathcal{T}_i$. Let

$$R_i' = R_i^0 \cup \{(\varphi_i(\{x, y\}), z) \mid \{x, y\} \in \mathcal{T}_i \text{ and}$$
$$\{x, y\} \setminus \{\varphi_i(\{x, y\})\} = \{z\}\}.$$

Again, that $R_i'$ is reflexive, complete, and antisymmetric follows using the same argument as that employed to establish these properties for $R_1'$.

We have now defined a profile $\langle R_i' \rangle_{i \in N}$ of reflexive, complete, and antisymmetric relations. To complete the proof that this profile is an END-rationalization of $D$, it has to be shown that (7.1) and (7.2) are satisfied.

To establish (7.1), suppose $x \in X$ and $(S, y) \in \Gamma$ are such that $x \in D(S, y)$. Because $\langle R_i \rangle_{i \in N}$ is an END-rationalization of $D$, it follows that $(x, y) \in R_i$ for all $i \in N$ and, because $R_i \subseteq R_i'$ by definition, we obtain $(x, y) \in R_i'$ for all $i \in N$.

Finally, we show that (7.2) is satisfied. By way of contradiction, suppose there exist $(S, y) \in \Gamma$, $x \in D(S, y)$, and $z \in S \setminus \{x\}$ such that $(z, x) \in R_i'$ for all $i \in N$. Because $z \neq x$, $(z, x) \notin \Delta$.

If $(z, x) \in R_i$ for all $i \in N$, we immediately obtain a contradiction to the assumption that $\langle R_i \rangle_{i \in N}$ is an END-rationalization of $D$.

If there exists $i \in N$ such that $(z, x) \in R_i^0 \setminus (R_i \cup \Delta)$, it follows that $(x, z) \in R_j'$ for all $j \in N \setminus \{i, \ldots, m\}$. Because $(z, x) \in R_j'$ for all $j \in N \setminus \{i, \ldots, m\}$ by assumption, this contradicts the antisymmetry of these relations.

The last remaining possibility is that there exists $i \in N$ such that $(z, x) \in R_i' \setminus R_i^0$. Let $k = \max\{i \in N \mid (z, x) \in R_i' \setminus R_i^0\}$. Because $(z, x) \notin R_k^0$, it follows that there exists $j \in N \setminus \{k, \ldots, m\}$ such that $(z, x) \notin R_j'$, contradicting our hypothesis that $(z, x) \in R_j'$ for all $j \in N$.

(e) We now show that the first implication in the theorem statement is strict. To do so, we employ an example used in Bossert and Sprumont (2003), which, in turn, is an adaptation of an example developed in Sprumont (2001) in a different context. Let $X = \{x^1, \ldots, x^{|N|+1}, y^1, \ldots, y^{|N|+1}\}$ and

$$\Gamma = \bigcup_{j=1}^{|N|+1} \left\{ (\{x^1, \ldots, x^{|N|+1}, y^j\}, y^j), (\{x^j, y^j\}, y^j) \right\}.$$

Define a selection function $D$ by $D(\{x^1, \ldots, x^{|N|+1}, y^j\}, y^j) = \{x^1, \ldots, x^{|N|+1}\} \setminus \{x^j\}$ and $D(\{x^j, y^j\}, y^j) = \{y^j\}$ for all $j \in \{1, \ldots, |N|+1\}$. $D$ is END-rationalized by the profile $\langle R_i \rangle_{i \in N}$ of transitive relations given by

$$R_i = \left\{ (x^j, y^k) \mid j, k \in \{1, \ldots, |N|+1\} \text{ and } j \neq k \right\}$$
$$\cup \left\{ (y^j, y^j) \mid j \in \{1, \ldots, |N|+1\} \right\}$$

for all $i \in N$ but there exists no END-rationalization of $D$ that is composed of orderings. By way of contradiction, suppose $\langle R_i' \rangle_{i \in N}$ is an END-rationalization of $D$ and the $R_i'$ are orderings on $X$. Because these relations are antisymmetric orderings, it follows that, for each $i \in N$, there exists a unique $x_i^* \in \{x^1, \ldots, x^{|N|+1}\}$ such that $(x^j, x_i^*) \in R_i'$ for all $j \in \{1, \ldots, |N|+1\}$; that is, $x_i^*$ is the worst element in $\{x^1, \ldots, x^{|N|+1}\}$ according to $R_i'$. Because the number of agents $|N|$ is less than the number of elements $|N|+1$ in $\{x^1, \ldots, x^{|N|+1}\}$, there exists at least one $k \in \{1, \ldots, |N|+1\}$ such that $x^k$ is not the worst element in $\{x^1, \ldots, x^{|N|+1}\}$ for any of the agents. Thus, we have $(x^k, x_i^*) \in R_i'$ for all $i \in N$. By (7.1), $(x_i^*, y^k) \in R_i'$ for all $i \in N$. Transitivity implies $(x^k, y^k) \in R_i'$ for all $i \in N$. Because $y^k \in D(\{x^k, y^k\}, y^k)$, this contradicts the efficiency requirement (7.2).

(f) To show that the second implication is strict, consider the following example. Let $X = \{x, y, z\}$, $\Gamma = \{(\{x, y\}, y), (\{x, z\}, z), (\{y, z\}, z)\}$, $D(\{x, y\}, y) = \{x\}$, $D(\{x, z\}, z) = \{z\}$, and $D(\{y, z\}, z) = \{y\}$. This selection function is END-rationalized by the profile $\langle R_i \rangle_{i \in N}$ of Suzumura-consistent relations defined by

$$R_i = \{(x, y), (y, z), (z, z)\}$$

for all $i \in N$. By way of contradiction, suppose $\langle R_i' \rangle_{i \in N}$ is an END-rationalization of $D$ with transitive relations $R_1', \ldots, R_n'$. By (7.1), we must have $(x, y) \in R_i'$ and $(y, z) \in R_i'$ for all $i \in N$ because $x \in D(\{x, y\}, y)$ and $y \in D(\{y, z\}, z)$. Transitivity implies $(x, z) \in R_i'$ for all $i \in N$, which contradicts (7.2) because $z \in D(\{x, z\}, z)$ and $x \in \{x, z\} \setminus \{z\}$.

(g) Finally, we show that the last implication is strict. Let $X = \{x, y, z\}$ and $\Gamma = \{(\{x, y\}, y), (\{x, z\}, x), (\{y, z\}, z)\}$, and define a selection function $D \colon \Gamma \to \mathcal{X}$ by $D(\{x, y\}, y) = \{x\}$, $D(\{x, z\}, x) = \{z\}$, and $D(\{y, z\}, z) = \{y\}$. This selection function is END-rationalized by the profile $\langle R_i \rangle_{i \in N}$ such that

$$R_i = \{(x, y), (y, z), (z, x)\}$$

for all $i \in N$. By way of contradiction, suppose $\langle R_i' \rangle_{i \in N}$ is an END-rationalization of $D$ that is composed of acyclical relations. By (7.1), it follows that we must have, for all $i \in N$, $(x, y) \in R_i'$ because $x \in D(\{x, y\}, y)$, $(y, z) \in R_i'$ because $y \in D(\{y, z\}, z)$, and $(z, x) \in R_i'$ because $z \in D(\{x, z\}, x)$. By antisymmetry, it follows that $(x, y) \in P(R_i')$, $(y, z) \in P(R_i')$, and $(z, x) \in P(R_i')$ for all $i \in N$, contradicting the acyclicity of the relations $R_i'$. ∎

## 7.4 Characterizing Efficient and Non-deteriorating Choice

Our next task is the characterization of the various notions of END-rationalizability distinguished in the above theorem. We provide characterizations of the three weakest versions. Interestingly, while the previously discussed single-agent versions of rationalizability are relatively straightforward to characterize if the rationalizing relation is required to be an ordering and difficulties typically arise if weaker coherence properties are imposed, the opposite is true for END-rationalizability: except for special cases in which the strongest notion of END-rationalizability coincides with the second-strongest version, the characterization of this property is an open problem. We provide a discussion of this issue following our characterization results.

A condition that is necessary and sufficient for E-Ø-T and its equivalent properties is obtained by a natural extension of selection congruence.

**Extended selection congruence**    For all $(S, z) \in \Gamma$ and for all $x, y \in X$,

$$[(x, y) \in tc(R_D) \text{ and } x \in S \text{ and } x \neq y] \Rightarrow y \notin D(S, z).$$

In addition to the restrictions imposed by selection congruence (which is the special case of this axiom obtained for $z = x$), extended selection congruence requires that if there is a chain of preferences involving distinct elements according to $R_D$, then the last element in the chain cannot be chosen if the first element of the chain is feasible; this applies even if the first element of the chain is not the reference alternative. Clearly, this additional requirement is imposed by the conjunction of transitivity, non-deterioration, and efficiency: transitivity and non-deterioration require that this chain of preferences be respected by all individual relations in the rationalizing profile and, in turn, efficiency rules out the choice of the last element in the chain in the presence of the first element. The following characterization follows from a result due to Bossert and Sprumont (2003).

**Theorem 7.8**  *Suppose $D: \Gamma \to \mathcal{X}$ is a selection function with an arbitrary non-empty domain $\Gamma \subseteq \{(S, y) \mid S \in \mathcal{X} \text{ and } y \in S\}$. $D$ satisfies any of* **E-R-T, E-Ø-T, E-R-Q, E-Ø-Q** *if and only if $D$ satisfies extended selection congruence.*

**Proof**  By Theorem 7.7, it is sufficient to establish the equivalence of **E-Ø-T** and extended selection congruence.

Suppose first that $\langle R_i \rangle_{i \in N}$ is an END-rationalization of $D$ such that the $R_i$ are transitive. By way of contradiction, suppose there exist $(S, z) \in \Gamma$ and $x, y \in X$ such that $(x, y) \in tc(R_D)$, $x \in S$, $x \neq y$, and $y \in D(S, z)$. Thus, there exist $K \in \mathbb{N}$ and $x^0, \ldots, x^K \in X$ such that $x = x^0$, $(x^{k-1}, x^k) \in R_D$ for all $k \in \{1, \ldots, K\}$, and $x^K = y$. By Theorem 7.5, $(x^{k-1}, x^k) \in R_i$ for all $i \in N$. Because the $R_i$ are transitive, it follows that $(x, y) \in R_i$ for all $i \in N$, which, together with the assumptions $x \in S, x \neq y$, and $y \in D(S, z)$, contradicts (7.2).

Now suppose $D$ satisfies extended selection congruence. Let

$$R_i = tc(R_D)$$

for all $i \in N$. Clearly, the $R_i$ are transitive. We complete the proof by establishing that $\langle R_i \rangle_{i \in N}$ is an END-rationalization of $D$.

The first step in accomplishing this task is to show that $R_i = tc(R_D)$ is antisymmetric. Suppose, by way of contradiction, that there exist two distinct alternatives $x, y \in X$ such that $(x, y) \in tc(R_D)$ and $(y, x) \in tc(R_D)$. Hence, there exist $K, L \in \mathbb{N}$, $x^0, \ldots, x^K \in X$, and $y^0, \ldots, y^L \in X$ such that $x = x^0$, $(x^{k-1}, x^k) \in R_D$ for all $k \in \{1, \ldots, K\}$, $x^K = y = y^0$, $(y^{\ell-1}, y^\ell) \in R_D$ for all $\ell \in \{1, \ldots, L\}$, and $y^L = x$. Without loss of generality, suppose $y^{L-1} \neq x$ (if not, replace $y^{L-1}$ with the highest-numbered $y^\ell$ that is different from $x$; this is always possible because $x \neq y$). By definition, we have $(x, y^{L-1}) \in tc(R_D)$. Because $(y^{L-1}, y^L) = (y^{L-1}, x) \in R_D$, there exists $S \in \mathcal{X}$ such that $(S, x) \in \Gamma$ and $y^{L-1} \in D(S, x)$. But this contradicts extended selection congruence because $x \in S$ and $x \neq y^{L-1}$.

Finally, we prove that (7.1) and (7.2) are satisfied. (7.1) follows immediately by definition of $R_D$ and the fact that $R_D \subseteq tc(R_D)$. Now suppose, by way of contradiction, that (7.2) is violated. Then there exist $(S, y) \in \Gamma$, $x \in D(S, y)$, and $z \in S \setminus \{x\}$ such that $(z, x) \in tc(R_D)$, contradicting extended selection congruence. ∎

Now we turn to a characterization of the axioms in the third box. The conjunction of two axioms turns out to be equivalent to these notions of END-rationalizability. The first property is selection congruence as defined earlier in the context of single-agent non-deteriorating choice. This property is needed in order to rule out strict preference cycles resulting from the non-deterioration requirement. However, a second property is needed in order to ensure that efficiency can be satisfied. This second axiom is the weakening of extended selection congruence that is obtained if the transitive closure of $R_D$ is replaced with $R_D$ itself.

**Weak extended selection congruence**   For all $(S, z) \in \Gamma$ and for all $x$, $y \in X$,

$$[(x, y) \in R_D \text{ and } x \in S \text{ and } x \neq y] \Rightarrow y \notin D(S, z).$$

Selection congruence and weak extended selection congruence are independent. To see that selection congruence does not imply weak extended selection congruence, suppose $X = \{x, y, z\}$, $\Gamma = \{(\{x, y\}, y), (X, y)\}$, $D(\{x, y\}, y) = \{x\}$, and $D(X, y) = \{y\}$. This selection function satisfies selection congruence, as is straightforward to verify. Because $x \in D(\{x, y\}, y)$, it follows that $(x, y) \in R_D$ and, together with $x \in X \setminus \{y\}$ and $y \in D(X, y)$, we obtain a violation of weak extended selection congruence. Now let $X = \{x, y, z\}$, $\Gamma = \{(\{x, y\}, y), (\{x, z\}, x), (\{y, z\}, z)\}$, $D(\{x, y\}, y) = \{x\}$, $D(\{x, z\}, x) = \{z\}$, and $D(\{y, z\}, z) = \{y\}$. This selection function satisfies weak extended selection congruence. Because $(x, z) \in tc(R_D)$, $x \neq z$, and $y \in D(\{x, z\}, x)$, selection congruence is violated.

We now obtain the following characterization result.

**Theorem 7.9**   *Suppose* $D\colon \Gamma \to \mathcal{X}$ *is a selection function with an arbitrary non-empty domain* $\Gamma \subseteq \{(S, y) \mid S \in \mathcal{X} \text{ and } y \in S\}$. *D satisfies any of* **E-R-S**, **E-Ø-S**, **E-R-A**, **E-Ø-A** *if and only if D satisfies selection congruence and weak extended selection congruence.*

**Proof**   By Theorem 7.7, it is sufficient to establish the equivalence of **E-Ø-A** and the conjunction of selection congruence and weak extended selection congruence.

Suppose first that $\langle R_i \rangle_{i \in N}$ is an END-rationalization of $D$ such that the $R_i$ are acyclical.

To show that selection congruence is satisfied, suppose, by way of contradiction, that there exist $S \in \mathcal{X}$ and $x, y \in X$ such that $(x, y) \in tc(R_D)$, $(S, x) \in \Gamma$, $x \neq y$, and $y \in D(S, x)$. Thus, there exist $K \in \mathbb{N}$ and $x^0, \ldots,$ $x^K \in X$ such that $x = x^0$, $(x^{k-1}, x^k) \in R_D$ for all $k \in \{1, \ldots, K\}$ and $x^K = y$. By Theorem 7.5, $(x^{k-1}, x^k) \in R_i$ for all $i \in N$. Because $x \neq y$, we can without loss of generality assume that the $x^k$ are pairwise distinct. Thus, the antisymmetry of the $R_i$ implies $(x^{k-1}, x^k) \in P(R_i)$ for all $i \in N$. Furthermore, $y \in D(S, x)$ implies $(y, x) \in R_D$ and, invoking Theorem 7.5 and antisymmetry again, it follows that $(y, x) = (x^K, x^0) \in P(R_i)$ for all $i \in N$. But this contradicts the acyclicity of the relations $R_i$.

To establish weak extended selection congruence, suppose, by way of contradiction, that there exist $(S, z) \in \Gamma$ and $x, y \in X$ such that $(x, y) \in R_D$, $x \in S$, $x \neq y$, and $y \in D(S, z)$. Theorem 7.5 implies $(x, y) \in R_i$ for all $i \in N$. Because $y \in D(S, z)$ and $x \in S \setminus \{y\}$, this contradicts (7.2).

We now prove the reverse implication. Suppose $D$ satisfies selection congruence and weak extended selection congruence. We complete the proof by establishing that $R_D$ is acyclical and that the profile such that $R_i = R_D$ for all $i \in N$ is an END-rationalization of $D$.

To establish the acyclicity of $R_D$, consider $K \in \mathbb{N}$ and $x^0, \ldots, x^K \in X$ such that $(x^{k-1}, x^k) \in P(R_D)$ for all $k \in \{1, \ldots, K\}$. This implies $(x^0, x^K) \in tc(R_D)$. By way of contradiction, suppose $(x^K, x^0) \in P(R_D)$. Clearly, this implies $x^0 \neq x^K$. Furthermore, by definition, there exists $S \in \mathcal{X}$ such that $(S, x^0) \in \Gamma$ and $x^K \in D(S, x^0)$. Because $x^0 \neq x^K$, this contradicts selection congruence.

Next, we show that $R_D$ is antisymmetric. Suppose, by way of contradiction, that there exist two distinct alternatives $x, y \in X$ such that $(x, y) \in R_D$ and $(y, x) \in R_D$. This implies that there exists $S \in \mathcal{X}$ such that $(S, x) \in \Gamma$ and $y \in D(S, x)$. Together with $(x, y) \in R_D$ and $x \neq y$, this contradicts selection congruence.

Finally, we prove that (7.1) and (7.2) are satisfied. (7.1) follows immediately by definition of $R_D$. Now suppose, by way of contradiction, that there exist $(S, y) \in \Gamma$, $x \in D(S, y)$, and $z \in S \setminus \{x\}$ such that $(z, x) \in R_D$. This is an immediate contradiction to weak extended selection congruence and, thus, (7.2) is satisfied as well. ∎

The weakest version of END-rationalizability is characterized by weak extended selection congruence alone. Because no coherence property is imposed in these notions of END-rationalizability, we do not require any restrictions concerning the transitive closure of $R_D$. Thus, we obtain the following result.

**Theorem 7.10** *Suppose $D: \Gamma \to \mathcal{X}$ is a selection function with an arbitrary non-empty domain $\Gamma \subseteq \{(S, y) \mid S \in \mathcal{X} \text{ and } y \in S\}$. $D$ satisfies any of E-RC-Ø, E-R-Ø, E-C-Ø, E-Ø-Ø if and only if $D$ satisfies weak extended selection congruence.*

**Proof** By Theorem 7.7, it is sufficient to establish the equivalence of E-Ø-Ø and weak extended selection congruence.

Suppose first that $\langle R_i \rangle_{i \in N}$ is an END-rationalization of $D$. To show that weak extended selection congruence is satisfied, suppose, by way of contradiction, that there exist $(S, z) \in \Gamma$ and $x, y \in X$ such that $(x, y) \in R_D$, $x \in S$, $x \neq y$, and $y \in D(S, z)$. Theorem 7.5 implies $(x, y) \in R_i$ for all $i \in N$. Because $y \in D(S, z)$ and $x \in S \setminus \{y\}$, this contradicts (7.2).

Now suppose $D$ satisfies weak extended selection congruence. We complete the proof by establishing that the profile given by $R_i = R_D$ for all $i \in N$ is an END-rationalization of $D$.

To show that $R_D$ is antisymmetric, suppose, by way of contradiction, that there exist two distinct alternatives $x, y \in X$ such that $(x, y) \in R_D$ and $(y, x) \in R_D$. This implies that there exists $S \in \mathcal{X}$ such that $(S, x) \in \Gamma$ and $y \in D(S, x)$. Together with $(x, y) \in R_D$ and $x \neq y$, this contradicts weak extended selection congruence.

That (7.1) is satisfied follows immediately by definition of $R_D$. Now suppose, by way of contradiction, that there exist $(S, y) \in \Gamma$, $x \in D(S, y)$, and $z \in S \setminus \{x\}$ such that $(z, x) \in R_D$. This is an immediate contradiction to weak extended selection congruence and, thus, (7.2) is satisfied as well.   ∎

As mentioned earlier, the requirement E-RC-T and its equivalents are more complex than the remaining notions of END-rationalizability. The reason why it is difficult to obtain a characterization result on arbitrary domains for an arbitrary set of agents and an arbitrary universal set of alternatives is that it is not possible to formulate a condition that applies to *all* combinations of the number $|N|$ of agents and the cardinality $|X|$ of the set of alternatives. The cases where a general characterization can be formulated are those in which E-RC-T is equivalent to E-Ø-T and, thus, Theorem 7.8 applies. For all other combinations of $|N|$ and $|X|$, it is not possible to obtain necessary and sufficient conditions that do not depend on $|N|$, and the formal problem that results is closely related to the problem of determining the dimension of a quasi-ordering; see, for instance, Dushnik and Miller (1941) and our discussion at the end of Chapter 4.

Clearly, extended selection congruence is necessary for E-RC-T because, as shown in Theorem 7.8, the axiom is necessary for E-Ø-T that obviously is implied by E-RC-T. The following theorem, due to Bossert and Sprumont (2003), identifies the combinations of $|N|$ and $|X|$ for which extended selection congruence is also sufficient for E-RC-T.

**Theorem 7.11**  *Suppose $N$ and $X$ are such that $|X| < 2(|N|+1)$ and $D: \Gamma \to \mathcal{X}$ is a selection function with an arbitrary non-empty domain $\Gamma \subseteq \{(S, y) \mid S \in \mathcal{X} \text{ and } y \in S\}$. D satisfies any of E-RC-T, E-C-T, E-RC-S, E-C-S, E-RC-Q, E-C-Q, E-RC-A, E-C-A if and only if D satisfies extended selection congruence.*

**Proof**  By Theorem 7.7, it is sufficient to restrict attention to E-RC-T.

That E-RC-T implies extended selection congruence follows immediately from Theorem 7.8 and the observation that E-RC-T implies E-Ø-T.

Now suppose $|X| < 2(|N|+1)$ and $D$ satisfies extended selection congruence. As in the proof of Theorem 7.8, it follows that $tc(R_D) \cup \Delta$ is reflexive and transitive, and the profile such that $R_i = tc(R_D) \cup \Delta$ for all $i \in N$ is an END-rationalization of $D$.

The following definitions are used in the remainder of the proof. The *dimension* of a quasi-ordering $R$ on $X$ is the smallest positive integer $r$ with the property that there exist $r$ orderings $R_1, \ldots, R_r$ whose intersection is $R$. For a real number $\alpha$, the largest integer less than or equal to $\alpha$ is denoted by $[\alpha]$.

Next, we show that the dimension of $tc(R_D) \cup \Delta$ does not exceed $|N|$. If $|X| \leq 3$, the dimension of $tc(R_D) \cup \Delta$ is less than or equal to two, which, in turn, is less than or equal to $|N|$. If $|X| \geq 4$, Hiraguchi's inequality (see Hiraguchi, 1955) implies that the dimension of $tc(R_D) \cup \Delta$ is less than or equal to $[|X|/2]$. Because $|X| < 2(|N|+1)$ implies $[|X|/2] \leq |N|$, it follows again that the dimension of $tc(R_D) \cup \Delta$ is less than or equal to $|N|$.

Thus, there exist antisymmetric orderings $R_1, \ldots, R_{|N|}$ (not necessarily distinct) on $X$ whose intersection is $tc(R_D) \cup \Delta$. It is now straightforward to verify that the profile $\langle R_i \rangle_{i \in N}$ is an END-rationalization of $D$.   ∎

As an immediate corollary of this result and Theorem 7.8, it follows that **E-$\emptyset$-T** and **E-RC-T** are equivalent whenever $|X| < 2(|N|+1)$.

The above theorem is tight in the sense that the assumption $|X| < 2(|N| + 1)$ cannot be weakened: whenever $|X| \geq 2(|N|+1)$, it is possible to find a selection function $D$ satisfying extended selection congruence and violating **E-RC-T**. This observation is also due to Bossert and Sprumont (2003) and it can be proven by employing the example of part (e) in the proof of Theorem 7.7.

We conclude this chapter with an analysis of the consequences of a specific domain assumption. In particular, we employ what Bossert and Sprumont (2003) refer to as *universal set domains*. These domains are such that, for every selection problem, the entire set $X$ is feasible and only the reference alternative is allowed to vary from one selection problem to another. Thus, $\Gamma$ is a universal set domain if and only if $S = X$ for all $(S, y) \in \Gamma$.

The assumption that $\Gamma$ is a universal set domain has remarkably strong consequences. Under this assumption, *all* notions of END-rationalizability coincide.

**Theorem 7.12**  *Suppose* $\beta, \beta' \in \{RC, R, C, \emptyset\}$, $\gamma, \gamma' \in \{T, Q, S, A, \emptyset\}$, *and* $D \colon \Gamma \to \mathcal{X}$ *is a selection function with a non-empty universal set domain* $\Gamma \subseteq \{(X, y) \mid y \in X\}$. *$D$ satisfies* E-$\beta$-$\gamma$ *if and only if $D$ satisfies* E-$\beta'$-$\gamma'$.

**Proof**  Suppose $D$ is a selection function defined on a universal set domain $\Gamma$. Given that all equivalences of Theorem 7.7 remain valid on universal set domains, it is sufficient to prove that E-∅-∅ implies E-C-T. Let $\langle R_i \rangle_{i \in N}$ be an END-rationalization of $D$. Define the relation $R^*$ on $X$ by

$$R^* = \big\{ (x, y) \mid x \in D(\Gamma) \text{ and } y \in X \setminus D(\Gamma) \big\}.$$

To see that $R^*$ is transitive, suppose $(x, y) \in R^*$ and $(y, z) \in R^*$. By definition of $R^*$, $(x, y) \in R^*$ implies $y \notin D(\Gamma)$ and $(y, z) \in R^*$ implies $y \in D(\Gamma)$, which is impossible. Therefore, transitivity is vacuously satisfied. Analogously, the definition of $R^*$ immediately implies that it is impossible to have both $(x, y) \in R^*$ and $(y, x) \in R^*$ and, therefore, $R^*$ is antisymmetric.

Next, we prove that $R_D \subseteq R^*$. Suppose $(x, y) \in R_D$. The definition of $R_D$ implies $(X, y) \in \Gamma$ and $x \in D(X, y)$. Thus, $x \in D(\Gamma)$. Because $\langle R_i \rangle_{i \in N}$ is an END-rationalization of $D$, it follows that $(x, y) \in R_i$ for all $i \in N$. If $y \in D(\Gamma)$, there exists $z \in X$ such that $(X, z) \in \Gamma$ and $y \in D(X, z)$. Because $x \in X \setminus \{y\}$, this contradicts the efficiency property (7.2) implied by E-∅-∅. Thus, $y \in X \setminus D(\Gamma)$ and, by definition, $(x, y) \in R^*$.

Let $R^{**}$ be an arbitrary complete, transitive, and antisymmetric relation defined on $X \setminus D(\Gamma)$, and let $R^0 = R^* \cup R^{**}$. Clearly, $R^0$ is a transitive and antisymmetric relation such that $R_D \subseteq R^* \subseteq R^0$. According to the relation $R^0$, the non-comparable pairs $(x, y)$ are all such that both $x$ and $y$ are in $D(\Gamma)$.

Now let $R_1^0$ be an arbitrary complete, transitive, and antisymmetric relation defined on $D(\Gamma)$, and let $R_2^0 = \cdots = R_{|N|}^0$ be the inverse of $R_1^0$; that is,

$$R_i^0 = \{ (x, y) \mid (y, x) \in R_1^0 \}$$

for all $i \in N \setminus \{1\}$. Define

$$R_i' = R^0 \cup R_i^0$$

for all $i \in N$. It is straightforward to verify that the $R_i'$ are complete, transitive, and antisymmetric. To conclude the proof that $\langle R_i' \rangle_{i \in N}$ is an END-rationalization of $D$, note first that (7.1) follows immediately from the observation that $R_D \subseteq R_i'$ for all $i \in N$. To establish (7.2), suppose $x \in D(\Gamma)$. This implies $(x, y) \in R^*$ and thus $(x, y) \in R_i'$ for all $y \in X \setminus D(\Gamma)$ and for all $i \in N$ and, by antisymmetry, no $y \in X \setminus D(\Gamma)$ can be such that $(y, x) \in R_i'$ for all $i \in N$. Furthermore, we have

$$(x, y) \in R_1' \text{ or } (x, y) \in R_2'$$

for all $y \in D(\Gamma) \setminus \{x\}$ by definition and, thus, $(y, x) \in R_i'$ for all $i \in N$ is not possible for any $y \in D(\Gamma) \setminus \{x\}$ either. ∎

Our final result in this chapter provides a characterization of END-rationalizability if $\Gamma$ is a universal set domain. In this case, the relevant congruence axiom is defined as follows.

**Universal selection congruence**   For all $(X, z) \in \Gamma$ and for all $x, y \in X$,

$$[(x, y) \in R_D \text{ and } x \neq y] \Rightarrow y \notin D(X, z).$$

This axiom characterizes the single version of END-rationalizability that exists in the presence of a universal set domain.

**Theorem 7.13**  *Suppose $D: \Gamma \to \mathcal{X}$ is a selection function with a non-empty universal set domain $\Gamma \subseteq \{(X, y) \mid y \in X\}$. $D$ satisfies E-$\beta$-$\gamma$ for any $\beta \in \{RC, R, C, \emptyset\}$ and any $\gamma \in \{T, Q, S, A, \emptyset\}$ if and only if $D$ satisfies universal selection congruence.*

**Proof**  By Theorem 7.12, it is sufficient to establish the equivalence of E-$\emptyset$-$\emptyset$ and universal selection congruence.

Suppose first that $\langle R_i \rangle_{i \in N}$ is an END-rationalization of $D$ and, by way of contradiction, suppose there exist $(X, z) \in \Gamma$ and $x, y \in X$ such that $(x, y) \in R_D$, $x \neq y$, and $y \in D(X, z)$. By Theorem 7.5, $(x, y) \in R_i$ and, by antisymmetry, $(x, y) \in P(R_i)$ for all $i \in N$. Because $y \in D(X, z)$ and $x \in X \setminus \{y\}$, this contradicts efficiency.

Now suppose $D$ satisfies universal selection congruence. To complete the proof, we show that the profile such that $R_i = R_D$ for all $i \in N$ is an END-rationalization of $D$.

First, we establish the antisymmetry of $R_D$. Suppose $(x, y) \in R_D$ for two distinct alternatives $x, y \in X$. If $(X, x) \notin \Gamma$, it is immediate that $(y, x) \notin R_D$. If $(X, x) \in \Gamma$, universal selection congruence implies $y \notin D(X, x)$.

That (7.1) is satisfied follows immediately from the definition of $R_D$. Finally, suppose (7.2) is violated. Then there exist $(X, y) \in \Gamma, x \in D(X, y)$, and $z \in X \setminus \{x\}$ such that $(z, x) \in R_D$. This contradicts universal selection congruence and, thus, (7.2) is satisfied.  ∎

# — 8 —

# External Norms and Rational Choice

## 8.1  Internal Coherence of Choice

As mentioned in Section 1.8, Sen (1993) argued against the convention of imposing internal requirements of coherence (such as those we discussed in earlier chapters) on observable choices. He then went on to investigate the implications of eschewing these internal choice coherence properties altogether and, instead, including considerations that may be considered external to choice as such. Recall that Sen (1993, p. 500) uses the following example to illustrate one of his points. Suppose a choice function $C$ whose domain includes the sets $\{x, y\}$ and $\{x, y, z\}$ is such that

$$C(\{x, y\}) = \{x\} \text{ and } C(\{x, y, z\}) = \{y\}.$$

As Sen rightly points out, this pair of choices violates most of the standard choice coherence conditions including the weak and the strong axioms of revealed preference, Arrow's choice axiom, and Richter's coherence properties. It is arguable (and, indeed, Sen, 1993, p. 501, argues) that this seeming inconsistency can be easily resolved if only we know more about the person's choice situation. For instance, if we use the interpretation spelled out in Chapter 1 where the alternatives in question are choices of a person from a fruit basket at a dinner table, rules of conduct the person desires to observe may lead her or him to choose in that fashion, in spite of the violation of internal coherence properties alluded to above.

On the face of it, Sen's argument to this effect may seem to go squarely against the theory of rationalizability à la Arrow (1959), Richter (1966, 1971), Hansson (1968), Sen (1971), Suzumura (1976a), and many others, where the weak axiom of revealed preference is a necessary condition for rationalizability. In this chapter, we present a concept of *norm-conditional rationalizability* and build a bridge between rationalizability theory and Sen's criticism. In essence, what emerges from our theory is the peaceful coexistence of a norm-conditional rationalizability theory and Sen's elaborate criticism against the internal coherence of choice. The purpose of this chapter is to provide an amended version of the traditional rational choice model that can accommodate Sen's criticism. This chapter is based on Bossert and Suzumura (2009b).

## 8.2    Norm-Conditional Choice

We introduce a model of choice where external norms are taken into consideration by specifying all pairs consisting of a feasible set and an element of this set with the interpretation that this element is prohibited from being chosen from this set by the relevant system of external norms. Norm-conditional rationalizability then requires the existence of a preference relation such that, for each feasible set in the domain of the choice function, the chosen elements are at least as good as all elements in the set *except* for those that are prohibited by the external norm. This approach is very general because no restrictions are imposed on how the system of external norms comes about—any specification of a set of pairs as described above is possible. The traditional model of rational choice is included as a special case—the case that obtains if the set of prohibited pairs is empty.

External norms can be expressed by identifying pairs of feasible sets and alternatives that are not to be chosen from these feasible sets. For example, suppose there is a feasible set $S = \{x, y\}$, where $x$ stands for selecting nothing and $y$ stands for selecting (a single) apple. Now consider the feasible set $T = \{x, y, z\}$ where there are two (identical) apples $y$ and $z$ available. The external norm not to take the last apple can easily and intuitively be expressed by requiring that the choice of $y$ from $S$ is excluded, whereas the choice of $y$ (or $z$) from $T$ is perfectly acceptable. In general, norms of that nature can be expressed by identifying all pairs $(S, y)$, where $y \in S$, such that $y$ is not supposed to be chosen from the feasible set $S$. To that end, we use a set $\mathcal{N}$, to be interpreted as the set of all pairs $(S, y)$ of a feasible set $S$ and an element $y$ of $S$ such that the choice of $y$ from $S$ is prevented by the external norm under consideration.

Given an external norm defined by $\mathcal{N}$, a *norm-conditional choice function* is a choice function $C$ such that $C(S) \subseteq S \setminus \{y \in S \mid (S, y) \in \mathcal{N}\}$ for all $S \in \Sigma$. To ensure that the standard non-emptiness requirement on $C$ does not conflict with the restrictions imposed by the norm $\mathcal{N}$, we consider only norms $\mathcal{N}$ such that, for all $S \in \Sigma$, there exists $x \in S$ satisfying $(S, x) \notin \mathcal{N}$. Thus, whenever we mention a norm $\mathcal{N}$ in this chapter, it is understood that it respects this restriction.

An alternative way of modeling external norms employs a *norm-embodying* relation, where a pair $(x, S)$ with $x \in S \subseteq X$ stands for the act of choosing $x$ from a choice environment $S$ given an underlying norm. The statement that the pair $((x, S), (y, T))$ is in this relation can then be interpreted to mean that choosing $x$ from the admissible choice environment $S$ is at least as good as choosing $y$ from $T$ in terms of conformity with the requisite external norm. The basic difference between such an approach and ours is that the former works with a *comparative* notion of norm satisfaction, whereas our model treats external norms as *constraints* on acceptable choice behavior. We do not view one setup as being superior to the other but we believe that our formulation in terms of constraints is more in the spirit of Sen's (1993) example because it allows us to rule out choice behavior that is not permitted in the sense of violating the requisite norm constraints. With an alternative model that is based on the relation "is at least as norm-conforming as," it seems to us that it is more difficult to capture the situations Sen had in mind.

Returning to Sen's (1993) example involving the norm "do not choose the last available apple," we can, for instance, define the universal set $X = \{x, y, z\}$, the domain $\Sigma = \{\{x, y\}, X\} \subseteq \mathcal{X}$, and the external norm described by the set $\mathcal{N} = \{((x, y), y)\}$. Thus, the external norm requires that $y \notin C(\{x, y\})$ but no restrictions are imposed on the choice $C(X)$ from the set $X$—that is, this external norm represents the requirement that the last available apple should not be chosen.

## 8.3   Norm-Conditional Rationalizability

In contrast with the classical model of rational choice, an element $x$ that is chosen by a choice function $C$ from a feasible set $S \in \Sigma$ need not be considered at least as good as *all* elements of $S$ by a rationalizing relation, but merely at least as good as all elements $y \in S$ such that $(S, y) \notin \mathcal{N}$. That is, if the choice of $y$ from $S$ is already prohibited by the norm, there is no need to demand that $x$ dominate such an element $y$ according to the rationalization. Needless to say, the chosen element $x$ itself must be admissible in the presence of the prevailing system of external norms.

To make this concept of norm-conditional rationalizability precise, let a system of external norms $\mathcal{N}$ and a feasible set $S \in \Sigma$ be given. An $\mathcal{N}$-*admissible set for* $S$, denoted by $A^{\mathcal{N}}(S) \subseteq S$, is defined by letting

$$A^{\mathcal{N}}(S) = \{x \in S \mid (S, x) \notin \mathcal{N}\}.$$

Note that, by assumption, $A^{\mathcal{N}}(S) \neq \emptyset$ for all possible $\mathcal{N}$ and for all $S \in \Sigma$.

We say that a choice function $C$ on $\Sigma$ is $\mathcal{N}$-*rationalizable* if and only if there exists a binary relation $R^{\mathcal{N}} \subseteq X \times X$ such that, for all $S \in \Sigma$,

$$C(S) = G(A^{\mathcal{N}}(S), R^{\mathcal{N}}).$$

In this case, we say that $R^{\mathcal{N}}$ $\mathcal{N}$-*rationalizes* $C$, or $R^{\mathcal{N}}$ is an $\mathcal{N}$-*rationalization* of $C$.

To facilitate our analysis of $\mathcal{N}$-rationalizability, a generalization of the notion of the direct revealed preference relation of a choice function is of use. We define

$$R_C^{\mathcal{N}} = \{(x, y) \mid \exists S \in \Sigma \text{ such that } [x \in C(S) \text{ and } y \in A^{\mathcal{N}}(S)]\}.$$

We refer to $R_C^{\mathcal{N}}$ as the *norm-conditional direct revealed preference relation* corresponding to $C$ and $\mathcal{N}$.

We consider three basic versions of norm-conditional rationalizability. The first is $\mathcal{N}$-rationalizability by itself, where an $\mathcal{N}$-rationalization $R^{\mathcal{N}}$ does not have to possess any additional property. This notion of rationalizability is equivalent to $\mathcal{N}$-rationalizability by a reflexive relation. The second is $\mathcal{N}$-rationalizability by a Suzumura-consistent relation (again, reflexivity can be added and an equivalent condition is obtained). Finally, we consider $\mathcal{N}$-rationalizability by a transitive relation, which, as in the classical case, turns out to be equivalent to $\mathcal{N}$-rationalizability by an ordering. Other notions of norm-conditional rationalizability could be examined, which would lead to results parallel to those obtained in the classical framework. For ease of exposition, we do not reproduce them here but note that they can be obtained in the same fashion as the ones we do report.

## 8.4   Characterization Results

The following three preliminary results are straightforward adaptations of their counterparts in the classical framework. They state that the norm-conditional direct revealed preference relation $R_C^{\mathcal{N}}$ must be respected by any $\mathcal{N}$-rationalization $R^{\mathcal{N}}$, that any Suzumura-consistent $\mathcal{N}$-rationalization

$R^{\mathcal{N}}$ must respect not only the norm-conditional direct revealed preference relation $R_C^{\mathcal{N}}$ but also its Suzumura-consistent closure $sc(R_C^{\mathcal{N}})$ and, finally, that any transitive $\mathcal{N}$-rationalization $R^{\mathcal{N}}$ must respect the transitive closure $tc(R_C^{\mathcal{N}})$ of $R_C^{\mathcal{N}}$.

**Theorem 8.1**   *Let $\mathcal{N}$ be a system of external norms and let $C$ be a choice function. If $R^{\mathcal{N}}$ is an $\mathcal{N}$-rationalization of $C$, then $R_C^{\mathcal{N}} \subseteq R^{\mathcal{N}}$.*

**Proof**   Suppose that $R^{\mathcal{N}}$ is an $\mathcal{N}$-rationalization of $C$ and $x, y \in X$ are such that $(x, y) \in R_C^{\mathcal{N}}$. By definition of $R_C^{\mathcal{N}}$, there exists $S \in \Sigma$ such that $x \in C(S)$ and $y \in A^{\mathcal{N}}(S)$. Because $R^{\mathcal{N}}$ is an $\mathcal{N}$-rationalization of $C$, we obtain $(x, y) \in R^{\mathcal{N}}$. Thus, $R_C^{\mathcal{N}} \subseteq R^{\mathcal{N}}$ must be true.   ∎

**Theorem 8.2**   *Let $\mathcal{N}$ be a system of external norms and let $C$ be a choice function. If $R^{\mathcal{N}}$ is a Suzumura-consistent $\mathcal{N}$-rationalization of $C$, then $sc(R_C^{\mathcal{N}}) \subseteq R^{\mathcal{N}}$.*

**Proof**   Suppose that $R^{\mathcal{N}}$ is a Suzumura-consistent $\mathcal{N}$-rationalization of $C$ and $x, y \in X$ are such that $(x, y) \in sc(R_C^{\mathcal{N}})$. By definition of the Suzumura-consistent closure of a binary relation,

$$(x, y) \in R_C^{\mathcal{N}} \tag{8.1}$$

or

$$(x, y) \in tc(R_C^{\mathcal{N}}) \text{ and } (y, x) \in R_C^{\mathcal{N}} \tag{8.2}$$

must hold. If (8.1) is true, $(x, y) \in R^{\mathcal{N}}$ follows from Theorem 8.1. If (8.2) applies, there exist $K \in \mathbb{N}$ and $x^0, \ldots, x^K \in X$ such that $x = x^0$, $(x^{k-1}, x^k) \in R_C^{\mathcal{N}}$ for all $k \in \{1, \ldots, K\}$, and $x^K = y$. By Theorem 8.1, $(x^{k-1}, x^k) \in R^{\mathcal{N}}$ for all $k \in \{1, \ldots, K\}$ and, thus, $(x, y) \in tc(R^{\mathcal{N}})$. Furthermore, $(y, x) \in R_C^{\mathcal{N}}$ implies $(y, x) \in R^{\mathcal{N}}$ by Theorem 8.1 again. If $(x, y) \notin R^{\mathcal{N}}$, it follows that $(y, x) \in P(R^{\mathcal{N}})$ in view of $(y, x) \in R^{\mathcal{N}}$. Because $(x, y) \in tc(R^{\mathcal{N}})$, this contradicts the Suzumura consistency of $R^{\mathcal{N}}$. Therefore, $(x, y) \in R^{\mathcal{N}}$. Thus, $sc(R_C^{\mathcal{N}}) \subseteq R^{\mathcal{N}}$ must be true.   ∎

**Theorem 8.3**   *Let $\mathcal{N}$ be a system of external norms and let $C$ be a choice function. If $R^{\mathcal{N}}$ is a transitive $\mathcal{N}$-rationalization of $C$, then $tc(R_C^{\mathcal{N}}) \subseteq R^{\mathcal{N}}$.*

**Proof**   Suppose that $R^{\mathcal{N}}$ is a transitive $\mathcal{N}$-rationalization of $C$ and $x, y \in X$ are such that $(x, y) \in tc(R_C^{\mathcal{N}})$. By definition of the transitive closure of a binary relation, there exist $K \in \mathbb{N}$ and $x^0, \ldots, x^K \in X$ such that $x = x^0$, $(x^{k-1}, x^k) \in R_C^{\mathcal{N}}$ for all $k \in \{1, \ldots, K\}$, and $x^K = y$. By Theorem 8.1, we obtain $x = x^0$, $(x^{k-1}, x^k) \in R^{\mathcal{N}}$ for all $k \in \{1, \ldots, K\}$, and $x^K = y$. Repeated application of the transitivity of $R^{\mathcal{N}}$ implies $(x, y) \in R^{\mathcal{N}}$. Thus $tc(R_C^{\mathcal{N}}) \subseteq R^{\mathcal{N}}$ must hold.   ∎

We are now ready to identify a necessary and sufficient condition for each one of these notions of $\mathcal{N}$-rationalizability of a choice function. To obtain a necessary and sufficient condition for simple $\mathcal{N}$-rationalizability, we follow Richter (1971) by generalizing the relevant axiom in his approach in order to accommodate an externally imposed system of norms $\mathcal{N}$. This leads us to the following axiom.

**$\mathcal{N}$-conditional direct revelation coherence**   For all $S \in \Sigma$ and for all $x \in A^{\mathcal{N}}(S)$,

$$(x, y) \in R_C^{\mathcal{N}} \text{ for all } y \in A^{\mathcal{N}}(S) \Rightarrow x \in C(S).$$

The next result establishes that this property is indeed necessary and sufficient for $\mathcal{N}$-rationalizability.

**Theorem 8.4**   *Let $\mathcal{N}$ be a system of external norms and let $C$ be a choice function. $C$ is $\mathcal{N}$-rationalizable if and only if $C$ satisfies $\mathcal{N}$-conditional direct revelation coherence.*

**Proof**   Suppose first that $R^{\mathcal{N}}$ is an $\mathcal{N}$-rationalization of $C$. Let $S \in \Sigma$ and $x \in A^{\mathcal{N}}(S)$ be such that $(x, y) \in R_C^{\mathcal{N}}$ for all $y \in A^{\mathcal{N}}(S)$. By Theorem 8.1, $(x, y) \in R^{\mathcal{N}}$ for all $y \in A^{\mathcal{N}}(S)$, which implies $x \in C(S)$ because $R^{\mathcal{N}}$ is an $\mathcal{N}$-rationalization of $C$.

Now suppose $C$ satisfies $\mathcal{N}$-conditional direct revelation coherence. We complete the proof by showing that $R^{\mathcal{N}} = R_C^{\mathcal{N}}$ is an $\mathcal{N}$-rationalization of $C$. Let $S \in \Sigma$ and $x \in A^{\mathcal{N}}(S)$.

Suppose first that $x \in C(S)$. By definition, it follows immediately that $(x, y) \in R_C^{\mathcal{N}} = R^{\mathcal{N}}$ for all $y \in A^{\mathcal{N}}(S)$.

Conversely, suppose that $(x, y) \in R_C^{\mathcal{N}} = R^{\mathcal{N}}$ for all $y \in A^{\mathcal{N}}(S)$. Now $\mathcal{N}$-conditional direct revelation coherence immediately implies $x \in C(S)$. Thus, $C$ is $\mathcal{N}$-rationalizable by $R^{\mathcal{N}} = R_C^{\mathcal{N}}$.   ∎

As is the case for the traditional model of rational choice on general domains, it is straightforward to verify that $\mathcal{N}$-rationalizability by a reflexive relation is equivalent to $\mathcal{N}$-rationalizability without any further properties of an $\mathcal{N}$-rationalization; this can be verified analogously to Richter (1971). However, adding completeness as a requirement leads to a stronger notion of $\mathcal{N}$-rationalizability; see again Richer (1971).

Next, we examine $\mathcal{N}$-rationalizability by a Suzumura-consistent relation, which is equivalent to $\mathcal{N}$-rationalizability by a reflexive and Suzumura-consistent relation. As in the traditional case, adding completeness, how-ever, leads to a stronger property, namely, one that is equivalent to $\mathcal{N}$-rationalizability by an ordering; see Bossert, Sprumont, and Suzumura (2005a) for an analogous observation in the traditional model.

The requisite necessary and sufficient condition is obtained from $\mathcal{N}$-conditional direct revelation coherence by replacing $R_C^{\mathcal{N}}$ with its Suzumura-consistent closure $sc(R_C^{\mathcal{N}})$.

**$\mathcal{N}$-conditional Suzumura-consistent closure coherence**    For all $S \in \Sigma$ and for all $x \in A^{\mathcal{N}}(S)$,

$$(x, y) \in sc(R_C^{\mathcal{N}}) \text{ for all } y \in A^{\mathcal{N}}(S) \Rightarrow x \in C(S).$$

We obtain

**Theorem 8.5**  *Let $\mathcal{N}$ be a system of external norms and let $C$ be a choice function. $C$ is $\mathcal{N}$-rationalizable by a Suzumura-consistent relation if and only if $C$ satisfies $\mathcal{N}$-conditional Suzumura-consistent closure coherence.*

**Proof**  The proof is analogous to that of Theorem 8.4. All that needs to be done is replace $R_C^{\mathcal{N}}$ with $sc(R_C^{\mathcal{N}})$ and invoke Theorem 8.2 instead of Theorem 8.1.  ∎

The final result of this chapter establishes a necessary and sufficient con-dition for $\mathcal{N}$-rationalizability by a transitive relation that is equivalent to $\mathcal{N}$-rationalizability by an ordering. We leave it to the reader to verify that the proof strategy employed by Richter (1966, 1971) in the traditio-nal case generalizes in a straightforward manner to the norm-dependent model when establishing that transitive $\mathcal{N}$-rationalizability is equivalent to $\mathcal{N}$-rationalizability by an ordering.

The requisite necessary and sufficient condition is obtained from $\mathcal{N}$-conditional direct revelation coherence by replacing $R_C^{\mathcal{N}}$ with its transitive closure $tc(R_C^{\mathcal{N}})$.

$\mathcal{N}$-conditional transitive closure coherence  For all $S \in \Sigma$ and for all $x \in A^{\mathcal{N}}(S)$,

$$(x, y) \in tc(R_C^{\mathcal{N}}) \text{ for all } y \in A^{\mathcal{N}}(S) \Rightarrow x \in C(S).$$

We obtain

**Theorem 8.6**  *Let $\mathcal{N}$ be a system of external norms and let $C$ be a choice function. $C$ is $\mathcal{N}$-rationalizable by a transitive relation if and only if $C$ satisfies $\mathcal{N}$-conditional transitive closure coherence.*

**Proof**  Again, the proof is analogous to that of Theorem 8.4. All that needs to be done is replace $R_C^{\mathcal{N}}$ with $tc(R_C^{\mathcal{N}})$ and invoke Theorem 8.3 instead of Theorem 8.1.  ∎

We conclude this chapter with a remark on a related concept. Sen (1997) provided an important step toward a norm-conditional theory of rationalizability through the concept of *self-imposed choice constraints*, excluding some alternatives from permissible choices. According to Sen's (1997, p. 769) scenario, "the person may first restrict the choice options ... by taking a 'permissible' subset $K(S)$, reflecting *self-imposed* constraints, and then seek the maximal elements $M(K(S), R)$ in $K(S)$." Despite an apparent family resemblance between Sen's concept of self-imposed choice constraints and our concept of norm-conditionality, Sen did not go as far as to bridge the idea of norm-induced constraints and the theory of rationalizability as we did in this chapter.

# — V —

# Topics in Social Choice Theory

# — 9 —

# Collective Choice Rules

## 9.1 Weakening Social Coherence Properties

Arrow's (1951, 1963) celebrated theorem regarding the impossibility of defining a collective choice rule possessing some seemingly innocuous properties is the most fundamental result in the theory of collective decision making. There have been numerous attempts to circumvent this impossibility, such as weakening some of Arrow's original properties or departing from the stringent informational assumption that only ordinally measurable and interpersonally non-comparable information on individual well-being is available. The route of escape from the negative conclusion of Arrow's theorem that we pursue in this chapter consists of relaxing the requirement that the social ranking be an ordering for all preference profiles under consideration. In particular, we allow for incompleteness and intransitivities in the social ranking but require that social rankings be Suzumura consistent. Large parts of this chapter are based on Bossert and Suzumura (2008a).

Ours is not the first approach based on weakenings of the requirements imposed on social rankings. In the same spirit, Sen (1969; 1970, theorem 5*3) characterized the *Pareto extension rule* under the assumption that social preferences are quasi-transitive but not necessarily transitive while retaining the completeness assumption. Weymark (1984, theorem 3) allowed social preferences to be incomplete but imposed full transitivity and, as a result, obtained a characterization of the *Pareto rule*.

In spite of its intuitive appeal, Suzumura consistency has received little attention in the literature on Arrovian social choice so far. It turns out that, in many circumstances, Suzumura consistency permits a larger class of possible collective choice rules as compared to those that are available if completeness is dropped as a requirement on a social relation but the full force of transitivity is retained. See also Cato and Hirata (2010) for further observations in this context.

A *collective choice rule* is a mapping that assigns, to each profile of individual preference orderings in its domain, a social preference relation. The axioms we impose on collective choice rules in this chapter are *unrestricted domain, strong Pareto, anonymity*, and *neutrality*. If there are at least as many alternatives as there are agents, an alternative characterization of the Pareto rule is obtained. The difference between our characterization and Weymark's (1984) is that we weaken the transitivity requirement imposed on the social relation to Suzumura consistency and strengthen Arrow's *independence of irrelevant alternatives* (not to be confused with Nash's 1950 property carrying the same label) to neutrality. If there are fewer alternatives than agents, additional rules satisfy the above axioms. We characterize all of them and obtain the above-mentioned new axiomatization of the Pareto rule as a special case. Especially in applications where there are many voters and relatively few candidates (this is the case for political elections, to name a prominent and important example), our result shows that it is possible to go considerably beyond the limitations of unanimity imposed by the Pareto rule. In particular, some *quota rules* are possible, in addition to others. This is achieved at relatively little cost because Suzumura consistency still ensures the existence of an ordering compatible with the social relation.

Our approach to the analysis of collective choice rules develops some new proof techniques; some of the tools previously developed cannot be applied in our setting. For example, Sen's (1979, 1995) *field expansion lemma,* which allows one to extend "local" observations to arbitrary collections of alternatives crucially relies on transitivity (or quasi-transitivity), and Suzumura consistency is not sufficient to obtain these types of results.

Throughout this and the following chapter, we assume that the set of alternatives $X$ contains at least three elements. The population is the set $N$ that is assumed to contain at least two elements. Furthermore, in this chapter, we assume $N$ to be finite and, without loss of generality, we write it as $N = \{1, \ldots, |N|\}$ in this case. The set of all orderings on $X$ is denoted by $\mathcal{R}$ and the set of all binary relations on $X$ is $\mathcal{B}$. A *profile* is a list $\mathbf{R} = \langle R_i \rangle_{i \in N}$, where $R_i \in \mathcal{R}$ for all $i \in N$. The set of all possible profiles is $\mathcal{R}^N$.

A *collective choice rule* is a mapping $F \colon \mathcal{D} \to \mathcal{B}$ where $\mathcal{D} \subseteq \mathcal{R}^N$ is the *domain* of this function, assumed to be non-empty. A *Suzumura-consistent collective choice rule* is a collective choice rule such that all social preferences are Suzumura consistent, a *reflexive, complete, and quasi-transitive collective choice rule* is a collective choice rule $F$ such that all social preferences are reflexive, complete, and quasi-transitive, and so on. A *social welfare function* is a collective choice rule such that all social preferences are orderings. Note that, because $\mathcal{D} \subseteq \mathcal{R}^N$, we retain the assumption that all admissible profiles are composed of individual preferences that are orderings. On the other hand, we consider environments in which social preferences may be incomplete and we permit some violations of transitivity. For each profile $\mathbf{R} \in \mathcal{D}, R = F(\mathbf{R})$ is the social preference corresponding to $\mathbf{R}$.

An example of a reflexive and transitive (and, thus, Suzumura consistent and quasi-transitive) collective choice rule is the *Pareto rule* $F^p \colon \mathcal{R}^N \to \mathcal{B}$ defined by $R^p = F^p(\mathbf{R})$, where

$$R^p = \{(x, y) \mid (x, y) \in R_i \text{ for all } i \in N\}$$

for all $\mathbf{R} \in \mathcal{R}^N$. The *Pareto extension rule* $F^e \colon \mathcal{R}^N \to \mathcal{B}$ is defined by $R^e = F^e(\mathbf{R})$, where

$$R^e = \{(x, y) \in X \times X \mid (y, x) \notin P(R^p)\}$$

for all $\mathbf{R} \in \mathcal{R}^N$. $R^e = F^e(\mathbf{R})$ is reflexive, complete, and quasi-transitive for all $\mathbf{R} \in \mathcal{R}^N$. However, $R^e$ is not necessarily Suzumura consistent (and, thus, not necessarily transitive).

We use $B(x, y; \mathbf{R})$ to denote the set of individuals $i \in N$ such that $x \in X$ is better for $i$ than $y \in X$ in the profile $\mathbf{R} \in \mathcal{R}^N$; that is, for all $x, y \in X$ and for all $\mathbf{R} \in \mathcal{R}^N$,

$$B(x, y; \mathbf{R}) = \{i \in N \mid (x, y) \in P(R_i)\}.$$

The following preliminary result, which is of use in the proof of our characterization theorem, establishes that the cardinalities of these sets satisfy a *triangle inequality*.

**Theorem 9.1**   *For all $x, y, z \in X$ and for all $\mathbf{R} \in \mathcal{R}^N$,*

$$|B(x, z; \mathbf{R})| \leq |B(x, y; \mathbf{R})| + |B(y, z; \mathbf{R})|.$$

**Proof**   Let $x, y, z \in X$ and $\mathbf{R} \in \mathcal{R}^N$. First, we prove that

$$B(x, z; \mathbf{R}) \subseteq B(x, y; \mathbf{R}) \cup B(y, z; \mathbf{R}). \tag{9.1}$$

Suppose $i \notin B(x, y; \mathbf{R}) \cup B(y, z; \mathbf{R})$. Because individual preferences are complete, this implies $(y, x) \in R_i$ and $(z, y) \in R_i$. By the transitivity of the individual preferences, $(z, x) \in R_i$ and, thus, $i \notin B(x, z; \mathbf{R})$, which proves (9.1).

Clearly, (9.1) implies

$$|B(x, z; \mathbf{R})| \le |B(x, y; \mathbf{R}) \cup B(y, z; \mathbf{R})|.$$

Furthermore, we obviously must have

$$|B(x, y; \mathbf{R}) \cup B(y, z; \mathbf{R})| \le |B(x, y; \mathbf{R})| + |B(y, z; \mathbf{R})|.$$

Combining the last two inequalities yields the desired result.  ∎

The following axioms are standard in the literature on Arrovian social choice theory.

**Unrestricted domain**  $\mathcal{D} = \mathcal{R}^N$.

**Weak Pareto**  For all $x, y \in X$ and for all $\mathbf{R} \in \mathcal{D}$,

$$(x, y) \in P(R_i) \text{ for all } i \in N \Rightarrow (x, y) \in P(R).$$

**Strong Pareto**  For all $x, y \in X$ and for all $\mathbf{R} \in \mathcal{D}$,

   (i) $(x, y) \in R_i$ for all $i \in N \Rightarrow (x, y) \in R$.
   (ii) $[(x, y) \in R_i$ for all $i \in N$ and $\exists j \in N$ such that $(x, y) \in P(R_j)] \Rightarrow$
        $(x, y) \in P(R)$.

**Non-dictatorship**  There exists no $i \in N$ such that, for all $x, y \in X$ and for all $\mathbf{R} \in \mathcal{D}$,

$$(x, y) \in P(R_i) \Rightarrow (x, y) \in P(R).$$

**Anonymity**  For all bijections $\rho: N \to N$ and for all $\mathbf{R}, \mathbf{R}' \in \mathcal{D}$,

$$R_i = R'_{\rho(i)} \text{ for all } i \in N \Rightarrow R = R'.$$

**Independence of irrelevant alternatives**  For all $x, y \in X$ and for all $\mathbf{R}, \mathbf{R}' \in \mathcal{D}$,

$[[(x, y) \in R_i \Leftrightarrow (x, y) \in R'_i]$ and $[(y, x) \in R_i \Leftrightarrow (y, x) \in R'_i]]$ for all $i \in N$
$\Rightarrow [[(x, y) \in R \Leftrightarrow (x, y) \in R']$ and $[(y, x) \in R \Leftrightarrow (y, x) \in R']]$.

**Neutrality**  For all $x, y, x', y' \in X$ and for all $\mathbf{R}, \mathbf{R}' \in \mathcal{D}$,

$[[(x, y) \in R_i \Leftrightarrow (x', y') \in R'_i]$ and $[(y, x) \in R_i \Leftrightarrow (y', x') \in R'_i]]$ for all $i \in N$
$\Rightarrow [[(x, y) \in R \Leftrightarrow (x', y') \in R']$ and $[(y, x) \in R \Leftrightarrow (y', x') \in R']]$.

As is straightforward to verify, the Pareto rule and the Pareto extension rule satisfy all of the axioms introduced above.

Unrestricted domain, weak Pareto, non-dictatorship, and independence of irrelevant alternatives are Arrow's (1951, 1963) original axioms. Strong Pareto is stronger than weak Pareto, anonymity is stronger than non-dictatorship, and neutrality is stronger than independence of irrelevant alternatives.

## 9.2   Earlier Results

To place our contribution within the relevant literature, we review the basic results that have been obtained by weakening the ordering requirement on social preferences.

Arrow's theorem, the most fundamental result in social choice theory, establishes the incompatibility of his four axioms if the collective choice rule is required to produce an *ordering* for each profile in its domain, that is, if $F$ is a social welfare function. In addition to Arrow's (1951, 1963) original demonstration, there are now numerous proofs available in the literature (for instance, Blackorby, Donaldson, and Weymark, 1984, employ diagrammatic arguments to establish the result) and we therefore state the theorem without a proof.

**Theorem 9.2**   *Suppose X contains at least three elements and N is finite and contains at least two elements. There exists no social welfare function satisfying unrestricted domain, weak Pareto, non-dictatorship, and independence of irrelevant alternatives.*

Sen (1969; 1970, theorem 5*3) characterized the Pareto extension rule by weakening the transitivity of the social ranking to quasi-transitivity while retaining the completeness assumption. Furthermore, he strengthened weak Pareto to strong Pareto and non-dictatorship to anonymity.

**Theorem 9.3**   *Suppose X contains at least three elements and N is finite and contains at least two elements. A reflexive, complete, and quasi-transitive collective choice rule F satisfies unrestricted domain, strong Pareto, anonymity, and independence of irrelevant alternatives if and only if $F = F^e$.*

Weymark (1984, theorem 3) disposed of completeness of the social ranking, which Arrow as well as Sen required, and showed that the Pareto rule is the only transitive collective choice rule that satisfies unrestricted domain, strong Pareto, anonymity, and independence of irrelevant alternatives.

**Theorem 9.4** *Suppose X contains at least three elements and N is finite and contains at least two elements. A transitive collective choice rule F satisfies unrestricted domain, strong Pareto, anonymity, and independence of irrelevant alternatives if and only if $F = F^P$.*

As a corollary to our characterization, we obtain an alternative axiomatization of the Pareto rule that is obtained by strengthening independence of irrelevant alternatives to neutrality and weakening transitivity of the social relation to Suzumura consistency. This special case is obtained whenever $|X| \geq |N|$. If $|X| < |N|$, further Suzumura-consistent collective choice rules are possible. This is in contrast to Sen's (1969; 1970, theorem 5*3) and Weymark's (1984) results that are valid for any finite $N$ with at least two elements and any $X$ with at least three elements.

## 9.3   Generalizations of the Pareto Rule

To describe all collective choice rules satisfying our requirements, we introduce some additional definitions. Let

$$\mathcal{L} = \{(w, \ell) \in \{0, \ldots, |N|\}^2 \mid |X|\ell < w + \ell \leq |N|\} \cup \{(0,0)\}$$

and, furthermore, define

$$\Lambda = \{L \subseteq \mathcal{L} \mid (w, 0) \in L \text{ for all } w \in \{0, \ldots, |N|\}\}.$$

For $L \in \Lambda$, define the *L-rule* $F^L \colon \mathcal{R}^N \to \mathcal{B}$ by $R^L = F^L(R)$, where

$$R^L = \{(x, y) \mid \exists (w, \ell) \in L \text{ such that } [|B(x, y; R)| = w$$
$$\text{and } |B(y, x; R)| = \ell]\}$$

for all $R \in \mathcal{R}^N$. The set $L$ specifies the pairs of numbers of agents who have to consider an alternative $x$ better (respectively worse) than an alternative $y$ in order to obtain a weak preference of $x$ over $y$ according to the profile under consideration. Clearly, because only the number of individuals matters and not their identities, the resulting rule is anonymous. Analogously, neutrality is satisfied because these numbers do not depend on the alternatives to be ranked. Strong Pareto follows from the requirement that the pairs $(w, 0)$ be in $L$ in the definition of $\Lambda$. As is shown in the proof of our characterization result, the social relation $R^L$ is Suzumura consistent due to the restrictions imposed on the pairs $(w, \ell)$ in the definition of $\mathcal{L}$.

Clearly, the Pareto rule is the special case that is obtained for $L = \{(w, 0) \mid w \in \{0, \ldots, |N|\}\}$. If $|X| \geq |N|$, this is *the only* $L$-rule. This is the case because only pairs $(w, \ell)$ where $\ell = 0$ are in $L$ in the presence of this inequality. To see this, suppose, to the contrary, that there exists $(w, \ell) \in L$ such that $\ell > 0$. Because $(w, \ell) \in L$, it follows that $|N| \geq w + \ell > |X|\ell > 0$. Combined with $|X| \geq |N|$, this implies $|N| > |N|\ell$, which is impossible if $\ell > 0$. Thus, if $|X| \geq N$, our characterization of the class of $L$-rules presented below provides an alternative characterization of the Pareto rule. This axiomatization differs from Weymark's (1984) in that independence of irrelevant alternatives is strengthened to neutrality and transitivity is weakened to Suzumura consistency. Note that if $|X| \geq |N|$, transitivity of the social relation is implied by the conjunction of Suzumura consistency and the axioms employed in our theorem.

If $|X| < |N|$, the Pareto rule is not the only $L$-rule. For example, consider the collective choice rule $F^L$ corresponding to the set $L = \{(w, 0) \mid w \in \{0, \ldots, |N|\}\} \cup \{(|N| - 1, 1)\}$. For $(w, \ell) = (|N| - 1, 1)$, we have $|N| = w + \ell > |X| = |X|\ell$ and, thus, the relevant inequalities are satisfied.

$L$-rules other than the Pareto rule do not necessarily produce transitive social preferences (but, of course, all social preferences are Suzumura consistent, as established in the main result of this chapter). For example, suppose $X = \{x, y, z\}$, $N = \{1, 2, 3, 4\}$,

$$L = \{(0, 0), (1, 0), (2, 0), (3, 0), (4, 0), (3, 1)\},$$

and consider the profile $\mathbf{R}$ defined by

$$R_1 = R_2 = \{(x, y), (x, z), (y, z)\},$$
$$R_3 = \{(z, x), (z, y), (x, y)\},$$
$$R_4 = \{(y, z), (y, x), (z, x)\}.$$

According to $R^L = F^L(\mathbf{R})$, $(x, y) \in P(R^L)$ and $(y, z) \in P(R^L)$ because $|B(x, y; \mathbf{R})| = |B(y, z; \mathbf{R})| = 3$ and $|B(y, x; \mathbf{R})| = |B(z, y; \mathbf{R})| = 1$. But $|B(x, z; \mathbf{R})| = |B(z, x; \mathbf{R})| = 2$ and, thus, $(x, z) \notin R^L$ so that $R^L$ is not transitive (not even quasi-transitive).

An interesting feature of the $L$-rules is that there may be "gaps" in the set of possible values of $w$ or $\ell$ within a rule. For instance, suppose $X = \{x, y, z\}$, $N = \{1, \ldots, 7\}$, and $L = \{(0, 0), (1, 0), (2, 0), (3, 0), (4, 0), (5, 0),$

$(6, 0), (7, 0), (5, 2)\}$. Consider the pair $(w, \ell) = (5, 2)$. We have $|N| = w + \ell = 7 > 6 = 3 \times 2 = |X|\ell > 0$ and, thus, $F^L$ is well-defined. In addition to the rankings generated by unanimity, five agents can ensure a superior ranking of an alternative over another against two agents with the opposite preference but, on the other hand, if six agents prefer $x$ to $y$ and one agent prefers $y$ to $x$, non-comparability results. $L$-rules exhibiting such gaps can be eliminated by adding a suitable version of *non-negative responsiveness*. See, for instance, Banks (1995) who employs such a property in the context of acyclical collective choice rules.

## 9.4   A Characterization

We now show that the $L$-rules are the only rules satisfying our axioms.

**Theorem 9.5** *Suppose $X$ contains at least three elements and $N$ is finite and contains at least two elements. A Suzumura-consistent collective choice rule $F$ satisfies unrestricted domain, strong Pareto, anonymity, and neutrality if and only if there exists $L \in \Lambda$ such that $F = F^L$.*

**Proof**   As mentioned earlier, that the $L$-rules satisfy unrestricted domain, strong Pareto, anonymity, and neutrality is straightforward to verify. It remains to establish that $R^L = F^L(\mathbf{R})$ is Suzumura consistent for all $L \in \Lambda$ and for all $\mathbf{R} \in \mathcal{R}^N$. Let $L \in \Lambda$ and suppose, by way of contradiction, that there exist $\mathbf{R} \in \mathcal{R}^N$, $K \in \mathbb{N} \setminus \{1, 2\}$, and $x^1, \ldots, x^K \in X$ such that $(x^{k-1}, x^k) \in R^L$ for all $k \in \{2, \ldots, K\}$ and $(x^K, x^1) \in P(R^L)$. Clearly, we can assume $K \leq |X|$ because redundant elements in the cycle can be eliminated. By definition of $R^L$, there exist $(w_1, \ell_1), \ldots, (w_K, \ell_K) \in L$ such that $|B(x^{k-1}, x^k; \mathbf{R})| = w_{k-1}$ and $|B(x^k, x^{k-1}; \mathbf{R})| = \ell_{k-1}$ for all $k \in \{2, \ldots, K\}$. Furthermore, we must have $|B(x^K, x^1; \mathbf{R})| = w_K$ and $|B(x^1, x^K; \mathbf{R})| = \ell_K$ with $w_K$ positive; if $w_K = 0$, we have $(w_K, \ell_K) = (0, 0)$ by definition of $\mathcal{L}$ and it follows that $(x^1, x^K) \in I(R^L)$, contrary to our hypothesis $(x^K, x^1) \in P(R^L)$.

If $\max \{\ell_1, \ldots, \ell_K\} = 0$, (repeated if necessary) application of Theorem 9.1 yields

$$|B(x^3, x^1; \mathbf{R})| \leq |B(x^3, x^2; \mathbf{R})| + |B(x^2, x^1; \mathbf{R})|,$$

$$\vdots$$

$$|B(x^K, x^1; \mathbf{R})| \leq |B(x^K, x^{K-1}; \mathbf{R})| + \cdots + |B(x^2, x^1; \mathbf{R})| = 0.$$

But this contradicts our earlier observation that $|B(x^K, x^1; \mathbf{R})| = w_K > 0$.

If max $\{\ell_1, \ldots, \ell_K\} > 0$, suppose this maximum is achieved at $\ell_k$ for some $k \in \{1, \ldots, K\}$. By definition of $\mathcal{L}$, $|X| \geq 3 > 0$ and $w_k + \ell_k > |X|\ell_k$ together rule out the possibility that $w_k + \ell_k > |X|w_k$ and, therefore, we must have $(\ell_k, w_k) \notin L$ and the preference corresponding to the $k^{\text{th}}$ element in the chain is strict. This, in turn, allows us to assume, without loss of generality, that $k = K$; this can be achieved with a simple relabeling of the elements in our chain if required. Invoking Theorem 9.1 again and using the maximality of $\ell_K$, we obtain

$$|B(x^3, x^1; \mathbf{R})| \leq |B(x^3, x^2; \mathbf{R})| + |B(x^2, x^1; \mathbf{R})| \leq 2\ell_K$$

$$\vdots$$

$$|B(x^K, x^1; \mathbf{R})| \leq |B(x^K, x^{K-1}; \mathbf{R})| + \cdots + |B(x^2, x^1; \mathbf{R})| \leq (K-1)\ell_K.$$

Because $K \leq |X|$, this implies

$$|B(x^K, x^1; \mathbf{R})| \leq (|X| - 1)\ell_K. \tag{9.2}$$

By assumption and by the definition of $\mathcal{L}$, we have $|B(x^K, x^1; \mathbf{R})| = w_K > (|X| - 1)\ell_K$, a contradiction to (9.2).

Now suppose $F$ is a Suzumura-consistent collective choice rule satisfying the axioms of the theorem statement. Let

$$L = \{(w, \ell) \mid \exists\, x, y \in X \text{ and } \mathbf{R} \in \mathcal{R}^N \text{ such that}$$

$$|B(x, y; \mathbf{R})| = w \text{ and } |B(y, x; \mathbf{R})| = \ell \text{ and } (x, y) \in R\}.$$

By anonymity and neutrality, $L$ is such that the relation $R$ is equal to $R^L$. It remains to show that $L \in \Lambda$. That $(w, 0) \in L$ for all $w \in \{0, \ldots, |N|\}$ follows from strong Pareto. Clearly, for all $(w, \ell) \in L$, $w + \ell \leq |N|$.

As an auxiliary result, we show that

$$w > \ell \tag{9.3}$$

for all $(w, \ell) \in L \setminus \{(0, 0)\}$. By way of contradiction, suppose that $w \leq \ell$ for some $(w, \ell) \in L \setminus \{(0, 0)\}$. Because $(w, \ell) \neq (0, 0)$ by assumption, this implies $\ell > 0$ and, by strong Pareto, $w > 0$. By unrestricted domain and the assumption $|X| \geq 3$, we can choose $x, y, z \in X$, and $\mathbf{R} \in \mathcal{R}^N$ so that

$$\{(x, y), (y, z)\} \subseteq P(R_i) \text{ for all } i \in \{1, \ldots, w\}$$

and

$$\{(y, z), (z, x)\} \subseteq P(R_i) \text{ for all } i \in \{\ell + 1, \ldots, \ell + w\}.$$

Furthermore, if $w < \ell$, let

$$\{(y, x), (x, z)\} \subseteq P(R_i) \text{ for all } i \in \{w + 1, \ldots, \ell\}$$

and if $w + \ell < |N|$, let

$$\{(x,y),(y,z)\} \subseteq I(R_i) \text{ for all } i \in \{w + \ell + 1, \ldots, |N|\}.$$

Because $|B(z,x;\mathbf{R})| = |B(x,y;\mathbf{R})| = w$ and $|B(x,z;\mathbf{R})| = |B(y,x;\mathbf{R})| = \ell$, we must have $(z,x) \in R$ and $(x,y) \in R$. By strong Pareto, it follows that $(y,z) \in P(R)$ and we obtain a contradiction to the Suzumura consistency of $R$. This establishes (9.3).

To complete the proof, we have to show that $w + \ell > |X|\ell$ for all $(w, \ell) \in L \setminus \{(0,0)\}$. By way of contradiction, suppose this is not true. Then there exists a pair $(w_0, \ell_0) \in L \setminus \{(0,0)\}$ such that $w_0 + \ell_0 \leq |X|\ell_0$ or, equivalently,

$$w_0 \leq (|X| - 1)\ell_0. \tag{9.4}$$

Combining (9.3), which is true for all $(w, \ell) \in L \setminus \{(0,0)\}$ and thus for $(w_0, \ell_0)$, with (9.4), we obtain

$$\ell_0 < w_0 \leq (|X| - 1)\ell_0. \tag{9.5}$$

Clearly, $\ell_0 = 0$ is incompatible with (9.5). Thus, $\ell_0 > 0$.

(9.3) immediately implies that, for any $(w, \ell) \in L \setminus \{(0,0)\}$, $(\ell, w) \notin L$. Thus, in particular, whenever $|B(x,y;\mathbf{R})| = w_0$ and $|B(y,x;\mathbf{R})| = \ell_0$, we must have $(x,y) \in P(R)$ and not merely $(x,y) \in R$.

We now distinguish two cases. The first of these occurs whenever $w_0$ is a positive multiple of $\ell_0$. That is, given (9.5), there exists $\beta \in \{3, \ldots, |X|\}$ such that $w_0 = (\beta - 1)\ell_0$ (and, thus, $w_0 + \ell_0 = \beta\ell_0$). By unrestricted domain, we can choose $\beta$ alternatives $x^1, \ldots, x^\beta \in X$ and a profile $\mathbf{R} \in \mathcal{R}^N$ such that

$$\{(x^1,x^2),\ldots,(x^{\beta-1},x^\beta)\} \subseteq P(R_i) \qquad \text{for all } i \in \{1,\ldots,\ell_0\},$$

$$\{(x^2,x^3),\ldots,(x^\beta,x^1)\} \subseteq P(R_i) \qquad \text{for all } i \in \{\ell_0 + 1,\ldots,2\ell_0\},$$

$$\vdots$$

$$\{(x^{\beta-1},x^\beta),(x^\beta,x^1)\} \subseteq P(R_i) \qquad \text{for all } i \in \{(\beta - 2)\ell_0 + 1,\ldots,(\beta - 1)\ell_0\}$$

and, if $\beta > 3$,

$$\{(x^1,x^2),\ldots,(x^{\beta-3},x^{\beta-2})\} \subseteq P(R_i) \quad \text{for all } i \in \{(\beta - 2)\ell_0 + 1,\ldots,(\beta - 1)\ell_0\},$$

$$\{(x^\beta,x^1),\ldots,(x^{\beta-2},x^{\beta-1})\} \subseteq P(R_i) \quad \text{for all } i \in \{(\beta - 1)\ell_0 + 1,\ldots,\beta\ell_0\}$$

and, if $|N| > w_0 + \ell_0 = \beta\ell_0$,

$$R_i = X \times X \text{ for all } i \in \{w_0 + \ell_0 + 1, \ldots, |N|\}.$$

We have $|B(x^{j-1}, x^j; \mathbf{R})| = (\beta - 1)\ell_0 = w_0$ and $|B(x^j, x^{j-1}; \mathbf{R})| = \ell_0$ for all $j \in \{2, \dots, \beta\}$ and, furthermore, $|B(x^\beta, x^1; \mathbf{R})| = (\beta - 1)\ell_0 = w_0$ and $|B(x^1, x^\beta; \mathbf{R})| = \ell_0$. Therefore, $(x^{j-1}, x^j) \in P(R)$ for all $j \in \{2, \dots, \beta\}$ and $(x^\beta, x^1) \in P(R)$, contradicting the Suzumura consistency of $R$.

Finally, we consider the case in which $w_0$ is not a positive multiple of $\ell_0$. Clearly, this is only possible if $\ell_0 > 1$. By (9.5), there exists $\alpha \in \{3, \dots, |X|\}$ such that

$$(\alpha - 2)\ell_0 < w_0 < (\alpha - 1)\ell_0. \tag{9.6}$$

By unrestricted domain, we can consider $\alpha$ alternatives $x^1, \dots, x^\alpha \in X$ and a profile $\mathbf{R} \in \mathcal{R}^N$ such that

$\{(x^2, x^3), \dots, (x^\alpha, x^1)\} \subseteq P(R_i)$  for all $i \in \{1, \dots, \ell_0\}$,

$\vdots$

$\{(x^{\alpha-1}, x^\alpha), (x^\alpha, x^1)\} \subseteq P(R_i)$  for all $i \in \{(\alpha - 3)\ell_0 + 1, \dots, (\alpha - 2)\ell_0\}$

and, if $\alpha > 3$,

$\{(x^1, x^2), \dots, (x^{\alpha-3}, x^{\alpha-2})\} \subseteq P(R_i)$  for all $i \in \{(\alpha - 3)\ell_0 + 1, \dots, (\alpha - 2)\ell_0\}$,

$\{(x^\alpha, x^1), \dots, (x^{\alpha-2}, x^{\alpha-1})\} \subseteq P(R_i)$  for all $i \in \{(\alpha - 2)\ell_0 + 1, \dots, w_0\}$,

$\{(x^1, x^2), \dots, (x^{\alpha-1}, x^\alpha)\} \subseteq P(R_i)$  for all $i \in \{w_0 + 1, \dots, 2w_0 - (\alpha - 2)\ell_0\}$,

$\{(x^1, x^\alpha), (x^\alpha, x^2), \dots, (x^{\alpha-2}, x^{\alpha-1})\} \subseteq P(R_i)$   for all $i \in \{2w_0 - (\alpha - 2)\ell_0 + 1, \dots, w_0 + \ell_0\}$

and, if $|N| > w_0 + \ell_0$,

$$R_i = X \times X \text{ for all } i \in \{w_0 + \ell_0 + 1, \dots, |N|\}.$$

This profile is well-defined because (9.6) implies

$$w_0 < 2w_0 - (\alpha - 2)\ell_0 < w_0 + \ell_0.$$

We have $|B(x^{j-1}, x^j; \mathbf{R})| = w_0$ and $|B(x^j, x^{j-1}; \mathbf{R})| = \ell_0$ for all $j \in \{2, \dots, \alpha\}$ and, furthermore, $|B(x^\alpha, x^1; \mathbf{R})| = w_0$ and $|B(x^1, x^\alpha; \mathbf{R})| = \ell_0$. Therefore, $(x^{j-1}, x^j) \in P(R)$ for all $j \in \{2, \dots, \alpha\}$ and $(x^\alpha, x^1) \in P(R)$, again contradicting the Suzumura consistency of $R$. ∎

The conclusion of Theorem 9.5 does not hold if merely independence of irrelevant alternatives rather than neutrality is imposed. Suppose $x^0$, $y^0 \in X$ are two distinct alternatives. Define a collective choice rule by letting

$$R = \{(x, y) \mid (x, y) \in R^p \text{ or } [(x, y) \notin R^p \text{ and } (y, x) \notin R^p$$
$$\text{and } \{x, y\} = \{x^0, y^0\}]\}$$

for all $\mathbf{R} \in \mathcal{R}^N$. This is a Suzumura-consistent collective choice rule satisfying unrestricted domain, strong Pareto, anonymity, and independence of irrelevant alternatives. However, neutrality is violated.

Suzumura consistency cannot be weakened to acyclicity in our characterization result. The collective choice rule defined by letting

$$R = \{(x, y) \mid (x, y) \in R^P \text{ or } |B(x, y; \mathbf{R})| = |B(y, x; \mathbf{R})| = 1\}$$

for all $\mathbf{R} \in \mathcal{R}^N$ produces acyclical social preferences and satisfies the axioms of Theorem 9.5. However, social preferences are not always Suzumura consistent. For example, suppose $X = \{x, y, z\}$ and $N = \{1, 2, 3\}$, and consider the profile $\mathbf{R}$ defined by

$$R_1 = \{(x, y), (x, z), (y, z)\},$$
$$R_2 = \{(z, x), (z, y), (x, y)\},$$
$$R_3 = X \times X.$$

According to $R = F(\mathbf{R})$, we obtain $(y, z) \in I(R), (z, x) \in I(R)$, and $(x, y) \in P(R)$, a social preference relation that is not Suzumura consistent.

# — 10 —

## Decisiveness and Infinite Populations

### 10.1 Decisive Coalitions, Filters, and Ultrafilters

The conclusion of Arrow's (1951, 1963) seminal theorem depends crucially on the assumption that the population under consideration is finite. Kirman and Sondermann (1972) and Hansson (1976) are among the first authors who consider the structure of decisive coalitions in the Arrovian framework. They establish that, in the general case where the population may be finite or infinite, the set of decisive coalitions forms an ultrafilter, given that social relations are assumed to be orderings and Arrow's axioms are satisfied. If the population is finite, all ultrafilters are principal ultrafilters and thus, by definition of the decisiveness property, dictatorial. If the population is infinite, there exist non-principal ultrafilters and these ultrafilters correspond to decisive coalition structures that are non-dictatorial. See Cato (2008) for discussions of alternative notions of decisiveness.

An interesting application of social choice theory with an infinite population consists of the design of intergenerational resource allocation mechanisms with an infinite horizon. Some important work in this area has been done by Ferejohn and Page (1978) and Packel (1980).

In this chapter (the last two sections of which are based on Bossert and Suzumura, 2008b), we examine the impact of weakening the social ordering requirement on decisive coalition structures. In addition, we reconsider Ferejohn and Page's (1978) and Packel's (1980) impossibility results and suggest an alternative way of circumventing these impossibilities.

We begin with statements of Hansson's (1976) fundamental results regarding the structure of decisive coalitions for collective choice rules satisfying Arrow's axioms, both under the assumption that social preferences are orderings and under the assumption that they are reflexive, complete, and quasi-transitive. Because the proofs of our results are similar, we do not provide formal demonstrations of Hansson's theorems but refer the reader to the original source for details.

The population is $N$, a set that may now be finite or infinite and is assumed to contain at least two elements. As in Chapter 9, we use $R$ to denote the social preference $F(\mathbf{R})$ assigned to a profile $\mathbf{R}$ in the domain of a collective choice rule $F$. Let $x, y \in X$ be distinct. A set of individuals $M \subseteq N$ (also referred to as a *coalition*) is *decisive for x over y for a collective choice rule F* (in short, $M$ is $d_F(x, y)$) if and only if, for all $\mathbf{R} \in \mathcal{R}^N$,

$$(x, y) \in P(R_i) \quad \text{for all } i \in M \Rightarrow (x, y) \in P(R).$$

A set $M \subseteq N$ is *decisive for F* if and only if $M$ is $d_F(x, y)$ for all distinct $x, y \in X$. Clearly, $N$ is decisive for any collective choice rule satisfying weak Pareto. If there is an individual $i \in N$ such that $\{i\}$ is decisive for $F$, individual $i$ is a *dictator for F*. Let $D_F$ denote the set of all decisive coalitions for a collective choice rule $F$.

Recall from Chapter 2 that a filter on $N$ is a collection $\mathcal{F}$ of subsets of $N$ such that

$f.1.$  $\emptyset \notin \mathcal{F}$.
$f.2.$  $N \in \mathcal{F}$.
$f.3.$  For all $M, M' \in \mathcal{F}, M \cap M' \in \mathcal{F}$.
$f.4.$  For all $M, M' \subseteq N, [[M \in \mathcal{F} \text{ and } M \subseteq M'] \Rightarrow M' \in \mathcal{F}]$.

An ultrafilter on $N$ is a collection $\mathcal{U}$ of subsets of $N$ such that

$u.1.$  $\emptyset \notin \mathcal{U}$.
$u.2.$  For all $M \subseteq N, [M \in \mathcal{U} \text{ or } N \setminus M \in \mathcal{U}]$.
$u.3.$  For all $M, M' \in \mathcal{U}, M \cap M' \in \mathcal{U}$.

Hansson's first result applies to social welfare functions, that is, collective choice rules that always generate social orderings. It shows that any social welfare function satisfying Arrow's axioms has a collection of decisive coalitions that forms an ultrafilter.

**Theorem 10.1**  *Suppose X contains at least three elements and N contains at least two elements. If a social welfare function F satisfies unrestricted do-*

*main, weak Pareto, and independence of irrelevant alternatives, then $D_F$ is an ultrafilter on $N$.*

Arrow's theorem now can be obtained as a corollary to this result. If $N$ is finite, all ultrafilters are principal. Therefore, there exists an individual $i \in N$ who is decisive. By definition of decisiveness, this individual is a dictator.

The implication of this theorem can be reversed in the sense that the ultrafilter structure is all we can get out of the Arrow axioms: for any ultra-filter $\mathcal{U}$ on $N$, there exists a social welfare function $F$ satisfying unrestricted domain, weak Pareto, and independence of irrelevant alternatives such that $D_F = \mathcal{U}$.

**Theorem 10.2** *Suppose $X$ contains at least three elements and $N$ contains at least two elements. For any ultrafilter $\mathcal{U}$ on $N$, there exists a social welfare function $F$ that satisfies unrestricted domain, weak Pareto, and independence of irrelevant alternatives such that $D_F = \mathcal{U}$.*

Hansson (1976) also considered the case in which transitivity of a social relation is weakened to quasi-transitivity but reflexivity and completeness continue to be imposed. In that case, the resulting structure of decisive co-alitions is not necessarily an ultrafilter but it is a filter. Again, the result is tight in the sense that the reverse implication is also true. Thus we obtain the following two theorems, also due to Hansson (1976).

**Theorem 10.3** *Suppose $X$ contains at least three elements and $N$ contains at least two elements. If a reflexive, complete, and quasi-transitive collective choice rule $F$ satisfies unrestricted domain, weak Pareto, and independence of irrelevant alternatives, then $D_F$ is a filter on $N$.*

**Theorem 10.4** *Suppose $X$ contains at least three elements and $N$ contains at least two elements. For any filter $\mathcal{F}$ on $N$, there exists a reflexive, complete, and quasi-transitive collective choice rule $F$ that satisfies unrestricted domain, weak Pareto, and independence of irrelevant alternatives such that $D_F = \mathcal{F}$.*

## 10.2 Decisiveness without Social Richness Assumptions

We now reexamine Hansson's (1976) observations involving transitive and quasi-transitive social relations satisfying the Arrow axioms in the absence

of reflexivity and completeness. Although the resulting decisiveness structures can be recovered following steps analogous to those employed by
Hansson himself, there is an interesting difference: once reflexivity and
completeness are dropped, the families of decisive coalitions associated with
transitive collective choice rules and with quasi-transitive collective choice
rules can no longer be distinguished. Intuitively, this is the case because
only strict preferences are necessarily imposed by weak Pareto and, in the
absence of completeness, an absence of strict preference does not imply a
weak preference in the reverse direction. Moreover, as a corollary to the
results of this section, it emerges that quasi-transitivity with reflexivity and
completeness is equivalent to quasi-transitivity without reflexivity and completeness, whereas transitivity without reflexivity and completeness results in
weaker structural properties of the family of decisive coalitions—namely,
the same structure that obtains for quasi-transitivity. It is worth noting
at this stage that the notion of a decisive coalition continues to be well-
defined; this is in contrast with alternative coherence properties discussed
briefly at the end of this section.

As a preliminary observation, we state and prove a version of Sen's *field
expansion lemma* (Sen, 1995, p. 4) that does not assume reflexivity or completeness.

**Theorem 10.5**   *Suppose $X$ contains at least three elements and $N$ contains
at least two elements. Let $F$ be a quasi-transitive collective choice rule that
satisfies unrestricted domain, weak Pareto, and independence of irrelevant
alternatives. Let $x, y \in X$ be distinct and let $M \subseteq N$. If $M$ is $d_F(x, y)$, then
$M \in D_F$.*

**Proof**   Let $F$ be a quasi-transitive collective choice rule that satisfies the
Arrow axioms, let $x, y \in X$ be distinct and let $M \subseteq N$ be $d_F(x, y)$. We have
to establish that $M$ is $d_F(z, v)$ for any choice of distinct alternatives $z$ and $v$.
Thus, we have to show that $M$ is

   (i)  $d_F(z, v)$ for all distinct $z, v \in X \setminus \{x, y\}$;
   (ii)  $d_F(x, z)$ for all $z \in X \setminus \{x, y\}$;
   (iii)  $d_F(z, y)$ for all $z \in X \setminus \{x, y\}$;
   (iv)  $d_F(z, x)$ for all $z \in X \setminus \{x, y\}$;
   (v)  $d_F(y, z)$ for all $z \in X \setminus \{x, y\}$;
   (vi)  $d_F(y, x)$.

(i) Because $F$ has an unrestricted domain, we can consider a profile $\mathbf{R} \in \mathcal{R}^N$ such that

$$\{(z,x),(x,y),(y,v)\} \subseteq P(R_i) \quad \text{for all } i \in M,$$
$$\{(z,x),(y,v)\} \subseteq P(R_i) \quad \text{for all } i \in N \setminus M.$$

By weak Pareto, $(z,x) \in P(R)$ and $(y,v) \in P(R)$. Because $M$ is $d_F(x,y)$, we have $(x,y) \in P(R)$. By quasi-transitivity, $(z,v) \in P(R)$. Because of independence of irrelevant alternatives, this social preference cannot depend on individual preferences over pairs of alternatives other than $z$ and $v$. The ranking of $z$ and $v$ is not specified for individuals outside of $M$ and, thus, $M$ is $d_F(z,v)$.

(ii) Consider a profile $\mathbf{R} \in \mathcal{R}^N$ such that

$$\{(x,y),(y,z)\} \subseteq P(R_i) \quad \text{for all } i \in M,$$
$$(y,z) \in P(R_i) \quad \text{for all } i \in N \setminus M.$$

Because $M$ is $d_F(x,y)$, we have $(x,y) \in P(R)$. By weak Pareto, $(y,z) \in P(R)$. By quasi-transitivity, $(x,z) \in P(R)$ and it follows as in the proof of part (i) that $M$ is $d_F(x,z)$.

(iii) Let $\mathbf{R} \in \mathcal{R}^N$ be such that

$$\{(z,x),(x,y)\} \subseteq P(R_i) \quad \text{for all } i \in M,$$
$$(z,x) \in P(R_i) \quad \text{for all } i \in N \setminus M.$$

By weak Pareto, $(z,x) \in P(R)$. Because $M$ is $d_F(x,y)$, we have $(x,y) \in P(R)$. By quasi-transitivity, $(z,y) \in P(R)$ and it follows as in the proofs of parts (i) and (ii) that $M$ is $d_F(z,y)$.

(iv) Let $\mathbf{R} \in \mathcal{R}^N$ be such that

$$\{(z,y),(y,x)\} \subseteq P(R_i) \quad \text{for all } i \in M,$$
$$(y,x) \in P(R_i) \quad \text{for all } i \in N \setminus M.$$

By (iii), $(z,y) \in P(R)$. Weak Pareto implies $(y,x) \in P(R)$ and, by quasi-transitivity, we obtain $(z,x) \in P(R)$. As in the earlier cases, it follows that $M$ is $d_F(z,x)$.

(v) Let $\mathbf{R} \in \mathcal{R}^N$ be such that

$$\{(y,x),(x,z)\} \subseteq P(R_i) \quad \text{for all } i \in M,$$
$$(y,x) \in P(R_i) \quad \text{for all } i \in N \setminus M.$$

By weak Pareto, $(y, x) \in P(R)$. By part (ii), we have $(x, z) \in P(R)$. By quasi-transitivity, $(y, z) \in P(R)$ and it follows that $M$ is $d_F(y, z)$.

(vi) Let $\mathbf{R} \in \mathcal{R}^N$ be such that

$$\{(y, z), (z, x)\} \subseteq P(R_i) \quad \text{for all } i \in M.$$

By part (v), $(y, z) \in P(R)$ and by part (iv), $(z, x) \in P(R)$. By quasi-transitivity, $(y, x) \in P(R)$ and it follows that $M$ is $d_F(y, x)$. ∎

Hansson's (1976) theorems on quasi-transitive collective choice rules remain valid even in the absence of reflexivity and completeness. Thus, we obtain the following result.

**Theorem 10.6** *Suppose $X$ contains at least three elements and $N$ contains at least two elements. If a quasi-transitive collective choice rule $F$ satisfies unrestricted domain, weak Pareto, and independence of irrelevant alternatives, then $D_F$ is a filter on $N$.*

**Proof** Suppose $F$ is a quasi-transitive collective choice rule that satisfies unrestricted domain, weak Pareto, and independence of irrelevant alternatives. We need to show that $D_F$ has the four properties of a filter.

$f.1$. If $\emptyset \in D_F$, we obtain $(x, y) \in P(R)$ and $(y, x) \in P(R)$ for any two distinct alternatives $x, y \in X$ and for any profile $\mathbf{R} \in \mathcal{R}^N$ such that all individuals are indifferent between $x$ and $y$, which is impossible. Thus, $\emptyset \notin D_F$.

$f.2$. This property is a consequence of weak Pareto.

$f.3$. Suppose $M, M' \in D_F$. Let $x, y, z \in X$ be pairwise distinct and let $\mathbf{R} \in \mathcal{R}^N$ be such that

$$\{(y, x), (z, x)\} \subseteq P(R_i) \quad \text{for all } i \in M \setminus M',$$
$$\{(z, x), (x, y)\} \subseteq P(R_i) \quad \text{for all } i \in M \cap M',$$
$$\{(x, y), (x, z)\} \subseteq P(R_i) \quad \text{for all } i \in M' \setminus M.$$

Because $M$ is decisive, we have $(z, x) \in P(R)$. Because $M'$ is decisive, we have $(x, y) \in P(R)$. By quasi-transitivity, $(z, y) \in P(R)$. This implies that $M \cap M'$ is $d_F(z, y)$ because the preferences of individuals outside of $M \cap M'$ over $z$ and $y$ are not specified. By Theorem 10.5, $M \cap M' \in D_F$.

$f.4$. This property follows immediately from the definition of decisiveness. ∎

As an immediate corollary of Theorem 10.6, it follows that if $F$ is a transitive rather than a quasi-transitive collective choice rule, the same conclusion holds: the family of decisive coalitions must form a filter in the presence of the three Arrow axioms.

We now establish the reverse implication of the above theorem. An even stronger result is valid: given any filter $\mathcal{F}$ on $N$, it follows that there exists a *transitive* (and not merely a quasi-transitive) collective choice rule $F$ satisfying the axioms such that $D_F = \mathcal{F}$.

**Theorem 10.7**   *Suppose $X$ contains at least three elements and $N$ contains at least two elements. For any filter $\mathcal{F}$ on $N$, there exists a transitive collective choice rule $F$ that satisfies unrestricted domain, weak Pareto, and independence of irrelevant alternatives such that $D_F = \mathcal{F}$.*

**Proof**   Let $\mathcal{F}$ be a filter on $N$. Define a collective choice rule $F$ by letting, for all $\mathbf{R} \in \mathcal{R}^N$ and for all $x, y \in X$,

$$(x, y) \in R \Leftrightarrow B(x, y; \mathbf{R}) \in \mathcal{F}.$$

We first prove that $R$ is transitive for all possible profiles $\mathbf{R}$. Suppose $\mathbf{R} \in \mathcal{R}^N$ and $x, y, z \in X$ are such that $(x, y) \in R$ and $(y, z) \in R$. By definition of $F$,

$$B(x, y; \mathbf{R}) \in \mathcal{F} \text{ and } B(y, z; \mathbf{R}) \in \mathcal{F}.$$

By $f.3$,

$$B(x, y; \mathbf{R}) \cap B(y, z; \mathbf{R}) \in \mathcal{F}.$$

Because individual preferences are transitive, it follows that

$$B(x, y; \mathbf{R}) \cap B(y, z; \mathbf{R}) \subseteq B(x, z; \mathbf{R})$$

and, by $f.4$, $B(x, z; \mathbf{R}) \in \mathcal{F}$. Thus, by definition of $F$, $(x, z) \in R$ as was to be established.

Clearly, unrestricted domain is satisfied by definition. That weak Pareto is satisfied follows immediately from $f.1$ and $f.2$. Independence of irrelevant alternatives is satisfied because the social ranking of any two alternatives $x$ and $y$ is defined exclusively in terms of the individual rankings of $x$ and $y$.

It remains to show that $D_F = \mathcal{F}$. As a first step, we show that $R$ is asymmetric for all possible profiles. By way of contradiction, suppose $\mathbf{R} \in \mathcal{R}^N$ and $x, y \in X$ are such that $(x, y) \in R$ and $(y, x) \in R$. By definition of $F$, this means that

$$B(x, y; \mathbf{R}) \in \mathcal{F} \text{ and } B(y, x; \mathbf{R}) \in \mathcal{F}.$$

By $f.3$,

$$B(x, y; \mathbf{R}) \cap B(y, x; \mathbf{R}) = \emptyset \in \mathcal{F},$$

contradicting $f.1$.

To prove that $D_F \subseteq \mathcal{F}$, suppose that $M \in D_F$. Let $\mathbf{R} \in \mathcal{R}^N$ and $x, y \in X$ be such that $(x, y) \in P(R_i)$ for all $i \in M$. By definition of a decisive coalition, this implies $(x, y) \in P(R)$ and, thus, $(x, y) \in R$. By definition of $F$, this implies $M \in \mathcal{F}$.

To complete the proof, suppose that $M \in \mathcal{F}$. Let $\mathbf{R} \in \mathcal{R}^N$ and $x, y \in X$ be such that $(x, y) \in P(R_i)$ for all $i \in M$. By definition of $F$, we obtain $(x, y) \in R$. Because $R$ is asymmetric, it follows that $(x, y) \in P(R)$. Thus, $M$ is decisive and hence $M \in D_F$. ■

Combining the last two theorems, it follows immediately that the class of transitive collective choice rules and the class of quasi-transitive collective choice rules have identical characterizations in terms of decisive coalitions. This contrasts with the case of collective choice rules that always generate reflexive and complete social relations where the two concepts are distinct.

If, in the absence of reflexivity and completeness, merely acyclicity or Suzumura consistency is imposed on social preferences, the approach involving decisive coalitions and filters employed so far in this chapter cannot be used. This is the case because the existence of such coalitions is not guaranteed and there is no equivalent of the field expansion lemma (Theorem 10.5) with acyclicity or with Suzumura consistency. Intuitively, this difference emerges because, unlike transitivity and quasi-transitivity, acyclicity and Suzumura consistency do not *force* certain additional pairs to be in a relation as a consequence of the presence of others but, rather, *prevent* certain pairs of alternatives to appear in the relation in order to avoid the respective cycles. For that reason, property $f.3$ of a filter cannot be established because it relies on the transitivity of $R$ or $P(R)$. Moreover, even property $f.4$ must be abandoned. To see that this is the case, consider the following example that extends an example in the previous chapter. Suppose $X = \{x, y, z\}$ and $N = \{1, \dots, 7\}$. Define a collective choice rule by letting, for all $\mathbf{R} \in \mathcal{R}^N$ and for all $x, y \in X$,

$$(x, y) \in R \Leftrightarrow [|B(y, x; \mathbf{R})| = 0 \text{ or } [|B(x, y; \mathbf{R})| = 5 \text{ and}$$
$$|B(y, x; \mathbf{R})| = 2]].$$

This collective choice rule is Suzumura consistent and satisfies unrestricted domain, weak Pareto, and independence of irrelevant alternatives. However, even though $(x, y) \in P(R_i)$ for all $i \in \{1, \ldots, 5\}$ and $(y, x) \in P(R_i)$ for all $i \in \{6, 7\}$ implies $(x, y) \in P(R)$, we obtain non-comparability of $x$ and $y$ rather than a strict preference for $x$ over $y$ if $(x, y) \in P(R_i)$ for all $i \in \{1, \ldots, 6\}$ and $(y, x) \in P(R_7)$. Thus, an expansion of a coalition that can force $x$ to be preferred to $y$ does *not* generate a coalition with that power. In addition, as established in the previous chapter, even the coalition $\{1, \ldots, 5\}$ cannot be considered decisive according to our earlier definition. Thus, the framework based on decisiveness and filters as families of decisive coalitions cannot be employed. In this context, it is worth noting that Banks (1995) employs a monotonicity property that strengthens independence of irrelevant alternatives. This property is akin to non-negative responsiveness, requiring that a strict preference for $x$ over $y$ must be preserved if we move to a profile where the set of those preferring $x$ to $y$ and the set of those considering $x$ at least as good as $y$ weakly expand. Clearly, this property rules out examples of the above nature. See also Blair and Pollak (1982) for discussions of acyclical collective choice in the presence of the richness properties reflexivity and completeness. As is the case for Banks (1995), Blair and Pollak (1982) restrict attention to the finite-population case.

## 10.3   Intergenerational Social Choice

Up to now, we did not explicitly consider any possible sequential relationships among the members of an infinite population. Ferejohn and Page (1978) introduced time explicitly into the analysis of intergenerational social choice in a multi-profile setting. Time flows only unidirectionally, and two members $i$ and $j$ of the society, to be called generation $i$ and generation $j$, are such that generation $j$ appears in the society after generation $i$ if and only if $i < j$. As a result of introducing this time structure of infinite population, Ferejohn and Page (1978) also opened up the possibility of combining Arrovian social choice theory and the theory of evaluating infinite intergenerational utility streams, which was initiated by Koopmans (1960) and Diamond (1965); see Asheim (forthcoming 2010) for a survey. In the remainder of this chapter, we reexamine the Ferejohn and Page approach.

Ferejohn and Page (1978) proposed a stationarity condition in an infinite-horizon multi-profile social choice model and showed that if a social welfare function satisfying Arrow's conditions and stationarity exists, generation one must be a dictator. As they noted themselves, the question whether such a social welfare function exists at all was left open by their analysis; what they showed was that *if* such a function exists, it must be dictatorial with generation one being the dictator. Packel (1980) answered the question Ferejohn and Page left open by establishing a strong impossibility result: even without independence of irrelevant alternatives and without assuming social preferences to be transitive, no collective choice rule can satisfy the remaining axioms, not even dictatorships of any kind.

We first prove that the negative implications of the Ferejohn-Page stationarity condition are even more far-reaching: there exist no collective choice rules satisfying unrestricted domain, weak Pareto, and stationarity. The same conclusion holds if individual preferences are assumed to be history-independent. No further restrictions whatsoever are imposed on social preferences—they need not possess any of the richness or coherence properties discussed in this monograph. By dropping reflexivity and completeness, we strengthen Packel's impossibility result even further.

Some additional notation is required in order to allow us to distinguish between per-period alternatives and streams of these per-period alternatives. Suppose now that $X_{pp}$ denotes a set of per-period alternatives containing at least three elements. We identify the (infinite) population $N$ with a sequence of generations indexed by the positive integers; that is, $N = \mathbb{N}$. As before, let $X$ be the universal set of alternatives, which now consists of streams of per-period alternatives $x = \langle x_i \rangle_{i \in N}$ where, for each $i \in N$, $x_i \in X_{pp}$ is the period-$i$ alternative experienced by generation $i$. We also refer to $x_i$ as the factor of $x$ relevant for generation $i$. The terms *individual* and *generation* are used interchangeably from now on because we abstract from intragenerational distribution issues.

That the set of feasible per-period alternatives is the same for all generations appears to be a rather restrictive assumption; for example, technological progress is likely to generate dramatically different feasible sets of consumption bundles several decades into the future. The above more restrictive formulation is chosen because it is needed in order to define Ferejohn and Page's (1978) version of stationarity and their relevant results using this property; this is the case because, to apply their axiom, some generations must be able to assess not only their own per-period alternatives but those of other generations as well. However, the new approach we develop in our analysis can easily accommodate a framework where the per-period feasible sets may be period-dependent. The reason is that our proposed model is based on axioms that do not require a generation $i$ to be capable of comparing per-period alternatives other than those relevant for $i$ or those relevant for all generations from $i$ onward.

We assume that each generation $i \in N$ has an ordering $R_i$ defined on the universal set of streams $X$. For $x \in X$, we define

$$x_{\geq i} = \langle x_j \rangle_{j \geq i} \in X$$

and, analogously, for $\mathbf{R} \in \mathcal{R}^N$,

$$\mathbf{R}_{\geq i} = \langle R_j \rangle_{j \geq i} \in \mathcal{R}^N.$$

Two subsets of the unrestricted domain $\mathcal{R}^N$ are of importance in what follows. We define the *forward-looking domain* $\mathcal{R}^N_{fwl} \subseteq \mathcal{R}^N$ by letting, for all $\mathbf{R} \in \mathcal{R}^N$, $\mathbf{R} \in \mathcal{R}^N_{fwl}$ if and only if, for each $i \in N$, there exists an ordering $Q_i$ on $X$ such that, for all $x, y \in X$,

$$(x, y) \in R_i \Leftrightarrow (x_{\geq i}, y_{\geq i}) \in Q_i.$$

Analogously, the *selfish domain* $\mathcal{R}^N_{self} \subseteq \mathcal{R}^N_{fwl} \subseteq \mathcal{R}^N$ is obtained by letting, for all $\mathbf{R} \in \mathcal{R}^N$, $\mathbf{R} \in \mathcal{R}^N_{self}$ if and only if, for each $i \in N$, there exists an ordering $\succeq_i$ on $X_{pp}$ such that, for all $x, y \in X$,

$$(x, y) \in R_i \Leftrightarrow (x_i, y_i) \in \succeq_i .$$

In addition to the Arrovian axioms of unrestricted domain, weak Pareto, and independence of irrelevant alternatives, the following properties are of relevance in this intergenerational context. The first two are domain restrictions.

**Forward-looking domain**   $\mathcal{D} = \mathcal{R}^N_{fwl}$.

**Selfish domain**   $\mathcal{D} = \mathcal{R}^N_{self}$.

**Pareto indifference**   For all $x, y \in X$ and for all $\mathbf{R} \in \mathcal{D}$,

$$(x, y) \in I(R_i) \quad \text{for all } i \in N \Rightarrow (x, y) \in I(R).$$

None of the above-defined axioms invoke the intertemporal structure imposed by our intergenerational interpretation. In contrast, the following *stationarity* property proposed by Ferejohn and Page (1978) is based on the unidirectional nature of time. The intuition underlying stationarity is that if two streams of per-period alternatives agree in the first period, their relative social ranking is unchanged if this common first-period alternative is eliminated. To formulate a property of this nature in a multi-profile setting, the profile under consideration for each of the two comparisons must be specified. In Ferejohn and Page's (1978) and Packel's (1980) contributions, the same profile is employed before and after the first-period alternative is eliminated. It seems to us that this leads to a rather demanding requirement because the preferences of the first generation continue to be taken into consideration even though the alternative relevant for this generation has been eliminated. Ferejohn and Page's (1978) stationarity axiom, which is due originally to Koopmans (1960) in a related but distinct context, is defined as follows.

**Stationarity**   For all $x, y \in X$ and for all $\mathbf{R} \in \mathcal{D}$, if $x_1 = y_1$, then

$$(x, y) \in R \Leftrightarrow (x_{\geq 2}, y_{\geq 2}) \in R.$$

Ferejohn and Page's (1978) result establishes that if a social welfare function $F$ satisfies unrestricted domain, weak Pareto, independence of irrelevant alternatives, and stationarity, then generation one is a dictator for $F$. Packel (1980, theorem 1) settled an open question posed by Ferejohn and Page (1978, p. 273) in the negative by showing that there does not exist any complete collective choice rule that satisfies unrestricted domain, weak Pareto, and stationarity. Neither transitivity nor independence of irrelevant alternatives are needed to establish this impossibility result.

Our first result in this section strengthens Packel's (1980) impossibility theorem. In particular, we show that, in addition to transitivity, reflexivity and completeness can be dropped and, moreover, the impossibility persists even on the forward-looking domain.

**Theorem 10.8**   *Suppose $X_{pp}$ contains at least three elements and $N = \mathbb{N}$. There exists no collective choice rule that satisfies forward-looking domain, weak Pareto, and stationarity.*

**Proof**   Suppose $F$ is a collective choice rule that satisfies the axioms of the theorem statement. Let $x^0, y^0 \in X_{pp}$ and let, for each generation $i$, $\succeq_i$ be an antisymmetric ordering on $X_{pp}$ such that $(y^0, x^0) \in P(\succeq_i)$ for all odd $i$ and $(x^0, y^0) \in P(\succeq_i)$ for all even $i$. Define a forward-looking profile $\mathbf{R}$ as follows. For all $x, y \in X$, let

$$(x, y) \in P(R_1) \Leftrightarrow [(x_1, y_1) \in P(\succeq_1) \text{ or } [x_1 = y_1 \text{ and } (x_3, y_3) \in P(\succeq_1)]].$$

Now let $(x, y) \in R_1$ if and only if $(y, x) \notin P(R_1)$. For all $i \in N \setminus \{1\}$ and for all $x, y \in X$, let

$$(x, y) \in R_i \Leftrightarrow (x_i, y_i) \in \succsim_i .$$

Clearly, the profile thus defined is in $\mathcal{R}_{fwl}^N$. Now consider the streams

$$x = (x^0, y^0, x^0, y^0, x^0, y^0, \dots) = (x^0, y),$$
$$y = (y^0, x^0, y^0, x^0, y^0, x^0, \dots) = (y^0, x),$$
$$z = (x^0, x^0, y^0, x^0, y^0, x^0, \dots) = (x^0, x).$$

Thus, $x_{\geq 2} = y$ and $z_{\geq 2} = x$. We have $(z, x) \in P(R_i)$ for all $i \in N$ and, by weak Pareto, $(z, x) \in P(R)$, which implies $(x, y) \in P(R)$ by virtue of stationarity. But $(y, x) \in P(R_i)$ for all $i \in N$, and we obtain a contradiction to weak Pareto.  ∎

Clearly, replacing forward-looking domain with unrestricted domain does not affect the validity of the above theorem. Furthermore, because no richness or coherence properties are imposed on social relations at all, there is nothing to be gained from using Suzumura consistency instead of any other coherence condition. Thus, in this instance, the impossibility is too fundamental to be solved by an adjustment of the coherence property employed.

Packel's (1980) approach to resolve this impossibility consisted of restricting the domain of a social welfare function to profiles where generation one's preferences are themselves stationary. This allowed him to obtain possibility results in that setting. In contrast, we think that the natural way to formulate a domain restriction in the intertemporal context is to assume that the preferences of any generation are restricted to depend on the outcome for this generation only. In that case, there do exist Arrow social welfare functions satisfying stationarity but they are all such that generation one has even more dictatorial power than established in the Ferejohn-Page result. Adding Pareto indifference as a requirement leads again to an impossibility. We conclude that the version of stationarity employed by Ferejohn and Page (1978) is too demanding and has some counterintuitive features. In response, we propose what we suggest is a more suitable multi-profile version of stationarity and characterize the lexicographic dictatorship where the generations are taken into consideration in chronological order.

The above impossibility can be resolved by replacing forward-looking domain with selfish domain. For example, the social welfare function $F$

defined by letting, for all $x, y \in X$ and for all $\mathbf{R} \in \mathcal{R}_{self}^N$, $(x, y) \in R$ if and only if

$$[(x_i, y_i) \in I(\succeq_1) \text{ for all } i \in N] \text{ or}$$
$$[\exists j \in N \text{ such that } [(x_i, y_i) \in I(\succeq_1) \text{ for all } i < j \text{ and } (x_j, y_j) \in P(\succeq_1)]]$$

satisfies selfish domain, weak Pareto, independence of irrelevant alternatives, and stationarity. However, it does not satisfy Pareto indifference. More generally, replacing forward-looking domain with selfish domain and adding Pareto indifference in Theorem 10.8 produces another impossibility.

**Theorem 10.9** *Suppose $X_{pp}$ contains at least three elements and $N = \mathbb{N}$. There exists no collective choice rule that satisfies selfish domain, weak Pareto, Pareto indifference, and stationarity.*

**Proof** Suppose $F$ is a collective choice rule that satisfies the axioms of the theorem statement. Let $x^0, y^0, z^0 \in X_{pp}$ and let, for each generation $i$, $\succeq_i$ be an ordering on $X_{pp}$ such that $(z^0, x^0) \in P(\succeq_i)$ and $(x^0, y^0) \in I(\succeq_i)$ for all odd $i$ and $(z^0, x^0) \in I(\succeq_i)$ and $(x^0, y^0) \in P(\succeq_i)$ for all even $i$. Define a selfish profile $\mathbf{R}$ as follows. For all $x, y \in X$ and for all $i \in N$, let

$$(x, y) \in R_i \Leftrightarrow (x_i, y_i) \in \succeq_i .$$

Clearly, the profile thus defined is in $\mathcal{R}_{self}^N$. Now consider the streams

$$x = (z^0, x^0, z^0, x^0, z^0, x^0, \dots),$$
$$y = (x^0, y^0, x^0, y^0, x^0, y^0, \dots),$$
$$z = (z^0, z^0, x^0, z^0, x^0, z^0, x^0, \dots) = (z^0, x),$$
$$v = (z^0, x^0, y^0, x^0, y^0, x^0, y^0, \dots) = (z^0, y).$$

Thus, $z_{\geq 2} = x$ and $v_{\geq 2} = y$. We have $(z, v) \in I(R_i)$ for all $i \in N$ and, by Pareto indifference, $(z, v) \in I(R)$, which implies $(x, y) \in I(R)$ by virtue of stationarity. But $(x, y) \in P(R_i)$ for all $i \in N$, and we obtain a contradiction to weak Pareto.  ∎

## 10.4  Multi-profile Stationarity

In view of the impossibilities presented in the previous section, we require less stringent intertemporal conditions than stationarity in order to obtain existence results in a multi-profile intergenerational infinite-horizon setting. In Ferejohn and Page's (1978) stationarity axiom, the same profile $\mathbf{R}$

is applied in both comparisons even though the period-one alternative is no longer present. This seems to us to be rather counterintuitive and, consequently, we propose the following version that takes this point into consideration by eliminating the first-period factor not only from the alternatives but also from the profile. When combined with selfish domain, this appears to be a natural version of the axiom. For $i \in N$, we use $R_{\geq i}$ to denote the social preference $F(\mathbf{R}_{\geq i})$ corresponding to the profile $\mathbf{R}_{\geq i}$.

**Multi-profile stationarity**   For all $x, y \in X$ and for all $\mathbf{R} \in \mathcal{D}$, if $x_1 = y_1$, then

$$(x, y) \in R \Leftrightarrow (x_{\geq 2}, y_{\geq 2}) \in R_{\geq 2}.$$

Unlike stationarity, multi-profile stationarity does not require generation $i$ to be able to compare per-period alternatives other than those relevant for period $i$ itself. Because this is the case for all other axioms as well, the following results remain true if the per-period sets of alternatives are period-dependent, thus providing a more realistic framework. For simplicity of presentation, we do not state these alternative versions explicitly and leave it to the reader to verify that if $X_{pp}$ is replaced with $X_{pp}^i$ for each $i \in N$, all arguments continue to go through, provided that each $X_{pp}^i$ contains at least three elements.

We now examine the implications of our multi-profile stationarity axiom. In particular, it allows us to characterize the *chronological dictatorship*. This variant of a lexicographic dictatorship consults generation one first but, in the case of indifference, then moves on to consult *generation two* regarding the ranking of two streams, and so on. Thus, there still is a strong dictatorship component but it is not as extreme as that generated by stationarity—and it is compatible with Pareto indifference. Moreover, the chronological dictatorship is a social welfare function and not merely a collective choice rule.

The chronological dictatorship $F^{cd}$ is defined as follows. For all $x, y \in X$ and for all $\mathbf{R} \in \mathcal{R}_{self}^N$, $(x, y) \in R^{cd}$ if and only if

$$[(x_i, y_i) \in I(\succeq_i) \text{ for all } i \in N] \text{ or}$$
$$[\exists j \in N \text{ such that } [(x_i, y_i) \in I(\succeq_i) \text{ for all } i < j \text{ and } (x_j, y_j) \in P(\succeq_j)]].$$

First, note that the field expansion lemma (Theorem 10.5) and Hansson's (1976) theorem remain valid on the selfish domain (and, of course, under the stronger assumption of $F$'s being a social welfare function and the maintained assumption that $N = \mathbb{N}$); this can be verified by inspecting the proofs provided earlier in this chapter. Thus we state the relevant results without a proof.

**Theorem 10.10**  *Suppose $X_{pp}$ contains at least three elements and $N = \mathbb{N}$. Let F be a social welfare function that satisfies selfish domain, weak Pareto, Pareto indifference, and independence of irrelevant alternatives. Let $x, y \in X$ be distinct and let $M \subseteq N$. If $M$ is $d_F(x, y)$, then $M \in D_F$.*

**Theorem 10.11**  *Suppose $X_{pp}$ contains at least three elements and $N = \mathbb{N}$. If a social welfare function F satisfies selfish domain, weak Pareto, Pareto indifference, and independence of irrelevant alternatives, then $D_F$ is an ultrafilter on $N$.*

The next step toward our characterization result consists of showing that Ferejohn and Page's (1978) dictatorship result is true even on a selfish domain *and* with multi-profile stationarity instead of stationarity.

**Theorem 10.12**  *Suppose $X_{pp}$ contains at least three elements and $N = \mathbb{N}$. If a social welfare function F satisfies selfish domain, weak Pareto, Pareto indifference, independence of irrelevant alternatives, and multi-profile stationarity, then generation one is a dictator for F.*

**Proof**  Suppose $F$ satisfies selfish domain, weak Pareto, Pareto indifference, independence of irrelevant alternatives, and multi-profile stationarity. By Theorem 10.11, $D_F$ is an ultrafilter on $N$. Suppose $N \setminus \{1\} \in D_F$.

Let $x^0$ and $y^0$ be two distinct elements of $X_{pp}$ and let $\succeq$ be an ordering on $X_{pp}$ such that $(x^0, y^0) \in P(\succeq)$. By selfish domain, we can define a profile $R \in \mathcal{R}_{self}^N$ by letting, for all $i \in N$ and for all $x, y \in X$,

$$(x, y) \in R_i \Leftrightarrow (x_i, y_i) \in \succeq .$$

Now consider the streams

$$x = (x^0, x^0, y^0, x^0, y^0, x^0, \ldots) = (x^0, y),$$
$$y = (x^0, y^0, x^0, y^0, x^0, y^0, \ldots) = (x^0, z),$$
$$z = (y^0, x^0, y^0, x^0, y^0, x^0, \ldots) = (y^0, y).$$

Recall that $N \setminus \{1\} \in D_F$. By part (iii) of Theorem 2.10, one of the two sets $\{2, 4, 6, \ldots\}$ and $\{3, 5, 7, \ldots\}$ must be decisive.

If $\{2, 4, 6, \ldots\}$ is decisive, we have $(x, y) \in P(R)$. By multi-profile stationarity,

$$(y, z) = (x_{\geq 2}, y_{\geq 2}) \in P(R_{\geq 2}),$$

contradicting the decisiveness of $\{2, 4, 6, \ldots\}$.

If $\{3, 5, 7, \ldots\}$ is decisive, we have $(y, x) \in P(R)$. By multi-profile stationarity,

$$(z, y) = (y_{\geq 2}, x_{\geq 2}) \in P(R_{\geq 2}),$$

contradicting the decisiveness of $\{3, 5, 7, \ldots\}$.

It follows that, in all cases, we obtain a contradiction to the assumption that $N \setminus \{1\} \in D_F$. Therefore, because $D_F$ is an ultrafilter, $u.2$ implies that $\{1\} \in D_F$ and generation one is a dictator. ∎

The final result of this chapter characterizes $F^{cd}$.

**Theorem 10.13** *Suppose $X_{pp}$ contains at least three elements and $N = \mathbb{N}$. A social welfare function $F$ satisfies selfish domain, weak Pareto, Pareto indifference, independence of irrelevant alternatives, and multi-profile stationarity if and only if $F = F^{cd}$.*

**Proof** That $F^{cd}$ satisfies the required axioms can be verified by the reader. To prove the converse implication, suppose $F$ satisfies selfish domain, weak Pareto, Pareto indifference, independence of irrelevant alternatives, and multi-profile stationarity. Because $F$ is a social welfare function (and, thus, social preferences are orderings), it is sufficient to show that, for all $x, y \in X$ and for all $\mathbf{R} \in \mathcal{R}_{self}^N$,

$$(x, y) \in I(R^{cd}) \Rightarrow (x, y) \in I(R) \tag{10.1}$$

and

$$(x, y) \in P(R^{cd}) \Rightarrow (x, y) \in P(R). \tag{10.2}$$

(10.1) follows immediately from Pareto indifference. To prove (10.2), suppose $j \in N$, $x, y \in X$, and $\mathbf{R} \in \mathcal{R}_{self}^N$ are such that

$$(x_i, y_i) \in I(\succeq_i) \text{ for all } i < j \text{ and } (x_j, y_j) \in P(\succeq_j).$$

If $j = 1$, let $z = y$; if $j \geq 2$, let $z = (x_1, \ldots, x_{j-1}, y_{\geq j})$. By Pareto indifference, $(y, z) \in I(R)$. Transitivity implies

$$(x, y) \in R \Leftrightarrow (x, z) \in R.$$

Together with the application of multi-profile stationarity $j - 1$ times, we obtain

$$(x, y) \in R \Leftrightarrow (x, z) \in R \Leftrightarrow (x_{\geq j}, z_{\geq j}) \in R_{\geq j} \Leftrightarrow (x_{\geq j}, y_{\geq j}) \in R_{\geq j}. \quad (10.3)$$

By Theorem 10.12, the relative ranking of $x_{\geq j}$ and $y_{\geq j}$ according to $R_{\geq j}$ is determined by the strict preference for $x$ over $y$ according to the first generation in the profile $R_{\geq j}$ (which is generation $j$ in R), so that $(x_{\geq j}, y_{\geq j}) \in P(R_{\geq j})$ and, by (10.3), $(x, y) \in P(R)$.   ∎

The results of this concluding part on social choice problems—as is the case for the results reported in this entire monograph—are intended to illustrate the possibilities of employing Suzumura consistency as an interesting and appealing alternative to transitivity. As we hope to have shown, while some impossibilities (such as those of Ferejohn and Page, 1978, and Packel, 1980) cannot be resolved by a mere weakening of the coherence properties imposed on relations, the move from transitivity to Suzumura consistency has the potential to resolve impossibilities or so-called paradoxes that have arisen in a variety of economic models.

References

Index

# References

Arrow, K. J. (1951, second ed. 1963). *Social Choice and Individual Values*. New York: Wiley.

Arrow, K. J. (1959). "Rational Choice Functions and Orderings." *Economica*, Vol. 26, pp. 121–127.

Asheim, G. B. (2010). "Intergenerational Equity." Forthcoming in *Annual Review of Economics*.

Asheim, G. B., W. Bossert, Y. Sprumont, and K. Suzumura (2010). "Infinite-Horizon Choice Functions." *Economic Theory*, Vol. 43, pp. 1–21.

Asheim, G. B., T. Mitra, and B. Tungodden (2007). "A New Equity Condition for Infinite Utility Streams and the Possibility of Being Paretian." In: J. E. Roemer and K. Suzumura, eds., *Intergenerational Equity and Sustainability*. Basingstoke, UK: Palgrave Macmillan, pp. 55–68.

Asheim, G. B., and B. Tungodden (2004). "Resolving Distributional Conflicts between Generations." *Economic Theory*, Vol. 24, pp. 221–230.

Baigent, N., and W. Gaertner (1996). "Never Choose the Uniquely Largest: A Characterization." *Economic Theory*, Vol. 8, pp. 239–249.

Banks, J. S. (1995). "Acyclic Social Choice from Finite Sets." *Social Choice and Welfare*, Vol. 12, pp. 293–310.

Basu, K., and T. Mitra (2003). "Aggregating Infinite Utility Streams with Intergenerational Equity: The Impossibility of Being Paretian." *Econometrica*, Vol. 71, pp. 1557–1563.

Basu, K., and T. Mitra (2007). "Utilitarianism for Infinite Utility Streams: A New Welfare Criterion and Its Axiomatic Characterization." *Journal of Economic Theory*, Vol. 133, pp. 350–373.

Berge, C. (1963). *Topological Spaces*. London: Oliver and Boyd.

Bernheim, B. D. (2009). "Behavioral Welfare Economics." *Journal of the European Economic Association*, Vol. 7, pp. 267–319.

Bernheim, B. D., and A. Rangel (2007). "Toward Choice-Theoretic Foundations for Behavioral Welfare Economics." *American Economic Review: Papers and Proceedings,* Vol. 97, pp. 464–470.

Bernheim, B. D., and A. Rangel (2009). "Beyond Revealed Preference: Choice-Theoretic Foundations for Behavioral Welfare Economics." *Quarterly Journal of Economics,* Vol. 124, pp. 51–104.

Blackorby, C., W. Bossert, and D. Donaldson (1995). "Multi-Valued Demand and Rational Choice in the Two-Commodity Case." *Economics Letters,* Vol. 47, pp. 5–10.

Blackorby, C., D. Donaldson, and J. A. Weymark (1984). "Social Choice with Inter-personal Utility Comparisons: A Diagrammatic Introduction." *International Economic Review,* Vol. 25, pp. 327–356.

Blair, D. H., G. Bordes, J. S. Kelly, and K. Suzumura (1976). "Impossibility The-orems without Collective Rationality." *Journal of Economic Theory,* Vol. 13, pp. 361–379. Reprinted in: K. J. Arrow and G. Debreu, eds. (2001), *The Foundations of 20th Century Economics, Vol. 3, Landmark Papers in General Equilibrium Theory, Social Choice and Welfare,* Cheltenham, UK: Edward Elgar, pp. 660–678.

Blair, D. H., and R. A. Pollak (1982). "Acyclic Collective Choice Rules." *Econometrica,* Vol. 50, pp. 931–943.

Bordes, G. (1976). "Consistency, Rationality and Collective Choice." *Review of Economic Studies,* Vol. 43, pp. 451–457.

Bossert, W. (1994). "Rational Choice and Two-Person Bargaining Solutions." *Journal of Mathematical Economics,* Vol. 23, pp. 549–563.

Bossert, W. (1999). "Intersection Quasi-Orderings: An Alternative Proof." *Order,* Vol. 16, pp. 221–225.

Bossert, W. (2001). "Choices, Consequences, and Rationality." *Synthese,* Vol. 129, pp. 343–369.

Bossert, W. (2008). "Suzumura Consistency." In: P. K. Pattanaik, K. Tadenuma, Y. Xu, and N. Yoshihara, eds., *Rational Choice and Social Welfare: Theory and Applications.* New York: Springer, pp. 159–179.

Bossert, W., and Y. Sprumont (2002). "Core Rationalizability in Two-Agent Exchange Economies." *Economic Theory,* Vol. 20, pp. 777–791.

Bossert, W., and Y. Sprumont (2003). "Efficient and Non-Deteriorating Choice." *Mathematical Social Sciences,* Vol. 45, pp. 131–142.

Bossert, W., and Y. Sprumont (2009). "Non-Deteriorating Choice." *Economica,* Vol. 76, pp. 337–363.

Bossert, W., Y. Sprumont, and K. Suzumura (2005a). "Consistent Rationalizability." *Economica,* Vol. 72, pp. 185–200.

Bossert, W., Y. Sprumont, and K. Suzumura (2005b). "Maximal-Element Rational-izability." *Theory and Decision,* Vol. 58, pp. 325–350.

Bossert, W., Y. Sprumont, and K. Suzumura (2006). "Rationalizability of Choice Functions on General Domains without Full Transitivity." *Social Choice and Welfare,* Vol. 27, pp. 435–458.

Bossert, W., Y. Sprumont, and K. Suzumura (2007). "Ordering Infinite Utility Streams." *Journal of Economic Theory,* Vol. 135, pp. 579–589.

Bossert, W., and K. Suzumura (2007a). "Domain Closedness Conditions and Rational Choice." *Order,* Vol. 24, pp. 75–88.

Bossert, W., and K. Suzumura (2007b). "Non-Deteriorating Choice without Full Transitivity." *Analyse & Kritik,* Vol. 29, pp. 163–187.

Bossert, W., and K. Suzumura (2008a). "A Characterization of Consistent Collective Choice Rules." *Journal of Economic Theory,* Vol. 138, pp. 311–320; Erratum in Vol. 140, p. 355.

Bossert, W., and K. Suzumura (2008b). "Multi-Profile Intergenerational Social Choice." Discussion Paper 08-2008, University of Montreal: CIREQ.

Bossert, W., and K. Suzumura (2009a). "Rational Choice on General Domains." In: K. Basu and R. Kanbur, eds., *Arguments for a Better World: Essays in Honor of Amartya Sen, Vol. I: Ethics, Welfare, and Measurement.* Oxford, UK: Oxford University Press, pp. 103–135.

Bossert, W., and K. Suzumura (2009b). "External Norms and Rationality of Choice." *Economics and Philosophy,* Vol. 25, pp. 139–152.

Bossert, W., and K. Suzumura (2010). "Rationality, External Norms and the Epistemic Value of Menus." Forthcoming in *Social Choice and Welfare.*

Brown, D. J. (1975). "Aggregation of Preferences." *Quarterly Journal of Economics,* Vol. 89, pp. 456–469.

Brown, D. J., and R. L. Matzkin (1996). "Testable Restrictions on the Equilibrium Manifold." *Econometrica,* Vol. 64, pp. 1249–1262.

Camerer, C. (1995). "Individual Decision Making." In: J. Kagel and A. Roth, eds., *Handbook of Experimental Economics.* Princeton, NJ: Princeton University Press, pp. 587–704.

Cato, S. (2008). "Quasi-Decisiveness, Quasi-Ultrafilter, and Social Quasi-Orderings." Working Paper, University of Tokyo: Graduate School of Economics.

Cato, S., and D. Hirata (2010). "Collective Choice Rules and Collective Rationality: A Unified Method of Characterizations." *Social Choice and Welfare,* Vol. 34, pp. 611–630.

Debreu, G. (1959). *Theory of Value: An Axiomatic Analysis of Economic Equilibrium.* New York: Wiley.

Diamond, P. (1965). "The Evaluation of Infinite Utility Streams." *Econometrica,* Vol. 33, pp. 170–177.

Diewert, W. E. (1973). "Afriat and Revealed Preference Theory." *Review of Economic Studies,* Vol. 40, pp. 419–425.

Donaldson, D., and J. A. Weymark (1988). "Social Choice in Economic Environments." *Journal of Economic Theory,* Vol. 46, pp. 291–308.

Donaldson, D., and J. A. Weymark (1998). "A Quasiordering Is the Intersection of Orderings." *Journal of Economic Theory,* Vol. 78, pp. 382–387.

Duggan, J. (1997). "Pseudo-Rationalizability and Tournament Solutions." Working Paper, University of Rochester: Department of Economics.

Duggan, J. (1999). "A General Extension Theorem for Binary Relations." *Journal of Economic Theory,* Vol. 86, pp. 1–16.

Dunford, N., and J. T. Schwartz (1957). *Linear Operators, Part I; General Theory.* New York: Interscience Publishers.

Dushnik, B. and E. W. Miller (1941). "Partially Ordered Sets." *American Journal of Mathematics,* Vol. 63, pp. 600–610.

Ferejohn, J., and T. Page (1978). "On the Foundations of Intertemporal Choice." *American Journal of Agricultural Economics,* Vol. 60, pp. 269–275.

Fishburn, P. C. (1970). "Arrow's Impossibility Theorem: Concise Proof and Infinite Voters." *Journal of Economic Theory,* Vol. 2, pp. 103–106.

Fisher, I. (1922). *The Making of Index Numbers.* Boston: Houghton Mifflin.

Frisch, R. (1926). "Sur un Problème d'Economie Pure." *Norsk Matematisk Forening Skrifter,* Vol. 1, pp. 1–40. English translation: "On a Problem in Pure Economics." In: J. S. Chipman, L. Hurwicz, M. K. Richter, and H. F. Sonnenschein, eds. (1971), *Preferences, Utility, and Demand.* New York: Harcourt Brace Jovanovich, pp. 386–423.

Gale, D. (1960). "A Note on Revealed Preference." *Economica,* Vol. 27, pp. 348–354.

Georgescu-Roegen, N. (1954). "Choice and Revealed Preference." *Southern Economic Journal,* Vol. 21, pp. 119–130.

Georgescu-Roegen, N. (1966). *Analytical Economics: Issues and Problems.* Cambridge, MA.: Harvard University Press.

Gul, F., and W. Pesendorfer (2007). "Welfare without Happiness." *American Economic Review: Papers and Proceedings,* Vol. 97, pp. 471–476.

Hansson, B. (1968). "Choice Structures and Preference Relations." *Synthese,* Vol. 18, pp. 443–458.

Hansson, B. (1976). "The Existence of Group Preference Functions." *Public Choice,* Vol. 38, pp. 89–98.

Hara, C., T. Shinotsuka, K. Suzumura, and Y. Xu (2008). "Continuity and Egalitarianism in the Evaluation of Infinite Utility Streams." *Social Choice and Welfare,* Vol. 31, pp. 179–191.

Hicks, J. R. (1939, second ed. 1946). *Value and Capital.* London: Oxford University Press.

Hicks, J. R. (no date; ca. 1955). "Another Shot at Welfare Economics, Lecture 1 and Lecture 2." Unpublished manuscript.

Hicks, J. R. (1956). *A Revision of Demand Theory.* London: Oxford University Press.

Hicks, J. R. (1959). *Essays in World Economics.* Oxford, UK: Clarendon Press.

Hicks, J. R. (no date; ca. 1963). "The Real Product: A Revision of 'Welfare Economics.'" Unpublished manuscript.

Hicks, J. R., and R. G. D. Allen (1934). "A Reconsideration of the Theory of Value." *Economica,* Vol. 14, pp. 52–76 and pp. 196–219.

Hiraguchi, T. (1955). "On the Dimension of Orders." *Scientific Report Kanazawa University,* Vol. 4, pp. 1–20.

Houthakker, H. S. (1950). "Revealed Preference and the Utility Function." *Economica,* Vol. 17, pp. 159–174.

Houthakker, H. S. (1965). "On the Logic of Preference and Choice." In: A.-T. Tymieniecka, ed., *Contributions to Logic and Methodology in Honour of J. M. Bochenski,* Amsterdam: North-Holland, pp. 193–205.

Inada, K.-I. (1954). "Elementary Proofs of Some Theorems about the Social Welfare Function." *Annals of the Institute of Statistical Mathematics,* Vol. 6, pp. 115–122.

Kahneman, D., J. L. Knetsch, and R. H. Thaler (1991). "The Endowment Effect, Loss Aversion, and Status Quo Bias." *Journal of Economic Perspectives,* Vol. 5, pp. 193–206.

Kalai, G., A. Rubinstein, and R. Spiegler (2002). "Rationalizing Choice Functions by Multiple Rationales." *Econometrica,* Vol. 70, pp. 2481–2488.

Kelley, J. L. (1955). *General Topology.* Princeton, NJ: D. Van Nostrand.

Kelly, J. S. (1987). "An Interview with Kenneth J. Arrow." *Social Choice and Welfare,* Vol. 4, pp. 43–62.

Kirman, A. P., and D. Sondermann (1972). "Arrow's Theorem, Many Agents, and Invisible Dictators." *Journal of Economic Theory,* Vol. 5, pp. 267–277.

Knetsch, J. L. (1989). "The Endowment Effect and Evidence of Nonreversible Indifference Curves." *American Economic Review,* Vol. 79, pp. 1277–1284.

Koopmans, T. C. (1960). "Stationary Ordinal Utility and Impatience." *Econometrica,* Vol. 28, pp. 287–309.

Kőszegi, B., and M. Rabin (2007). "Mistakes in Choice-Based Welfare Analysis." *American Economic Review: Papers and Proceedings,* Vol. 97, pp. 477–481.

Laspeyres, E. (1871). "Die Berechnung einer mittleren Waarenpreissteigerung." *Jahrbücher für Nationalökonomie und Statistik,* Vol. 16, pp. 296–315.

Lensberg, T. (1987). "Stability and Collective Rationality." *Econometrica,* Vol. 55, pp. 935–961.

Lensberg, T. (1988). "Stability and the Nash Solution." *Journal of Economic Theory,* Vol. 45, pp. 330–341.

Little, I. M. D. (1949). "A Reformulation of the Theory of Consumer's Behaviour." *Oxford Economic Papers,* Vol. 1, pp. 90–99.

Luce, R. D. (1956). "Semiorders and the Theory of Utility Discrimination." *Econometrica,* Vol. 24, pp. 178–191.

Luce, R. D., and H. Raiffa (1957). *Games and Decisions.* New York: Wiley.

Majumdar, M., and A. K. Sen (1976). "A Note on Representing Partial Orderings." *Review of Economic Studies,* Vol. 43, pp. 543–545.

Masatlioglu, Y., and E. A. Ok (2005). "Rational Choice with Status Quo Bias." *Journal of Economic Theory,* Vol. 121, pp. 1–29.

Mas-Colell, A. (1982). "Revealed Preference after Samuelson." In: G. R. Feiwel, ed., *Samuelson and Neoclassical Economics.* Amsterdam: Kluwer, pp. 72–82.

Mas-Colell, A., and H. Sonnenschein (1972). "General Possibility Theorems for Group Decisions." *Review of Economic Studies,* Vol. 39, pp. 185–192.

Munro, A., and R. Sugden (2003). "On the Theory of Reference-Dependent Preferences." *Journal of Economic Behavior and Organization,* Vol. 50, pp. 407–428.

Nash, J. F. (1950). "The Bargaining Problem." *Econometrica,* Vol. 18, pp. 155–162.

Paasche, H. (1874). "Über die Preisentwicklung der letzten Jahre nach den Hamburger Börsennotirungen." *Jahrbücher für Nationalökonomie und Statistik,* Vol. 23, pp. 168–178.

Packel, E. (1980). "Impossibility Results in the Axiomatic Theory of Intertemporal Choice." *Public Choice,* Vol. 35, pp. 219–227.

Pareto, V. (1906, second ed. 1909). *Manuale di Economia Politica, con una Introduzione alla Scienza Sociale.* Milano: Societa Editrice Libraria.

Peters, H., and P. Wakker (1991). "Independence of Irrelevant Alternatives and Revealed Group Preferences." *Econometrica,* Vol. 59, pp. 1787–1801.

Peters, H., and P. Wakker (1994). "WARP Does Not Imply SARP for More than Two Commodities." *Journal of Economic Theory,* Vol. 62, pp. 152–160.

Plott, C. R. (1973). "Path Independence, Rationality, and Social Choice." *Econometrica,* Vol. 41, pp. 1075–1091.

Pollak, R. A. (1990). "Distinguished Fellow: Houthakker's Contributions to Economics." *Journal of Economic Perspectives,* Vol. 4, pp. 141–156.

Rabin, M. (1998). "Psychology and Economics." *Journal of Economic Literature,* Vol. 36, pp. 11–46.

Raiffa, H. (1968). *Decision Analysis.* Reading, MA: Addison-Wesley.

Ramsey, F. P. (1928). "A Mathematical Theory of Savings." *Economic Journal,* Vol. 38, pp. 543–559.

Ray, I., and L. Zhou (2001). "Game Theory via Revealed Preferences." *Games and Economic Behavior,* Vol. 37, pp. 415–424.

Richter, M. K. (1966). "Revealed Preference Theory." *Econometrica,* Vol. 41, pp. 1075–1091.

Richter, M. K. (1971). "Rational Choice." In: J. S. Chipman, L. Hurwicz, M. K. Richter, and H. F. Sonnenschein, eds., *Preferences, Utility, and Demand.* New York: Harcourt Brace Jovanovich, pp. 29–58.

Robbins, L. (1932, second ed. 1935). *An Essay on the Nature and Significance of Economic Science.* London: Macmillan.

Robertson, D. H. (1952). *Utility and All That and Other Essays.* London: George Allen & Unwin.

Rose, H. (1958). "Consistency of Preference: The Two-Commodity Case." *Review of Economic Studies,* Vol. 25, pp. 124–125.

Rubinstein, A., and L. Zhou (1999). "Choice Problems with a 'Reference' Point." *Mathematical Social Sciences,* Vol. 37, pp. 205–209.

Sagi, J. S. (2006). "Anchored Preference Relations." *Journal of Economic Theory,* Vol. 130, pp. 283–295.

Samuelson, P. A. (1938a). "A Note on the Pure Theory of Consumer's Behaviour." *Economica,* Vol. 5, pp. 61–71.

Samuelson, P. A. (1938b). "A Note on the Pure Theory of Consumer's Behaviour: An Addendum." *Economica,* Vol. 5, pp. 353–354.

Samuelson, P. A. (1947, second ed. 1983). *Foundations of Economic Analysis.* Cambridge, MA: Harvard University Press.

Samuelson, P. A. (1948). "Consumption Theory in Terms of Revealed Preference." *Economica,* Vol. 15, pp. 243–253.

Samuelson, P. A. (1950). "The Problem of Integrability in Utility Theory." *Economica,* Vol. 17, pp. 355–385.

Samuelson, P. A. (1953). "Consumption Theorems in Terms of Overcompensation rather than Indifference Comparisons." *Economica,* Vol. 20, pp. 1–9.

Samuelson, W., and R. Zeckhauser (1988). "Status Quo Bias in Decision Making." *Journal of Risk and Uncertainty,* Vol. 1, pp. 7–59.

Sanchez, M. (2000). "Rationality of Bargaining Solutions." *Journal of Mathematical Economics,* Vol. 33, pp. 389–399.

Schwartz, T. (1976). "Choice Functions, 'Rationality' Conditions, and Variations of the Weak Axiom of Revealed Preference." *Journal of Economic Theory,* Vol. 13, pp. 414–427.

Sen, A. K. (1969). "Quasi-Transitivity, Rational Choice and Collective Decisions." *Review of Economic Studies,* Vol. 36, pp. 381–393.

Sen, A. K. (1970). *Collective Choice and Social Welfare.* San Francisco: Holden-Day.

Sen, A. K. (1971). "Choice Functions and Revealed Preference." *Review of Economic Studies,* Vol. 38, pp. 307–317.

Sen, A. K. (1973). "Behaviour and the Concept of Preference." *Economica,* Vol. 40, pp. 241–259.

Sen, A. K. (1979). "Personal Utilities and Public Judgements: Or What's Wrong with Welfare Economics?" *Economic Journal,* Vol. 89, pp. 537–558.

Sen, A. K. (1993). "Internal Consistency of Choice." *Econometrica,* Vol. 61, pp. 495–521.

Sen, A. K. (1995). "Rationality and Social Choice." *American Economic Review,* Vol. 85, pp. 1–24. Reprinted in: A. K. Sen (2002). *Rationality and Freedom.* Cambridge, MA: Belknap Press of Harvard University Press, pp. 261–299.

Sen, A. K. (1997). "Maximization and the Act of Choice." *Econometrica,* Vol. 65, pp. 745–779.

Shafir, E., and A. Tversky (1995). "Decision Making." In: D. N. Osherson and E. E. Smith, eds., *Invitation to Cognitive Science: Thinking.* Cambridge, MA: MIT Press, pp. 77–109.

Shubik, M. (1982). *Game Theory in the Social Sciences: Concepts and Solutions.* Cambridge, MA: MIT Press.

Sidgwick, H. (1907). *The Methods of Ethics, 7th ed.* London: Macmillan.

Simon, H. A. (1955). "A Behavioral Model of Rational Choice." *Quarterly Journal of Economics,* Vol. 69, pp. 99–118.

Simon, H. A. (1956). "Rational Choice and the Structure of the Environment." *Psychological Review,* Vol. 63, pp. 129–138.

Slutsky, E. (1915). "Sulla Teoria del Bilancio del Consumatore." *Giornale degli Economisti e Rivista di Statistica,* Vol. 51, pp. 1–26. English translation: "On the Theory of the Budget of the Consumer." In: G. J. Stigler and K. E. Boulding, eds. (1952), *Readings in Price Theory.* Homewood, IL: Richard D. Unwin, pp. 27–56.

Sprumont, Y. (2000). "On the Testable Implications of Collective Choice Theories." *Journal of Economic Theory,* Vol. 93, pp. 205–232.

Sprumont, Y. (2001). "Paretian Quasi-Orders: The Regular Two-Agent Case." *Journal of Economic Theory,* Vol. 101, pp. 437–456.

Stigum, B. P. (1973). "Revealed Preference—A Proof of Houthakker's Theorem." *Econometrica,* Vol. 41, pp. 411–423.

Suzumura, K. (1976a). "Rational Choice and Revealed Preference." *Review of Economic Studies,* Vol. 43, pp. 149–158.

Suzumura, K. (1976b). "Remarks on the Theory of Collective Choice." *Economica,* Vol. 43, pp. 381–390.

Suzumura, K. (1977). "Houthakker's Axiom in the Theory of Rational Choice." *Journal of Economic Theory,* Vol. 14, pp. 284–290.

Suzumura, K. (1978). "On the Consistency of Libertarian Claims." *Review of Economic Studies,* Vol. 45, pp. 329–342.

Suzumura, K. (1983). *Rational Choice, Collective Decisions and Social Welfare.* New York: Cambridge University Press.

Suzumura, K. (2000). "Welfare Economics beyond Welfarist-Consequentialism." *Japanese Economic Review,* Vol. 51, pp. 1–32.

Suzumura, K. (2004). "An Extension of Arrow's Lemma with Economic Applications." Working Paper, Hitotsubashi University: Institute of Economic Research.

Szpilrajn, E. (1930). "Sur l'Extension de l'Ordre Partiel." *Fundamenta Mathematicae*, Vol. 16, pp. 386–389.

Tarski, A. (1941). *Introduction to Logic and the Methodology of the Deductive Sciences.* New York: Oxford University Press.

Thaler, R. (1980). "Toward a Positive Theory of Consumer Choice." *Journal of Economic Behavior and Organization*, Vol. 1, pp. 39–60.

Thomson, W. (2010). *Bargaining Theory: The Axiomatic Approach.* New York: Academic Press, forthcoming.

Thomson, W., and T. Lensberg (1989). *Axiomatic Theory of Bargaining with a Variable Number of Agents.* Cambridge, MA: Cambridge University Press.

Tversky, A., and D. Kahneman (1991). "Loss Aversion in Riskless Choice: A Reference-Dependent Model." *Quarterly Journal of Economics*, Vol. 106, pp. 1039–1061.

Tyson, C. J. (2008). "Cognitive Constraints, Contraction Consistency, and the Satisficing Criterion." *Journal of Economic Theory*, Vol. 138, pp. 51–70.

Uzawa, H. (1956). "Note on Preference and Axioms of Choice." *Annals of the Institute of Statistical Mathematics*, Vol. 8, pp. 35–40.

Uzawa, H. (1960). "Preference and Rational Choice in the Theory of Consumption." In: K. J. Arrow, S. Karlin, and P. Suppes, eds., *Mathematical Methods in the Social Sciences, 1959.* Stanford, CA: Stanford University Press, pp. 129–148.

Varian, H. R. (1982). "The Nonparametric Approach to Demand Analysis." *Econometrica*, Vol. 50, pp. 945–973.

Varian, H. R. (2006). "Revealed Preference." In: M. Szenberg, L. Ramrattan, and A. A. Gottesman, eds., *Samuelsonian Economics and the Twenty-First Century.* Oxford, UK: Oxford University Press, pp. 99–115.

Weymark, J. A. (1984). "Arrow's Theorem with Social Quasi-Orderings." *Public Choice*, Vol. 42, pp. 235–246.

Xu, Y. (2007). "Norm-Constrained Choices." *Analyse & Kritik*, Vol. 29, pp. 329–339.

Zhou, L. (1997). "Revealed Preferences: The Role of the Status Quo." Working Paper, Duke University: Department of Economics.

# Index

A-congruence, 133
Acyclicity, 3, 35, 37, 42, 61, 72, 76, 87, 89, 91, 123, 129, 133, 135, 142, 144, 148, 149, 156, 158, 159, 161
Allen, R. G. D., 11
Anonymity, 28, 176, 177, 178, 180
Antisymmetry, 32, 148
Arbitrary domain, 19, 59, 61, 72, 76, 77, 78, 79, 81, 83, 85, 87, 89, 91, 93, 97, 101, 104, 107, 108, 119, 141, 142, 144, 145, 148, 149, 154, 156, 157, 158
Arrow, K. J., 3, 12, 16, 18, 20, 28, 29, 42, 46, 117, 118, 128, 162, 173, 177, 185
Arrow's choice axiom, 118, 119, 121, 122
Arrow's impossibility theorem. See Arrow's theorem
Arrow's lemma, 46
Arrow's theorem, 28, 177
Asheim, G. B., 31, 193
Asymmetric factor, 9, 32
Asymmetry, 5, 32
Axiom of choice, 43

Baigent, N., 25
Banks, J. S., 28, 29, 180, 193
Base domain, 128, 129, 130, 132, 133, 134, 135
Basu, K., 30, 31
Berge, C., 34, 52
Bernheim, B. D., 6, 28
Binary relation. See Relation
Blackorby, C., 13, 177
Blair, D. H., 19, 28, 29, 193

Bordes, G., 19
Bossert, W., 6, 13, 23, 25, 31, 46, 57, 60, 79, 83, 85, 87, 89, 91, 93, 97, 101, 104, 107, 108, 116, 117, 123, 128, 130, 139, 144, 146, 147, 152, 154, 158, 159, 163, 168, 173, 185
Brown, D. J., 28, 29, 147

Camerer, C., 22, 139
Cato, S., 174, 185
Choice function, 16, 58, 59, 61, 72, 76, 77, 78, 79, 81, 83, 85, 87, 89, 91, 93, 97, 101, 104, 107, 108, 119, 121, 122, 123, 129, 130, 132, 133, 134, 135, 166, 167, 168, 169
Chronological dictatorship, 199, 201
Closedness under intersection, 117, 121
Closedness under union, 117, 122, 123, 135
Coherence, 36
Collective choice rule, 174, 177, 178, 180, 187, 188, 190, 191, 196, 198
Compatibility, 42
Completeness, 33, 38, 41, 42, 61, 72, 76, 81, 85, 89, 91, 101, 104, 108, 123, 129, 130, 132, 133, 134, 135, 142, 144, 145, 149, 157, 158, 159, 161, 177, 187
Composition, 47
Congruence, 117, 119, 121, 122
Consistency. See Suzumura consistency

Debreu, G., 9
Decisiveness, 186, 187, 188, 190, 191, 200
Diagonal relation, 33

Diamond, P., 30, 193
Dictatorship, 186, 200
Diewert, W. E., 19
Direct exclusion, 83, 85, 87, 89, 91, 93, 97,
    101, 109
Direct irreversibility, 84, 85, 109
Direct revealed preference relation, 16, 58,
    59, 133, 141, 148
Direct revealed strict preference
    relation, 16
Direct revelation coherence, 78, 119, 121,
    122, 132, 133, 134
Distinctness exclusion, 101, 109
Distinctness irreversibility, 89, 101, 109
Donaldson, D., 13, 46, 116, 122, 177
Duggan, J., 22, 46
Dunford, N., 52
Dushnik, B., 46, 110, 158

Efficient and non-deteriorating
    rationalizability. *See*
    END-rationalizability
END-rationalizability, 147, 148, 149, 154,
    156, 157, 158, 159, 161
Extended selection congruence, 154, 158
Extension, 42

Ferejohn, J., 31, 185, 193, 194, 195, 196, 197,
    198, 200, 202
Field expansion lemma, 188
Filter, 52, 187, 190, 191
Fishburn, P. C., 29
Fisher, I., 10
Forward-looking domain, 195, 196
Free ultrafilter, 53
Frisch, R., 7

Gaertner, W., 25
Gale, D., 13, 15
Georgescu-Roegen, N., 7, 8
G-rationalizability, 58, 59, 61, 76, 77, 78,
    79, 81, 83, 85, 87, 89, 91, 93, 97, 101, 104,
    107, 108, 109, 123, 129, 130, 132, 133,
    134, 135
Greatest element, 41, 42
Greatest-element rationalizability.
    *See* G-rationalizability
Gul, F., 28

Hansson, B., 20, 29, 30, 31, 43, 121, 122, 162,
    185, 187, 190, 199
Hara, C., 31
Hicks, J. R., 11, 26, 27, 28
Hiraguchi, T., 159
Hiraguchi's inequality, 159
Hirata, D., 174
Houthakker, H. S., 12, 13, 14, 16
Houthakker's axiom of revealed
    preference, 17

Inada, K.-I., 47
Independence of irrelevant alternatives, 176,
    177, 178, 187, 188, 190, 191,
    200, 201
Indifference relation, 33
Indirect exclusion, 104, 109
Indirect irreversibility, 91, 104, 109
Indirect revealed preference relation.
    *See* Revealed preference relation
Indirect revealed strict preference
    relation, 16
Intermediate congruence, 118, 119, 121, 122

Kahneman, D., 22, 23
Kalai, G., 22, 23
Kelley, J. L., 52
Kelly, J. S., 3, 19
Kirman, A. P., 29, 30, 185
Knetsch, J. L., 22
Koopmans, T. C., 30, 193, 196
Kőszegi, B., 28

Laspeyres, E., 10
Lensberg, T., 116
Little, I. M. D., 8, 26
L-rule, 178, 180
Luce, R. D., 24, 35

Majumdar, M., 9
Masatlioglu, Y., 23, 140
Mas-Colell, A., 21, 28, 29
Matzkin, R. L., 147
Maximal element, 41, 42
Maximal-element rationalizability.
    *See* M-rationalizability
Miller, E. W., 46, 110, 158
Mitra, T., 30, 31

Money pump, 4, 38

M-rationalizability, 58, 59, 72, 76, 81, 85, 91, 104, 108, 129, 131, 132, 133, 134, 135

Multi-profile stationarity, 199, 200, 201

Munro, A., 22

Nash, J. F., 116, 119, 174

$\mathcal{N}$-conditional direct revelation coherence, 167

$\mathcal{N}$-conditional Suzumura-consistent closure coherence, 168

$\mathcal{N}$-conditional transitive closure coherence, 169

ND-rationalizability, 140, 141, 142, 144, 145

Neutrality, 176, 180

Non-comparability relation, 33

Non-comparable factor, 33

Non-deteriorating rationalizability. See ND-rationalizability

Non-dictatorship, 176, 177

Norm-conditional choice function, 163

Norm-conditional direct revealed preference relation, 165, 166

Norm-conditional rationalizability. See $\mathcal{N}$-rationalizability

$\mathcal{N}$-rationalizability, 165, 166, 167, 168, 169

Ok, E. A., 23, 140

Ordering, 33, 38, 47

Ordering extension, 5, 42, 43, 45, 47

Paasche, H., 10

Packel, E., 31, 185, 194, 196, 197, 202

Page, T., 31, 185, 193, 194, 195, 196, 197, 198, 200, 202

Pareto, V., 11

Pareto extension rule, 175, 177

Pareto indifference, 195, 198, 200, 201

Pareto rule, 175, 178

Pesendorfer, W., 28

Peters, H., 13, 116

Plott, C. R., 19, 28

Pollak, R. A., 17, 19, 28, 29, 193

Principal ultrafilter, 53

Q-congruence, 131, 132

Quasi-ordering, 33, 43

Quasi-transitivity, 35, 37, 61, 72, 76, 93, 97, 101, 104, 123, 129, 132, 135, 142, 144, 148, 149, 154, 158, 159, 161, 177, 187, 188, 190

Rabin, M., 22, 28

Raiffa, H., 4, 5, 24

Ramsey, F. P., 30

Rangel, A., 6, 28

Ray, I., 146

Reflexivity, 33, 38, 41, 42, 61, 72, 76, 78, 79, 81, 83, 85, 87, 91, 97, 104, 107, 108, 123, 129, 130, 131, 132, 133, 134, 135, 142, 144, 145, 149, 154, 156, 157, 158, 159, 161, 177, 187

Relation, 3, 32, 34, 37, 38, 39, 41, 42, 45, 47, 59, 77, 141, 148

Restriction, 46, 47

Revealed preference relation, 16

Revelation exclusion, 93, 97, 109

Revelation irreversibility, 86, 87, 93, 97, 109

Richness, 33

Richter, M. K., 20, 21, 62, 78, 80, 117, 118, 131, 132, 144, 162, 167, 168

Robbins, L., 6, 7

Robertson, D. H., 20

Rose, H., 12, 15

Rubinstein, A., 22, 23, 140

Sagi, J. S., 22

Samuelson, P. A., 7, 8, 10, 11, 12, 13, 14, 15, 19, 21, 26, 59

Samuelson, W., 22

Samuelson's weak axiom of revealed preference, 11

Sanchez, M., 116

Schwartz, J. T., 52

Schwartz, T., 19

Selection congruence, 144, 156

Selection function, 140, 141, 142, 144, 145, 148, 149, 154, 156, 157, 158, 159, 161

Self-irreversibility, 97, 109

Selfish domain, 195, 198, 200, 201

Sen, A. K., 9, 18, 20, 23, 24, 25, 28, 29, 36, 118, 128, 162, 164, 169, 173, 174, 177, 178, 188

Shafir, E., 22, 139

Shinotsuka, T., 31
Shubik, M., 117
Sidgwick, H., 30
Simon, H. A., 23, 139
Slutsky, E., 11
Social welfare function, 175, 177, 186, 187, 200, 201
Sondermann, D., 29, 30, 185
Sonnenschein, H., 28, 29
Spiegler, R., 22, 23
Sprumont, Y., 6, 23, 31, 57, 60, 79, 85, 91, 104, 128, 130, 139, 144, 146, 147, 152, 154, 158, 159, 168
Stationarity, 196, 198
Stigum, B. P., 15
Strict preference relation, 33
Strong axiom of revealed preference, 17
Strong Pareto, 176, 177, 178, 180
Subrelation, 42
Sugden, R., 22
Suzumura, K., 4, 5, 6, 19, 20, 23, 25, 29, 31, 36, 38, 45, 47, 57, 60, 79, 83, 85, 87, 89, 91, 93, 97, 101, 104, 107, 108, 117, 123, 128, 130, 139, 162, 163, 168, 173, 185
Suzumura consistency, 4, 36, 37, 38, 39, 45, 47, 61, 72, 76, 77, 79, 81, 91, 107, 108, 129, 130, 131, 133, 135, 142, 144, 148, 149, 156, 158, 159, 161, 166, 168, 180
Suzumura-consistent closure, 39, 77
Suzumura-consistent closure coherence, 79, 119, 121, 122
Suzumura-consistent closure irreversibility, 107, 109
Symmetric factor, 32
Symmetry, 32
Szpilrajn, E., 5, 42
Szpilrajn's theorem, 43

Tarski, A., 3
T-congruence, 130, 131

Thaler, R. H., 22
Thomson, W., 116
Transitive closure, 16, 34, 39, 77
Transitive closure coherence, 80, 81, 119, 121, 122
Transitive closure irreversibility, 108, 109
Transitivity, 33, 34, 61, 72, 76, 77, 81, 104, 108, 129, 130, 131, 132, 135, 142, 144, 148, 149, 154, 158, 159, 161, 166, 169, 178, 191
Tungodden, B., 31
Tversky, A., 22, 23, 139
Tyson, C. J., 22

Ultrafilter, 52, 53, 187, 200
Universal indifference relation, 141
Universal selection congruence, 161
Universal set domain, 159, 161
Unrestricted domain, 176, 177, 178, 180, 187, 188, 190, 191
Uzawa, H., 15, 16

Varian, H. R., 19, 21

Wakker, P., 13, 116
Weak axiom of revealed preference, 17
Weak congruence, 118, 119, 121, 122
Weak extended selection congruence, 155, 156, 157
Weak Pareto, 176, 177, 187, 188, 190, 191, 196, 198, 200, 201
Weak preference relation, 33
Weak selection congruence, 145
Weymark, J. A., 28, 29, 46, 116, 122, 173, 174, 177, 178, 179

Xu, Y., 25, 31

Zeckhauser, R., 22
Zhou, L., 23, 140, 146
Zorn's lemma, 43

Harvard University Press is a member of Green Press Initiative
(greenpressinitiative.org), a nonprofit organization working to
help publishers and printers increase their use of recycled paper
and decrease their use of fiber derived from endangered forests.
This book was printed on recycled paper containing 30%
post-consumer waste and processed chlorine free.